Perry And
and

PERRY ANDERSON, MARXISM AND THE NEW LEFT

Paul Blackledge

The Merlin Press

© Paul Blackledge, 2004
The author asserts the right to be identified as the
author of this work

First published 2004 by The Merlin Press Ltd.
PO Box 30705
London WC2E 8QD
www.merlinpress.co.uk

British Library Cataloguing in Publication Data
is available from the British Library

ISBN. 0850365325

All rights reserved. No part of this publication may be
reproduced, stored in a retrieval system, or transmitted,
in any form or by any means, electronic, mechanical,
photocopying, recording or otherwise, without the
prior permission of the publisher.

Printed in Great Britain by Antony Rowe Ltd., Chippenham

To the memory of my mother, Margaret
(15th September 1944 – 7th March 1988)

Contents

	Acknowledgements	viii
	Introduction	ix
1.	Anderson and the First New Left	1
2.	The Second New Left	12
3.	Towards Revolutionary Socialism	35
4.	A Revolutionary Strategy for the West	68
5.	A Flawed Synthesis	87
6.	The Retreat from Revolution	112
7.	Postmodern Renewals	147
8.	Conclusion	167
	Chronology	172
	Select Bibliography	176
	Notes	191
	Index	205

ACKNOWLEDGEMENTS

This book could not have been written without the help of Alex Callinicos and Zoë Anne Marsden: Zoë deserves especial thanks for her unstinting support. I would also like to register my appreciation for the kind assistance I received from Colin Barker, Ian Birchall, Sebastian Budgen, Matthew Caygill, Karl Claxton, Neil Davidson, John Davies, Sue Dodsworth, Gregory Elliott, Kristyn Gorton, Adrian Howe, Bob Looker, Andy Parkes, Evans Pierre, Giuseppe Tassone, Willie Thompson, Ben Watson and Tony Zurbrugg. Johnny and Matthew Marsden deserve special thanks for their unstinting lack of interest. My interest in Anderson, perversely enough, developed out of research I did towards the completion of my MA thesis on the part played by the ideology of amateurism in the split between rugby league and rugby union in 1895. While Anderson's name does not appear in the version of that essay that was eventually published in *The International Journal of the History of Sport*, his spirit continues to haunt it. An earlier version of this book was presented as a D.Phil. thesis to the Department of Politics at the University of York, and some of the themes taken up within it have been published in the journals *Contemporary Politics*, *Historical Materialism* and *Studies in Marxism*.

INTRODUCTION

Perry Anderson is among the most important and influential Marxists of his generation. He first came to prominence in 1960, as the New Left of 1956 was reaching the apogee of its influence, when, as a young Oxford undergraduate, he wrote a number of well-received essays for New Left publications. Despite the power and originality of these interventions, it would have seemed perverse at the time to suggest that within a couple of years of writing these articles he would inherit the editorial chair of the New Left's most influential journal, *New Left Review (NLR)*, and from then onwards would play a pivotal role in turning a magazine in crisis into the premier journal of academic Marxism in the English-speaking world. However, this is the role that he played in the two decades from 1962. In 1983 he passed on the editors position at the *NLR* to his long time collaborator Robin Blackburn, and shortly afterwards, while remaining on the *Review's* editorial committee, he moved on to take a chair in history at UCLA. In 2000, much to the surprise of the academic Marxist community, *NLR* was re-launched with Anderson back at the helm. However, much had changed in the four decades since he first attempted to reorient the fragments of Britain's first New Left after its collapse in the early 1960s; and while Anderson remained a stern critic of capitalism, he no longer believed that socialism was its viable alternative. Rather, he argued, Marxists should accept that the parameters within which history can turn at the present conjuncture were much more circumscribed than Marx had anticipated: not socialism, but more humane forms of capitalism were the only practical alternative to triumphant neo-liberalism. Following the logic of this position Anderson has argued that while *NLR* should obviously stand against any form of accommodation with capitalism, it should do so without falling into the alternate trap of regurgitating what he regards as ultra-left consolationary rhetoric. *NLR* should, by contrast, face the ruling system with 'uncompromising realism' and 'support any local movements or limited reforms, without pretending that they alter the nature of the system' (Anderson 2000, 14). This perspective is a long way from the Maoism and Guevarism that Anderson briefly espoused in the 1960s, and the Trotskyism that he championed in the 1970s and early 1980s. In this book I aim to trace Anderson's evolution towards that early radicalism with an eye to the ideas and events that influenced his idiosyncratic interpretation of Trotskyism, so as to make sense of, and immanently criticise, his later trajectory and his contemporary political perspective.

But why study Anderson? Two immediate answers spring to mind. First, Anderson has produced, over the last four decades, some of the most important political and theoretical contributions to Marxism in the Anglophone world. Thus, his analysis of Britain's economic and political decline has been highly influential upon those who have argued for constitutional reform in the UK; while he has also published both a seminal work on Western Marxism, and, in an essay on Gramsci, possibly the most sophisticated political critique of the *Prison Notebooks*. In addition to these summits he has subjected British Marxism, through the medium of one of its most illustrious practitioners, Edward Thompson, to its most articulate assessment, and has authoritatively engaged with Parisian irrationalism. Thus far his record is stunning enough, and this is before we mention his magnificent overview of the history of the European State system from classical antiquity to the epoch of bourgeois revolutions. Alongside a seminal essay on modernism and an equally important contribution to the debate over the nature of postmodernity, his *oeuvre* stretches from Plato to Pollock, from Marx to Habermas, and from Alexander to Louis XIV. Not for nothing has he been proclaimed an Olympian.[1]

However, the importance of his own work only constitutes the tip of the iceberg of Anderson's influence on the Anglophone Left: he has also played the key role as 'intellectual gatekeeper', through his editorship of *NLR*, New Left Books, and Verso (Fulbrook and Skocpol 1984). Thus, Anderson's editorial judgements on which Marxists to publish have shaped the way that a generation of left academics has understood historical materialism. Moreover, while Continental theorists helped to shape his Marxism, he and they then helped to shape the Marxism of a much broader range of intellectuals over the last few decades. For it was Anderson's *NLR* that acted for many English speakers as the first source of contact with the work of such Continental sages as Gramsci, Althusser, Colletti, Sartre, Lévi-Strauss, Poulantzas, Marcuse, and Lukács. Anderson's influence has therefore been much wider than even the reception of his own work would suggest; for many who would share few, if any, of his political perspectives have learnt much from the Marxists who were first published in *NLR*, or by NLB and Verso.

However, despite the near universal admiration for his *oeuvre*, Anderson himself remains, as Gregory Elliott attests, something of a mystery (Elliott 1998, xi). Elliott has done something to overcome this enigma in his excellent book *Perry Anderson: The Merciless Laboratory of History*. However, despite the many undoubted strengths of Elliott's work, he is perhaps too close politically to his subject to fully articulate an immanent critique of his ideas. Specifically, Anderson's thought has evolved to accept a highly pessimistic interpretation of the contemporary political conjuncture that Elliott broadly shares. In this book, by contrast, I seek to develop an understanding of Anderson's political and theoretical evolution over the last four decades that is aimed at challenging this reading of the present conjuncture. In this sense my book is a political intervention into the present (Anderson 1980, 2). Methodologically, I locate Anderson's trajectory within the context of debates on the left since 1960, with the aim of developing an immanent critique of it.

This book is organised around analyses of what I believe to be relatively distinct episodes in Anderson's career. I excavate the foundations for the evolution of his Marxism since 1960 in seven broad chapters. Throughout the book I attempt to locate Anderson's political and theoretical trajectory within the context of his relationship to other prominent thinkers. In particular, I show how his Marxism related to the broader academic and leftist milieus around him, and how he both attempted to influence, and was influenced by, these milieus. My thesis therefore operates not simply as a piece of intellectual history, but rather attempts to situate his trajectory within that of the broader culture within which he operated.

In chapter one I examine the evolution of Anderson's Marxism from within Britain's first New Left milieu. In this chapter I stress both the culturalist slant of Anderson's Marxism in this period, and his acceptance of Isaac Deutscher's general interpretation of Cold War politics: a framework that implied his Marxism was necessarily revisionist in a number of important ways. In chapter two I discuss Anderson's attempt to develop a viable socialist strategy for Britain after the collapse of the first New Left. Here I examine his move to incorporate into his understanding of historical materialism ideas associated with a series of Continental theorists – initially Sartre, Gramsci and Lukács – whom he identified as producers of sophisticated theory which British socialists could profitably use to produce a more robust strategic political thought. In chapter three I analyse his move towards revolutionary socialism. We shall see that this trajectory had roots both in Anderson's evolving understanding of Marxism, and in his relationship to the radicalised generation of the 1960s. Specifically, I show how Althusserian Marxism opened a theoretical door to revolutionary politics for Anderson, from which he made an unorthodox Trotskyist interpretation of the upheavals of 1968. In chapter four I discuss Anderson's attempt to utilise his newly developed Marxist framework to formulate a viable revolutionary socialist strategy for the West. In this chapter I argue that the foundations of his new strategic analysis were not as secure as he hoped. In chapter five I outline the politics he developed in an attempt to solve the problem of a viable revolutionary socialist strategy for the West. Here we see a shift in Anderson's theoretical frame of reference as Anglophone Marxists – most importantly G.A. Cohen – begin to take the place at the centre of his interpretation of historical materialism previously occupied by their continental cousins. At this point I analyse Anderson's attempt to formulate a strategic perspective built upon a synthesis of subject and structure in a historical materialist theory of agency. In chapter six I give an overview of Anderson's retreat from revolutionary to reformist politics, showing how his understanding of orthodox Marxism, in the context of a series of defeats for the Western labour movement, the crisis of Keynesianism and the collapse of the Soviet Union, opened up the possibility that his thought might take this particular trajectory. In chapter seven I discuss his analysis of the contemporary political conjuncture, and his attempt to intervene in this culture through the re-launch of *NLR*. I discuss this moment in his career within the context of his move to the American academy from where his key intellectual reference points became Fredric Jameson and Robert Brenner. I conclude with an overview of his theoretical and political trajectory since the 1960s, and argue that while the direction of his political trajectory can be read as a coherent attempt to follow a path suggested to him through a combination of Deutscher's revisions of Marxism, alongside Western Marxist pessimism regarding working-class agency, it is not one that other socialists need to follow.

A Note on the Text

Throughout the text I have assumed Anderson's authorship of the introductory *Themes* sections to the issues of *NLR* that he edited. Anderson has also published a number of anonymous essays in *NLR* and my sources for attributing these essays to him have been substantiated in the text. These anonymously published texts are important to my thesis as they were the only essays that Anderson published between 1968 and 1974: it is essential to analyse these if we are to comprehend his political and theoretical evolution during that period. I have also had access to a number of Anderson's unpublished essays. I have not quoted directly from these texts as they were not written for publication, and, in any case, they do not add substantively to our knowledge of Anderson's oeuvre. I have, however, referenced them sparingly were it has been necessary to substantiate my arguments and claims. In any event, Anderson later published many of the theses developed in these essays in not too dissimilar forms. I have referenced these similarities in the text, and have also summarised some of the arguments of these essays where it help to clarify my argument. Finally, Anderson published two collections of essays in 1992 – *English Questions* and *A Zone of Engagement*. These books contain a range of Anderson's essays that were initially published between 1964 and 1992. Given that these collections are the easiest sources for these essays, it is to them that I have made reference in the text. References to the original publication details can be found in the bibliography.

CHAPTER ONE

ANDERSON AND THE FIRST NEW LEFT

In the 1950s the political bipolarity of the Cold War was refracted within Britain's organised working-class politics through the media of the Communist and Labour parties. The Labour Party, then as now, hegemonised the British left. However, this position did not go unchallenged; in particular the Communist Party (CP), which positioned itself as the left opposition to Labour, was strong within the trade union movement. Unsurprisingly, the CP had long since proved its willingness to perform any number of elaborate political contortions at the behest of its mentors in Moscow, while, more counter-intuitively, the Labour Party leadership had developed a parallel relationship with Washington. This situation was, of course, not conducive to the development of an independent left capable of articulating a political programme that went beyond Cold War dualism.

The Asia-Africa Conference at Bandung in 1955 provided the first sign of an alternative to this bipolar worldview. At this conference, what later became known as the Third World declared itself for the first time as a major independent player in world affairs. If this event opened a crack in the world order, the events of 1956 – Khrushchev's secret speech, his invasion of Hungary and the Anglo-French invasion of Egypt – together created a space for widespread criticism of the world order as a whole. In striking deep at the heart of the international system these events opened a space from which independent political forces could emerge in Britain. As a response a 'New Left' was born which sought to map a third way between the West and the East, and their left-wing political allies: social democracy and Stalinism. Two journals, the *New Reasoner (NR)* and the *Universities and Left Review (ULR)*, which were to merge in 1959 to form *New Left Review (NLR)*, represented the most visible signs of the new space created on the English political scene. However, while the events of 1956 marked the point at which an independent left first emerged in post-war Britain, it was a further eighteen months or so before a movement erupted that offered this milieu the opportunity to test its politics against those of the Labour and Communist Parties. The force that brought a new generation of activists onto the streets, and then into the New Left meeting rooms, was the Campaign for Nuclear Disarmament (CND); whose marches from early 1958 saw thousands of the dissatisfied youth come into conflict, not only with the government, but also with the leaderships of the Labour and Communist Parties.[2] While CND was born as a response to the immediate threat of nuclear war, its membership was forged in large part from a layer created through the preceding social and economic evolution of British society. So, while the post-war economic boom generated previously unheard of levels of affluence, it did so unevenly and within the context of growing structures of international inequality: factors which helped foster an increasing sense of alienation in youth. This context generated its own disillusioned progeny who, in Britain, were personified by Jimmy Porter in John Osborne's play *Look Back in Anger*. Cynical of official politics, this generation provided the base of the New Left, after CND had provided a cathartic release of their frustrations with the status quo that had developed over the preceding decade. Indeed, this constituency provided the material underpinning of the New Left's hope that it might act as both an alternative to the establishment, and to the official organs of the old left.

By 1962 the New Left was – in Britain at any rate – a spent force. Perry Anderson cut his political teeth as one of the younger members of this milieu, and in this chapter I examine his early relationship to the first New Left. However, as the New Left was a broad milieu, I have chosen to examine just those of its constituent elements that were most influential on the development of Anderson's early thought. Specifically, Raymond Williams and Isaac Deutscher helped shape Anderson's political and theoretical horizons. This is not to say that Anderson accepted uncritically every dot and comma written by these thinkers; rather, they tended to frame the culture within which his Marxism developed. In particular Deutscher's view that the Cold War was an inter-systemic conflict, in which socialists should critically side with the East, became a long-term identifying motif of Anderson's Marxism; while Williams' strategic ideas informed the form, if not the content, of Anderson's early politics.

ANDERSON IN THE FIRST NEW LEFT

The early New Left saw in the delegates at the Bandung conference a possible alternative pole of attraction to the bipolarity of the Cold War. With the goal of following this lead they sought to push British policy makers towards a 'positive neutralist' foreign policy, which would include both a break with NATO, and the formation of alliances with neutral third world states (Worsley 1960). Unfortunately, despite its intuitive appeal, the utopian core of this strategy soon became apparent as Soviet-US tensions increased, the Sino-Indian conflict erupted, and the malign role of the UN in the Congo was exposed. Indeed, in the wake of these events this element of New Left thinking was quickly forgotten (Sedgwick 1976, 142). Regrettably, the New Left did not develop a fully rounded international perspective with which to replace positive neutralism. However, they did maintain a honourable tradition of support for dissident groups in the East, and for national liberation movements in the South; and, in so far as they underpinned this stance with a coherent theory of international relations, this was articulated by Isaac Deutscher.

Deutscher, while not an editor of any of the key journals of the New Left, was nonetheless perhaps the one figure to whom almost all of its key figures looked as an inspiration; both as a lifelong political activist and as one of the most intelligent commentators on Eastern European affairs. Deutscher's background was in the Polish Communist Party and later the Left Opposition, before he parted company with Trotsky over the formation of the Fourth International in 1938 (Deutscher 1987c, 513). As the author of majestic biographies of Stalin and Trotsky, of East European birth, and sharing much of the politics of the New Left, he almost naturally became the New Left's authority on Eastern Europe (Williams 1979, 90; Kozak 1995, 280; Stedman Jones 1972, 109).[3] Thus, he was published in the first issue of the *Universities & Left Review* (*ULR*), and his speech to a *ULR*-organised gathering in April 1957 was perhaps one of the New Left's largest, with more than 600 attending (Dworkin 1997, 56). Moreover, it was from a platform organised by *ULR* that Deutscher famously prophesied the 'red sixties' (Widgery 1974, 132).[4] As early as 1966, Anderson argued 'who would deny that the only Marxist intellectual of world eminence in Britain today is Isaac Deutscher' (Anderson 1966, 23). Two years later Anderson repeated and reinforced this claim when he suggested that Deutscher was 'the greatest living Marxist historian of his time' (Anderson 1992e, 65). Twelve years further on he again wrote that he had taken his 'earliest knowledge of the USSR from Isaac Deutscher' (Anderson 1980, 151).[5] Given the importance of Anderson's interpretation of Stalinism to his subsequent political and theoretical evolution, to understand his Marxism we must first understand Deutscher.

From Deutscher, Anderson learnt that recognising the post-capitalist[6] character of the Soviet Union, implied revising some key tenets of classical Marxism. Deutscher noted that the social transformations in the East European countries and China after the war were very different from that which had occurred in Russia: 'The old Bolsheviks ... believed in revolution from below ... The revolution now carried into eastern Europe was primarily a revolution from above' (Deutscher 1968, 539). In order to maintain the congruence of these two models, Deutscher worked a major transformation of Marxist theory. First, he challenged Marx's understanding of socialist agency. For Marx the heart of socialism was the proposition that the emancipation of the working class is the act of the working class itself (Draper 1978). In arguing that revolutions from above and below were not qualitatively distinct, Deutscher broke with this central tenet of Marxism, and implied that the socialist project has no necessary anchorage in any particular form of agency. Second, Deutscher challenged the traditional Marxist theory of revolution: 'In the classical Marxist scheme of things revolution was to occur when the productive forces of the old society had so outgrown its property relations as to burst the old social framework ... [this] conception of the revolution was thereby turned upside down' by the events of 1917 and 1945 (Deutscher 1987c, 514). The key strength of Deutscher's position was therefore that he understood that accepting a postcapitalist characterisation of the Soviet Union necessarily implied a major revision of classical Marxism. Similarly, Anderson's acceptance of Deutscher's general framework implied that he too would need to revise both Marx's account of socialist agency and his theory of history.

If accepting the socialist nature of the USSR implied a revision of Marxism, so too did the New Left's analysis of contemporary capitalism. Deutscher was strategically silent with regard to socialist practice in the West: indeed his global perspective implied that 'the only dignified attitude the intellectual ex-communist can take is to rise *au-dessus de la mêlée* ... he may withdraw into the watch-tower' (Deutscher 1984, 57). By contrast, the New Left's most eloquent theorists had much to say about strategy in Britain. In particular Raymond Williams mapped the general terrain of New Left strategic thought, to which others added.

The fundamental problem that the New Left faced was how to overcome the apathy of the post-war 'affluent' generation, whose knowledge of the world was increasingly received through the mass media. Williams, in *Culture and Society* (1958) and *The Long Revolution* (1961), attempted to come to terms with the novelty of the post-war world, and to develop a new, non-dogmatic, politics for the left. He challenged the Leavisite distinction between mass civilisation and minority culture, while, condemning Stalinist determinism and its corollary, the patronising view that workers were the mere objects of history. For both Eastern and Western ideologues, Williams argued, workers were transformed into the 'masses', 'a new word for mob ... gullibility, fickleness, herd prejudice, lowness of taste and habit ... a perpetual threat to culture' (Williams 1982, 252 ff & 298). Central to Williams' rejection of this patronising concept was his refutation of narrow and elitist models of culture, and his elevation of the practices of the working class into the realm of the cultural itself. This theoretical manoeuvre had direct political consequences: with Marx and against traditional Western intellectuals, Williams insisted that workers could not be dismissed as a-cultural brutes; however, in opposition to traditional interpretations of historical materialism, he argued that the middle and upper classes had much to offer the socialist movement. In particular, he suggested that bourgeois individualism, once shorn of its possessive aspects, would be a central element of a future socialist culture. Thus, when proletarian collectivism was combined with bourgeois individualism, this could produce a common socialist culture. This combination would not be unproblematic; there would be for instance the difficulty of 'achieving diversity without creating separation'. However, it was not an impossible dream: 'The real barrier is in the mind' (Williams 1982, 334 & 336). Peter Sedgwick suggested that through such formulations Williams replaced a 'conflict model of society (of the sort which has been traditional among socialists and even radical reformers) with a communications model, in which the unity of humankind is primordially broken, not by a clash of rival social interests, but by blockages and faulty linkages in moral perception' (Sedgwick 1976, 137). This theoretical shift was associated with a move by the bulk of the New Left towards an openly reformist political perspective, evidenced in its 1962 submission to the Pilkington Committee on Television.[7] In this submission the dominant New Left approaches to culture and politics were synthesised in a document within which the concept of quality was deployed to criticise the majority of television production, while holding out the possibility that better programmes could be made that could underpin the enlargement of the welfare state into, what McIlroy has called, a 'cultural welfare state' (McIlroy quoted in Kenny 1995, 104). As we shall see, while Anderson did not share the detail of this perspective, Williams' goal of creating a common culture was one that informed his early politics.

After the original explosion of New Left activity at Oxford in 1956, a second, smaller, new wave of leftists, including Anderson, emerged in the university, who, from 1960, published the magazine *New University*. Anderson wrote one essay for the magazine – *Cuba, Free Territory of America* – which was authored jointly with Robin Blackburn and published alongside Anderson's translation of a piece on the Cuban Revolution by Sartre.

Anderson and Blackburn aimed to locate the specificity of the Cuban revolutionary dynamic. The most significant characteristic of the Cuban Revolution, they argued, lay in the lack of an organising party at its centre. The Cubans could win a revolution without a revolutionary party because they had 'an ultra developed system of communications', and 'an extensive professional class, a good many intellectuals and within a strictly limited range, some technicians. These human skills in themselves were enough to mark off Cuba radically from the run of underdeveloped countries'. Indeed, Cuba's free communications network overcame the need for a party, as a free flowing real human interaction introduced a new openness. Similarly, the lack of formal democracy could be explained as a result of the fear of closure through formalisation. The revolution was thus 'a humanism' (Anderson & Blackburn 1960, 18-23).

By contrast with this humanism, Anderson argued, in the first of two essays that he had published in *NLR* under the old committee – *Sweden: Mr. Crosland's Dreamland*, that, despite numerous reforms, alienated social relations dominated the Swedish social democratic state, such that, despite the fact that 'planning in Sweden is one of the points at which the far shore of a socialist community is most evidently almost touched by existing society', class divisions in Sweden remained very real (Anderson 1961a, 8). Moreover, class divisions, in and of themselves, represent a universal loss, which violated all human relations: 'The essence of man is social ... It is only by way of the most delicate and complex responsive relations with others that the individual can achieve fulfilment' (Anderson 1961b, 36). Anderson thus painted a picture of class as a material category through which all of our lives are distorted, irrespective of the particular class to which we belong (Anderson 1961a, 7). The solution to these lacunae in middle and working-class lives was obvious to Anderson. As both sides lost from the class nature of society, both were in a sense one-dimensional, only through their transcendental merging could they become whole. What was to be the medium of this merger? Anderson answered that parliament, rather than any particular institution of the working class, could represent this new form of collectivism: 'the bourgeois institution par excellence, parliament, has proved notably extendable, in fact in a series of ever wider franchises perhaps more recognizably so than any specifically working-class institution' (Anderson 1961b, 36).

Indeed, in contrast to Williams' argument that the Labour Party and the trade unions embodied the collectivist idea, Anderson suggested that these institutions were 'markedly authoritarian'. They were also class restrictive: both were almost wholly working-class organisations. Moreover, the public attitudes of workers could be characterised by 'indifference, intolerance, chauvinism, sexual bigotry, callousness and even relish in social punishment'. Despite this claim, Anderson did not suggest that the proletariat had nothing to offer a new socialist culture: the working class could offer 'a particular affective structure of the family and a particular type of small scale community, which together go to produce the distinctive maturity and emotional weight of so many working people'. By contrast, the middle class combined culture, which they could offer the new society, with a divorce 'from any wholeness of feeling' (Anderson 1961b, 36). So, in his first published essay in *NLR*, Anderson advocated a left parliamentary socialist strategy which would marry the best elements of working and middle-class cultures.

This reformist perspective was developed further in an essay, *The Politics of the Common Market*, jointly authored with *NLR's* original editor Stuart Hall. Together they traced Europe's historical trajectory as a means of mapping a strategic socialist politics with which to answer the issues raised by the formation of the Common Market. This question, they argued, could not 'be solved by an internal struggle on the left. It is an issue before the British people as a whole ... which the British community has to make'. A national debate which 'opens up for the socialist movement in this country the possibility of capturing the initiative' (Anderson & Hall 1961, 1).

Anderson and Hall's subsequent analysis was underpinned by two assumptions. First, the Common Market was 'heavily weighted in the favour of European business'. Second, there was more to the treaty of Rome than its letter; its logic tended towards political as well as economic unification. Membership of the community would 'severely limit the manoeuvrability of any British government, a Labour government most especially'. Thus, reform programmes like those of 1945-48 would be undermined, and, moreover, while authority, in contemporary Britain, lay with parliament, in the Common Market there would be an 'intangible problem of locating power' (Anderson & Hall 1961, 8-9).

Furthermore, any supranational Western European state would formalise the division of Germany and therefore prolong the Cold War for decades. This would occur simultaneously with the acceleration of the integration of Western Europe with America in a low tariff zone, finalising the division of the world into Cold War camps. Such a zone would also, through the colonies, act as a force for the propagation of the market in the Third World, splitting independent states and neo-colonies and pulling the latter into a free trade zone and forcing the former to bargain for neo-colonial status. Europe together would thus act as imperial Europe of old, but would offer a 'more powerful way of controlling the undeveloped countries than any single country could do in the past' (Anderson & Hall 1961, 11-12).

Despite this claim, Anderson and Hall argued that in Britain the ideology of 'Little Englandism' was, for socialists, the main enemy; and that entry into Europe would be a progressive step, if it were the only alternative to the status quo, albeit that it 'may not take us nearly far enough' (Anderson & Hall 1961, 13). However, alternate options did exist, including a minimum and a more radical strategy. The minimum strategy was built upon the foundations set by the policy of 'positive neutralism', and, while moderate, it was important because it would be disastrous to go as we are. Fortunately, Britain's role in the Commonwealth and in the European Free Trade Area (EFTA) had created the basis for 'a genuine internationalism' for the 1970s and 1980s. Links with these countries should be deepened, as EFTA's neutralism, and the links to the emergent nations of the third world through the Commonwealth, could put Britain into a position where it could act as a force for international peace and progress. The more radical programme would join to the Commonwealth and EFTA the independent 'emergent powers' themselves. Together they could pool the world's 'industrial, agricultural and capitalist resources which could be mobilised ... for a common assault ... on common problems' (Anderson & Hall 1961, 14).

Thus, the key barrier to socialist advance at the macro level was seen to be Cold War bipolarity, while at a micro level it was the ideology of 'little Englandism'. Entry into the Common Market was seen as a risky means of undermining 'little Englandism'. In addition to this, a more radical internationalism could open up the possibility of the creation of a non-aligned socialist alternative to the superpower rivalry. Anderson and Hall advocated entry into Europe if that was the only alternative on offer. However, they argued for a socialist solution to Britain's crisis that went far beyond the 'internalism' of the Common Market and those representatives of big business and the government which were in favour of entry (Anderson & Hall 1961, 13). Should socialists form a party to propagate this message? The implication of Anderson's essay on Cuba was that while such an organisation would be unnecessary in principle, in practice it would be essential in Britain. But what sort of party was required? The beginning of Anderson's answer to this question was hinted at in an article that he wrote for the first issue of *NLR* after the bulk of the old board had departed.

In 1992 Anderson noted that alongside a coded contrast between Britain and France, his early work was characterised by a second contrast between continental – particularly Italian – radicalism and English moderation (Anderson 1992a, 6). This contrast is evident in his 1962 introduction to the debates of the central committee of the Italian Communist Party (PCI). Significantly, Anderson gave a positive appraisal of the evolution of the PCI from 1956 to 1961. In 1956 the PCI experienced a flush of independence in the wake of Khrushchev's secret speech, which was rescinded after the Soviet invasion of Hungary. However, after this invasion the tendencies towards democratisation and destalinisation 'discretely and gradually' worked themselves out, to the point where, by 1962, Anderson could claim that the PCI enjoyed a 'political stance which is now absolutely distinctive in the World Communist movement' (Anderson 1962a, 153).

Anderson suggested that it had been the good fortune of the PCI to have 'enjoyed in the writings of Gramsci the unique advantage of a sophisticated and indigenous Italian Marxism' (Anderson 1962a, 152). This ideological legacy furnished the PCI with the theoretical tools necessary to guide it between two alternate unpromising strategies of either revisionist decay into a form of social democracy, or the collapse of the party into sterile sectarianism (Anderson 1962a, 156). Both extremes would have meant that the PCI would forfeit its chance to lead the Italian people to socialism: the first by dropping the struggle for socialism itself; the second by refusing to hegemonise the middle ground in Italian politics.

In this essay Anderson showed that where Deutscher had analysed the regeneration of the Soviet Union under Khrushchev, he perceived in the trajectory of the Italian Communist Party a corollary of this international development. Moreover, in Italy this tendency was more pronounced because, where 'Deutscher had recently remarked that the one thing that these [Soviet anti-Stalinist] ideas lacked was any real focus ... [by contrast] the debate of the Central Committee of the PCI ... had this focus' (Anderson 1962a, 157-160). Thus, in a proto-Eurocommunist argument, Anderson suggested that a socialist transformation of society could be executed by an organisation of a type similar to the regenerated PCI.

PORTUGAL: MARXISM, FUNCTIONALISM AND VOLUNTARISM

As we shall see in the next chapter, the New Left had entered a period of deep crisis by 1962. In this context Stuart Hall resigned as the editor of *NLR* after issue 12. The next issue, which carried Anderson's essay on the PCI, was a double edition, edited by a committee of four that included Anderson and two of his future long-term collaborators.[8] It was with issue 15 that Anderson finally took over the editorial chair of *NLR*. Moreover, it was in this issue that he began to publish the most important work of his early period, *Portugal and the End of Ultra-Colonialism*. In this essay he wove together the various elements of his social theory into a version of Marxism, through which he attempted to examine both the specific characteristics of the developing national liberation movement in Angola – a conflict that was threatening not only the Portuguese empire but also the Portuguese state itself – and any generally relevant lessons that this struggle suggested for other anti-imperialist movements (Anderson 1962d, 83). He concluded, presciently, that the attempted insurrection in Angola of 1961 signalled that 'the end of an epoch is imminent' (Anderson 1962d, 112). While telescoping events somewhat, this prognosis was generally correct. There was, however, a weakness in Anderson's attempt to fully integrate the political, sociological and historical moments of his analysis.

The essay itself is neatly divided into three sections published over three issues of *NLR*, and each corresponding to an element of his Marxism. The first was an overview of the historical trajectory of the Portuguese empire; the second was an examination of the class structure in the empire; and the third an analysis of the national liberation movements erupting within it.

Anderson announced his Marxism in a short methodological note at the end of the essay. Here, he argued, while he appeared to have broken with good academic practice by combining synchronic with diachronic moments of his thesis, his aim was to unite these two elements, the structural and the developmental. Furthermore, the only intellectual system within which the two were united rigorously was Marxism: 'the only thought which has rigorously united developmental and structural analysis: it is at once pure historicity and radical functionalism. This synthesis remains unique'. His essay was thus a self-consciously Marxist analysis, but also one that that owed much to Levi-Strauss (Anderson 1962d, 113 & Anderson 1961b, 36). Indeed, the language that Anderson used to frame his Marxism – 'diachronic' and 'synchronic' – suggested that it was strongly influenced by Lévi-Strauss' structuralism, then hegemonic on the West Bank, as the mood in French intellectual circles had turned away from existentialist Marxism (Poster 1975, 306).

Unfortunately, despite Lévi-Strauss's formal acceptance of the utility of history, 'in reality he has never brought structural analysis to bear on diachronic phenomena' (Merquior 1986, 90). In this sense his thought paralleled that of Saussure, for whom, while the study of the diachronic had in fact contributed to the 'regeneration' of the study of linguistics, the synchronic was the proper area of the scientific study of language: 'the linguist must take the study of linguistic structure as his primary concern' (Saussure 1983, 19 & 25). Regrettably, the dualism between diachronic and synchronic in Saussure's formulation is in practice made 'absolutely insurmountable' (Volosinov 1986, 54). Thus, history was lost from this system. If this was true of both Saussure's and Lévi-Strauss's systems, then it also appeared to be true of Anderson's early Marxism. Indeed, while he criticised Parsons' functionalism, he admitted that his own sociology 'followed a functionalist analysis of the Portuguese colonial system'. This, he admitted, could not 'properly account for the demise of a system'. However, he insisted, 'the lack of documentation of African nations and resistance made this inevitable' (Anderson 1962d, 114). Maybe this was so. The outcome was, however, a functionalism within which Anderson's juxtaposition of history and sociology, while rich in detail, explained nothing of the revolt itself.

Despite this lacuna in his argument, this essay, unlike his earlier texts, was explicitly written as a defence of revolutionary action. Did this mean that, along with his new adherence to Marxism, Anderson had shifted to the left politically? The answer to this question must be a qualified 'no'. For he assumed that the world system was divided into three distinct zones, each linked by 'competitive confrontation', to which three distinct socialist perspectives applied: 'world history is now immediately single and indivisible as never before; but its agents have become multiple' (*NLR* 18 1962, 1).

Following the logic of this suggestion, Anderson signalled the future trajectory of *NLR* in his introduction to issue 20: comparative studies of the advanced capitalist countries were to be undertaken to deepen the internationalist spirit of the British left. Moreover, these studies would 'deepen our understanding of the fundamental structure of capitalism by exploring all its contingent possibilities ... to perceive ... the specific nature of British society today' (*NLR* 20 1963, 1). The culmination of this comparative project was to be Anderson's analysis of English history. The structure of this essay, as we shall see, followed directly from that of the essay on Portugal.

CHAPTER TWO

THE SECOND NEW LEFT

The New Left's rejection of Stalinism after 1956 quickly elided into a rejection of Leninism, which, in turn, slipped into a rejection of the strategy of building any socialist organisation independent of the Labour Party. Indeed, for the main actors of the New Left milieu, Edward Thompson's dismissal of the project of building a distinct New Left organisation after 1956 read as common sense. Thompson famously suggested that 'the New Left does not offer an alternative faction, party or leadership to those now holding the field ... The bureaucracy will hold the machine; but the New Left will hold the passes between it and the younger generation': in fact, Thompson insisted, socialist intellectual work was best accomplished by not joining any organisation (Thompson 1959a, 15-17; 1957, 34). However, in a less well known remark published two years after these early arguments, Thompson, in his parting editorial for the last edition of the *New Reasoner*, before it merged with *Universities and Left Review* to form *NLR*, wrote that 'we think that the time has come for our readers, together with the readers of *ULR*, to pass over from diffuse discussion to political organisation. ... We must now put this thinking to **use**, and carry it outward to the younger generation, and inward to the traditional labour movement. In particular we must establish far more contact between the New Left and the industrial working class' (Thompson 1959b, 5-6). Indeed, Thompson insisted that new activists 'must learn from the steady attention to organisation, and from the true moral realism which has enabled men, year in and year out, to meet each situation as it has arisen' (Thompson 1959c, 55).

This new perspective reflected something of the dilemma in which the New

Left had found itself by 1959: Thompson's rejection of the case for building an independent New Left organisation was progressively coming into conflict with the way that the this milieu was increasingly acting as a *de facto* organisational alternative to both the Communist and Labour parties. This was no truer than in West Fife, where an attempt was made by Lawrence Daly to build an electoral alternative to both the Labour and Communist parties (Kenny 1995, 40). The New Left generally supported this development, but this support was equivocal. John Saville, for instance, argued that it was the unique features of West Fife's political culture that facilitated Daly's stand, and he concluded therefore that no national generalisation of Daly's strategy could be justified (Saville 1959). Many of the New Left's leading intellectuals followed Saville, to argue that while they would support Daly, this did not imply a universal break with the Labour Party. Moreover, this tactical perspective was lent something of a reformist theoretical strategic underpinning by Thompson, who, despite his revolutionary rhetoric, imagined a very unrevolutionary 'peaceful' British revolution (Thompson 1960a, 302).

In fact, by 1960, Thompson suggested that it was not only possible to transform the Labour Party into an agency of socialist advance, but that this potential was being realised as he wrote: 'Labour is ceasing to offer an alternative way of governing existing society, and is beginning to look for an alternative society' (Thompson 1960b, 19). He argued, therefore, that the New Left's role should be to encourage this process, while remaining aware that if his more optimistic scenario for the transformation of the Labour Party was frustrated 'then new organisations will have to be created' (Thompson 1960b, 29). So, by the late 1950s Thompson, and the mainstream within the New Left, had moved to accept both the viability and desirability of working to transform the Labour Party into an organisation capable of realising the transition to socialism. This optimistic appraisal of the prospects for reforming the Labour Party inclined the New Left activists to throw themselves into the fight against the Party's right wing after Labour's defeat in the 1959 general election. Thus, 'many who had previously been sceptical of Labour became involved in the struggle to convert the party to unilateralism after 1959: a trend that was reinforced by the appearance of a new, radical edge to Labour's rhetoric after 1960' (Kenny 1995, 131 & 43).

Unfortunately, at its heart, this perspective greatly underestimated the power of the right wing of the Party machine. Indeed, the entire perspective collapsed in 1961, when, at that year's Labour Party conference in Scarborough, the left was crushed on the issue of unilateral nuclear disarmament by the votes of the trade union bureaucracy (Cliff & Gluckstein 1996, 274-6; Anderson 1965a, 9). This defeat need not have spelt the end of the New Left, had it not previously fixed its colours so firmly to the mast of Labour Party reform in the years up to 1961. Regrettably, it had, and therefore the defeat of the Labour left at that year's conference entailed the subsequent collapse of the New Left.[9] The defeat at Scarborough was all the more dispiriting for the New Left as it came in the wake of two years of almost continuous advance in the Party: as Raymond Williams remembered it 'the reversal of the vote on nuclear disarmament in 1961 came as an astounding blow. There was no idea of the strengths of the labour machine, or of the political skill with which the right was able to organise for victory within it' (Williams 1979, 365). This defeat, according to Peter Sedgwick, marked the end of the first New Left as a political movement (Sedgwick 1976, 134 & 144).

TOWARDS WESTERN MARXISM

Anderson's response to the crisis of the first New Left was qualitatively superior to that of most other mainstream members of that milieu. These, beyond a minority that joined one or other of the Trotskyist groups, generally either drifted out of politics or, more likely, into an expanding academy; while he, by contrast, attempted to place British socialist strategic thinking on a firmer theoretical footing. As we noted in the last chapter, Anderson had called for the publication of a series of comparative studies of the advanced capitalist countries from which to found a strategic politics in those states. The culmination of this process was the publication of his essay, *Origins of the Present Crisis*, in 1964.[10] In *Origins*, and a series of connected essays, Anderson sought to locate the source of the contemporary crisis of British capitalism within the context of its historical trajectory. Second, he attempted to outline Britain's sociological structure with the aim of examining the mechanisms through which this affected the crisis. Third, he developed a political programme that was grounded in these historical and sociological analyses. Moreover, he did all of this from a perspective that was synthesised from insights borrowed from a number of 'Western Marxists'.

The theoretical structure of *Origins* is only implied within the text itself: Gramsci is mentioned once, while Sartre receives two footnotes and Lukács, Magri and Merleau-Ponty one each. However, in *Socialism and Pseudo-Empiricism* (1966) Anderson defended the peculiar application of 'Western Marxism' deployed in *Origins* to examine English history and society, and thus made his debt to these thinkers more explicit. Moreover, he defended his decision to look abroad for inspiration, as 'in Britain ... there has been no coherent Marxist thought at all'. Western Marxism was not, however, a homogeneous tradition – 'the preoccupations and accents of Lukács, Gramsci and Sartre alone differ enormously' (Anderson 1966, 31-2) – but Anderson did attempt to weave a coherent theory from insights of several of its leading representatives.

Isaac Deutscher criticised *Origins* as a 'national nihilist' work (Anderson 1992a, 5); by which he meant that Anderson, in his understandable desire to overcome the strategic weaknesses associated with the New Left, had unwarrantedly dismissed much of Britain's socialist heritage. This criticism speaks to a valid limitation in Anderson's work, but what is striking to the contemporary reader of *Origins* is precisely its silent national frame of reference. This, as Bob Looker has argued, was the common sense which united both Anderson, and his main domestic critic, Edward Thompson. Despite the seeming gulf between their works, 'Anderson and Thompson both saw "the national" as the natural – hence unexamined – level at which to debate the issues' (Looker 1988, 28). Anderson took this national frame of reference from Sartre, Lukács and above all Gramsci (cf Anderson 1992a, 3-4). These in *The Communists and Peace, The Destruction of Reason* and the *Prison Notebooks* had all attempted to analyse the specificities of their own national social formations, so as to better underpin more viable domestic socialist politics. Anderson's immediate goal, as he took over the reins of *NLR*, was to follow this lead.

The Communists and Peace, published in *Les Temps Modernes* between 1952 and 1954, was Sartre's attempt to historically underpin his fellow-travelling relationship to French Communism in the mid-1950s. That Anderson took up its themes is indicative of just how far he had retreated from the early attempts of the New Left to develop an independent left in Britain after 1956, for Sartre himself rejected this approach for a more explicitly anti-Stalinist and independent position after 1956 (Sartre 1969). It is therefore somewhat ironic that Anderson looked to Sartre's pre-1956 politics to underpin a socialist strategy for Britain in the 1960s.

Sartre argued his case in an exchange with 'Germain': Ernest Mandel. Paralleling many British socialist critiques of the Labour Party, Mandel had argued that the French Communist Party (PCF) had, on a number of occasions since the Second World War, done 'violence to the instincts and the revolutionary dynamism of millions of militants' (Sartre 1968, 105). If this were true, then Sartre, as a principled socialist, would have been compelled to realign himself with the independent left. To preclude what was to him, at the time, such an unpalatable conclusion, he set about trying to show that far from betraying the French working class, the PCF faithfully represented that class. Thus, in contrast to what he suggested was Mandel's Trotskyist 'idealism', Sartre argued, 'I don't concern myself with what would be desirable nor with the ideal relationship which the party-in-itself sustains with the Eternal Proletariat; I seek to understand what is happening in France today before our very eyes' (Sartre 1968, 120).

To be bourgeois, asserted Sartre, was easy; one simply needed to choose the right parents and then to exist. To be proletarian, on the other hand, a worker must, by contrast, fight against his existence: there must be praxis. Moreover, this praxis must have an organisational form, and this must be a political party: unions could not play this role because they reflected only the sectional interests of the workers, and fought merely with effects rather than causes (Sartre 1968, 128 & 181). However, Sartre went beyond even this radical claim to argue that 'without the CP the French Proletariat would not have an empirical history' (Sartre 1968, 134). Thus, to criticise the bureaucratisation of the CP was anachronistic; the PCF merely reflected the state of the workers' struggles, and if the workers threw up bureaucratic structures then so be it: these are proved necessary by their existence (Sartre 1968, 213). Thus, in contrast to Mandel's claims about the revolutionary nature of the working class, Sartre maintained that a concrete analysis of the peculiarities of French history was essential if the left was to understand the peculiarities of France's class struggle (Sartre 1968, 134-5). The detail of Sartre's historical analysis need not detain us; suffice to say that the history he painted was, prefiguring Anderson's history of England, a totalised process which provided the basis for the particular French psyche.[11]

Paralleling Sartre's history of France, Lukács detailed a totalised national history of Germany, as a means of firmly underpinning contemporary politics. In *The Destruction of Reason* (1954), he examined Germany's national characteristics, with a view to explaining the rise of the Nazis. Lukács accepted the Stalinist claim that Nazism represented the interests of monopoly capital, but attempted to overcome the crudities of this argument through an analysis of the growth of an irrationalist ideology in Germany from the nineteenth century onwards. However, while his model was undoubtedly more sophisticated than the orthodox Stalinist interpretation of the rise of Hitler, *The Destruction of Reason* paralleled the traditional Stalinist interpretation of this process in explaining Hitler's victory as an inevitable consequence of the telos of German history, against which the left – and here he influenced Anderson's later resignatory analysis of British politics – was powerless to resist (Lukács 1980, 76-7).

If Sartre's and Lukács' ideas informed Anderson's thesis, Gramsci was the most important influence on Anderson's thought in this period. Indeed Anderson has explicitly acknowledged that, in the early 1960s, *NLR* 'found in Gramsci two central themes which spoke to our situation. He was the first Marxist to trace the national features of his own capitalist society back to the peculiar forms, as he saw it, of the bourgeois revolution which had ushered it in; and the first revolutionary to acknowledge the need for a specific strategy for socialism in the industrialised West, after the advent of universal suffrage' (Anderson 1992a, 3).

It was Gramsci's critique of Trotskyism that most appealed to the young

Anderson. Regarding the Comintern 'debate' over Trotsky's theory of permanent revolution, Gramsci suggested that each Western state had a peculiar structure of hegemony, which in turn necessitated a specific national strategy for socialism. Thus, Stalin had asked the right questions when examining the relations between the international situation and 'national aspects', while Trotsky's analyses were too general and 'cosmopolitan' (Gramsci 1971, 240 and 237). Therefore, in contrast to his understanding of Trotsky, and with infinitely more skill than Stalin, Gramsci sought to underpin national socialist strategies with sophisticated analyses of national hegemonic structures; understood as the products of national histories.

Gramsci argued in the *Prison Notebooks* that in Italy, and more generally across the West, it was through intellectuals that the system of hegemony operated within civil society; they 'are the dominant group's deputies exercising the subaltern functions of social hegemony and political government' (Gramsci 1971, 12). Gramsci argued that if revolutionaries were to win the struggle for socialism they should therefore engage in a two-sided struggle, both against the state, and against the influence of bourgeois ideas within civil society (Gramsci 1971, 19-20). However, the revolution, which Gramsci analysed, was the Italian Risorgimento: a 'passive revolution', through which the Italian bourgeois intelligentsia had formed a counter-hegemonic bloc to win their bourgeois revolution (Gramsci 1971, 105 ff). Gramsci generalised from this case to suggest a universal distinction between corporate and hegemonic classes: the former, epitomised by the American trades unions, existed as a distinct class in society which had no pretensions to political power; a hegemonic class, by contrast, was one which challenged for political power both ideologically and economically. Moreover, unsystematically in the *Prison Notebooks*, Gramsci compared the passive revolution with the Marxist concept of the united front, to suggest that the Russian Revolution had marked 'a decisive turning point in the history of the art and science of politics', after which wars of position replaced violent revolutions as the medium of social transformation. So, Gramsci (in some formulations at least) argued the concept of the passive revolution, taken from his reading of Italian history, could be utilised to help explain the structure of the (passive) socialist revolution in the West (Gramsci 1971, 235). This perspective was especially important in informing the proto-Eurocommunism of Anderson's *Problems of Socialist Strategy*.[12]

In synthesising these elements to produce his own interpretation of Britain's decline, *Origins* was a bravura display of both Anderson's intelligence and his grasp of contemporary political thought. Moreover, it is an article whose influence can still be felt on political debates today.[13] Ironically, however, despite both the breadth of continental sources registered by Anderson in his attempt to formulate a new programme for the left, and the rancour of the polemic to which Edward Thompson would subject *Origins*, the actual political conclusions to which he gravitated were to all intents and purposes identical to those held by Thompson. In particular, both had, by 1963, come to the conclusion that Harold Wilson was to act as the agent of the first steps of the socialist transformation in Britain.[14] *Origins* is therefore perhaps of more interest for the theoretical influences that shaped its execution and for its analysis of English society, than it is for the rather anodyne short-term political conclusions to which Anderson gravitated in this period. However, as we shall see, his longer-term political programme was much more interesting.

A HISTORY OF ENGLAND

Anderson began *Origins* with a critique of all previous works in English which had discussed Britain's widely experienced crisis. Listing several, he described them as 'ephemeral in the most literal sense: they have no historical dimension'. This, he argued, was not only true of those works written by authors of the right, but also of the, more useful yet still ultimately flawed, works of left-wing critics such as Anthony Crosland and Raymond Williams: these had all produced mere sociology. And while they had met with more or less success in uncovering various elements of Britain's social structure, none had developed a total structural analysis of contemporary Britain. Anderson set out to correct these errors. His aim was to outline, schematically and in approximate form, 'the global evolution of the class structure ... the anchorage of any socialist theory of contemporary Britain' (Anderson 1992d, 15-16).

Anderson's history of England, is a history of the failure of the British bourgeoisie fully to modernise the British state, and, as a corollary of this, it is a history of the aristocracy's successful struggle to maintain its control over the levers of state power (Johnson 1980, 59 & 61). England, Anderson wrote, 'had the first, most mediated, and least pure bourgeois revolution of any major European country'. Furthermore, this revolution represented not the triumph of a new bourgeoisie, but rather the victory of one segment of the landowning aristocracy over another. Indeed, the civil war was fought 'primarily ... within and not between classes'. Moreover, while the parliamentary landlords were capitalists they did not constitute a bourgeoisie. So while the revolution broke the obstacles to capitalist advance, it did so without altering England's 'social structure', such that, consequentially, a pre-capitalist ideology remained hegemonic: 'The ideological legacy of the revolution was almost nil ... Puritanism was a useless passion' (Anderson 1992d, 17-19).

So much for the English Revolution, Anderson then moved from the seventeenth century to the nineteenth in his search for the next key conjuncture through which he explained the present malaise. It was at this juncture that the distinction that he drew between the bourgeoisie and the capitalists took centre stage. England had experienced industrialisation, and thus the growth of an industrial bourgeoisie, in a period of growing international political reaction. The threat of Napoleon, coupled with that of a rising working class, had pushed the leadership of the bourgeoisie towards a rapprochement with the capitalist aristocracy, creating in the English ruling class a 'unique fusion' of aristocracy and bourgeoisie (*NLR* ed. 1965, 19).[15] While this fusion was premised upon these global processes, it was mediated through the education system. The Arnoldians created a new 'gentleman' in the public schools in the second half of the nineteenth century as the bourgeoisie ran out of oppositional steam after the repeal of the corn laws in 1846, allowing the aristocracy to become their 'vanguard' (Anderson 1992d, 22). The repeal of the Corn Laws was another pivotal point in Anderson's 'conjunctural constellation', for it was at this point that the bourgeoisie ended its crusade against aristocratic privilege and sold its birthright for title and land. It was able to do this because, while the aristocracy was not a bourgeoisie, it was a capitalist class. Thus, 'no fundamental antagonistic contradiction between the old aristocracy and the new bourgeoisie' existed (Anderson 1992d, 20). In this, Anderson suggested, lay 'the most important single key to modern English history'.[16]

The corollary of England's early industrialisation was the growth of the world's first proletariat. Unfortunately, this proletariat was 'premature', for it developed before an indigenous socialism had time to mature. Too early for Marx, the English workers were thus intellectually ill-equipped to take on the British state in the great battles of Chartism. Tragically, therefore, Chartism ended in defeat. After 1848 there was a 'caesura' in British working-class life, so that when proletarian militancy did again spring up at the end of the century, the key beneficiary was Labourism not Marxism. Labourism was itself underpinned by imperialism, as, between the eras of Chartism and the New Unionism, Britain had moved onto an imperial footing. Moreover, while imperialism was a capitalist phenomenon, by extolling the virtues of militarism, it reinforced and set the 'personality type of the governing class' as 'aristocratic, amateur and "normatively" agrarian' (Anderson 1992d, 23-24).[17] Thus imperialism was the third conjuncture in Anderson's constellation that fixed Britain's aristocratic class in a hegemonic position. For imperialism swept all classes and parties along in its train, ideologically incorporating them into the aristocratic worldview: a process reflected in the new religion of monarchy which swept through Britain from around 1880 until the First World War. The bourgeoisie, cowed after 1846, was finally incorporated during this period of imperial expansion under the Queen Empress. Similarly, the working class was caught up in the imperialist enthusiasm in the last decades of the nineteenth century. Anderson was aware of the existence of anti-imperialist tendencies on the left, but ignored them, describing the organisations that extolled these beliefs as sects. These failed traditions thus played little part in his analysis of Britain's crisis. By way of contrast, he noted the strong Marxist influence on the formation of the modern labour movements in Germany, France, Italy and Sweden (Anderson 1992d, 27).

Finally, Anderson stressed that, alone of the European states, England had suffered no defeat or revolution between 1914 and 1945. Ironically, the defeats suffered by the other European powers, coupled with their experience of revolutionary upheavals, led to the modernisation of these states. Thus, while all around were modernised, England was never forced to break with the past. The resultant continuation of the hegemony of the aristocracy, Anderson suggested, was reflected in the choice of the Conservatives rather than the Liberals as the natural party of government in the twentieth century. Indeed, while England's economic base had been transformed over the last few centuries, its superstructure remained intact. The economy was a bastion of industrial capitalism, but the aristocracy had managed through a cumulative series of four favourable conjunctures to maintain its hegemony over the whole of society. Workers, meanwhile, had been industrially militant, but had never challenged for leadership of the state: they were 'separate but subordinate' (Anderson 1992d, 29).

ENGLAND'S SOCIAL STRUCTURE

Anderson's history of England ended with the ideological incorporation of both the industrial bourgeoisie and the proletariat into the worldview of the aristocracy. It was upon this historical footing that he then attempted to outline a powerful sociological analysis of Britain. He initiated this project with an explicit acknowledgment of one theoretical debt, and an implication of a second. Gramsci, he suggested, provided the best possible model for explaining the English social structure: 'The power structure of English society today can be most accurately described as an immensely elastic and all embracing hegemonic order'. He went on to define hegemony as 'the dominance of one social bloc over another, not simply by means of force or wealth, but by a social authority whose ultimate sanction and expression is a profound cultural supremacy' (Anderson 1992d, 30). If Anderson made his debt to Gramsci explicit in this section of *Origins*, the section subtitle, '*History and Class Consciousness: Hegemony*', strongly implied a Lukácsian frame of reference. In *History and Class Consciousness* Lukács argued that, as the bourgeoisie had come to power both as an ideological and an economic force, it was essential for the proletariat to challenge it at these two levels (Lukács 1971, 65 & 69). Moreover, while, at the time that he wrote *History and Class Consciousness*, Lukács expected the proletariat to play a revolutionary role, he also postulated the possibility that it might not. In periods of transition, he suggested, there occurs both a 'qualitative increase in the forms of reification', while simultaneously, 'there is the increasing undermining of the forms of reification'. Indeed, 'as [this] antagonism becomes more acute two possibilities open up for the proletariat. It is given the opportunity to substitute its own positive contents for the emptied and bursting husks. But also it is exposed to the danger that for a time at least it might adapt itself ideologically to conform to these, the emptiest and most decadent forms of bourgeois culture' (Lukács 1971, 208). At a juncture of this type, Lukács posited, 'decisive will be the role played by ideology in determining the fate of the proletarian revolution' (Lukács 1971, 261-2). Thus Lukács marries the Marxist category of revolutionary proletariat, with an explanation for non-revolutionary proletarian behaviour, even in periods of crisis. This insight, alongside Gramsci's demarcation between hegemonic and corporate consciousness, provides part of the basis of Anderson's critique of Williams' conceptualisation of working-class culture (Anderson 1992d, 36). For while Anderson accepted that proletarian culture was dense; in contrast to Williams, he maintained that the British working class was a corporate body, securely locked into the system of hegemony.

Anderson argued that this hegemonic order was mediated through at least four elements: social relations, ideology, leadership and rejects. The social relations, to which Anderson alluded, was the peculiar manner in which Britain's social structure was, and is, dominated by 'a seemingly feudal hierarchy of orders and ranks'. These relations acted as a 'powerful mystification of real social relations'. So, although workers spoke a language of 'them and us', their leaders 'tended to absorb false, feudal consciousness' (Anderson 1992d, 30-31). Therefore, when workers and their party attacked 'snobbery' etc. in English society their grievances had been displaced from the real relations that oppressed them towards mythological foes.

As to the second of these elements, Anderson suggested that the English ideology was characterised by its adherence to traditionalism and empiricism: with the former deriving from the aristocracy, while the latter was the immature offspring of the bourgeoisie. These, together, trapped England in the past, as traditionalism linked the present with a mythological history, while empiricism tied the future to the present (Anderson 1992d, 31). The leaders of this nation were furthermore a product of the empire. This fostered a 'patrician political style', as action counted for nothing while gesture made the man. The amateurism of the English upper class, Anderson suggested, was both a consequence of this style, and helped prevent the English ruling class from breaking out of its historic decline.

There had been one attempt made to furnish a total bourgeois ideology which aimed to oust this system: utilitarianism. However, this ideology was rejected, and never became hegemonic. Its failure reflected both the weaknesses of the nineteenth-century bourgeoisie, and also its own internal weakness as an ideology. Too bleakly materialistic, utilitarianism was prevented '*ipso facto* from creating that cultural and value system which is the mark of a hegemonic ideology' (Anderson 1992d, 32).

How did this system of hegemony operate inside the working class? Developing themes gleaned from Gramsci, and in opposition to Williams' interpretation of working-class culture, Anderson answered that English working-class life was characterised by 'an unmovable corporate class consciousness and almost no hegemonic ideology' (Anderson 1992d, 33). Two forces tended in this direction: the first was the intensity of the 'them and us' ideology, which prevented the English proletariat from developing a 'universal ideology'; second, no major group of intellectuals had moved to join the labour movement to help it form such a universal ideology. Both of these forces were determined by the overall structure of the system of hegemony; for as it was forced to make its own way in a pre-Marxist world, the English proletariat had relied on its own meagre resources, which proved inadequate to the task of creating a socialist ideology. Meanwhile, no alternative intelligentsia had been allowed to develop in England beyond the aristocratic leadership. Thus, the intelligentsia was 'homogeneous and cohesive'. Cowed by the experience of the French revolution, the English bourgeoisie and its intellectuals thus offered the proletariat no ideology from which it could underpin its struggle for hegemony. What the workers did get through the Fabians was a second-rate version of utilitarianism – 'the most stunted bourgeois ideology of all'. In England, therefore, 'a supine bourgeoisie', Anderson famously wrote, 'produced a subordinate proletariat' (Anderson 1992d, 35).

The subordination of the working class was primarily ideological. So, Anderson explained, the economic power of the British proletariat had been incorporated into the state, and thus did not pose a threat to bourgeois hegemony: dense workers' organisations exist but the will to universalise these institutions 'has only rarely existed' (Anderson 1992d, 36). Anderson therefore suggested, paralleling Sartre's argument noted above, that such famous defeats for the labour movement as 1926, 1931 and 1951 could not adequately be described as betrayals. More accurately, he argued following Tawney's analysis of 1931, defeat 'was in the logic of history' (Anderson 1992d, 38). This argument reinforced Anderson's claim that those left groups which had fought for another goal, most importantly the Communist Party in the 1920s, were in fact sects that did not represent real social forces in the labour movement. Labourism was the organic expression of the English working class and was ideologically incapable of overcoming the structural limitations of English society. This, Anderson suggested, may have been unfortunate, but it was the only realistic assessment upon which a left-wing politics could be based.

Therefore, Anderson concluded, the 'hegemonic system works as a total order ... Democracy was the ransom of hegemony' (Anderson 1992d, 42). However, democracy mystified the real location of power; this did not lie in parliament but followed the Conservative Party in and out of office. If they were in No 10 then that was the seat of power, if they were in opposition then they exercised their power from elsewhere. Moreover, parliamentary democracy existed within a peculiar English power structure, a 'triangular topography'. Power in all Western countries was polycentric, however, in each country this structure was unique. In Britain the triangular topography was made up of, first, a relatively insignificant bureaucratic and military strut: a consequence of Britain's peculiar island history. Second, there was an immensely strong economic strut, which controlled parliament via such mechanisms as the 'flight of capital'. In Britain, and in the West more generally, it was, however, mainly through a third strut, the 'means of communications', that power was exercised (Anderson 1992d, 41 & 39).

Specifically in England the public school and university system, coupled with the oligopoly of the press, 'is decisive for the perpetuation of the hegemony of the "upper class"' (Anderson 1992d, 41). So the legislature, nominally unconstrained by a written constitution, is, in practice, more constrained than any other. Parliamentary sovereignty was thus an illusion, which masked the real structures of power in Britain. So, while the capitalist aristocracy had allowed the franchise to be extended, it had done so precisely because it understood that it had developed such an effective mechanism of ideological incorporation, such that workers, and the bourgeoisie before them, could not conceive of a qualitatively different world. This hegemonic order was not, however, absolutely inelastic. Rather, it allowed shifts to the left and right – for instance, the 1945 Labour government shifted the order to the left. However, these shifts occurred within an overall 'equilibrium' which was 'crushingly capitalist', and from which no easy escape was possible.

ANDERSON'S POLITICS

The political conclusions outlined in *Origins* were developed at the highest level of abstraction; detail was provided in two further articles written by Anderson over the next year, *Critique of Wilsonism* and *Problems of Socialist Strategy*. These two essays served distinct purposes. The first was designed to inform contemporary socialist attitude to the Labour government; while, the second outlined the elements of a future possible socialist practice, once one had become feasible in a modernised Britain. Interestingly, these political essays were not reprinted alongside *Origins* and the rest of Anderson's articles on English history and politics in the 1992 collection, *English Questions*. As Gregory Elliott has argued, this is a significant fact if only because the exclusion of these essays from *English Questions* obscures the transformation in the nature of Anderson's project between the 1960s and 1990s (Elliott 1998, 31). In the 1960s, Anderson's historical and sociological essays were written to clarify a viable socialist strategic perspective. However, with the publication of *English Questions*, Anderson appears to have accepted that this project was no longer viable. Interestingly this was the implied conclusion of his analysis in *Origins*. In this section I discuss how he was able to draw optimistic political conclusions from his pessimistic analysis of Britain's history and sociology.

In *Origins*, Anderson argued that English society, in the post-war years, was experiencing increasing 'entropy' as a consequence of the relative decline of Britain's economy (Anderson 1992d, 43). There were a number of reasons for this condition. Britain was running against an international statist economic tide, while the City had become a yoke around the neck of industry as its international orientation drained resources away from the national economy. Furthermore, the City and Treasury were staffed by the old amateurish aristocratic class who were quite unfit for the job of rational management of the economy. Meanwhile, British managers had sold their bourgeois instincts 'for the accent of a gentleman'. Additionally, domestic plant had never been destroyed during the two world wars and, therefore, British industry had never been forced to modernise on a scale comparable to its continental competitors. Finally, the British elite had missed its one chance to extricate itself from this mess when, in 1957, it turned down the offer of a leading role in the newly formed Common Market. With her eyes still firmly fixed on empire, Britain missed its opportunity to 'renovate ... without a major political and social crisis at home' (Anderson 1992d, 45).

This did not imply that Anderson believed that Britain was doomed to disintegrate. Rather, as the crisis was forcing difficult questions on the British elite it opened up a space for a realistic socialist intervention into contemporary politics. As we saw in his essay on Europe, Anderson believed that it was the duty of the left to offer realistic solutions to national political problems, and in 1964 he believed that a realistic left alternative to the growing entropy would address two problems. First, it could prescribe the necessary conditions for the modernisation of Britain; second, this modernisation would not only solve the contemporary economic crisis, it would also create the necessary political conditions out of which a potentially hegemonic left could evolve. Thus, the crisis of the 1960s had, for the first time, created an opportunity for the left to influence policy – though not an opportunity for socialist advance. The left could, in these circumstances, attempt to complete 'the unfinished work of 1640 and 1832', with the longer-term project of the socialist transformation of Britain deferred until this initial stage had been completed.

The British state was therefore in need of modernisation. Whether or not this option was chosen was not written in the stars, but depended on the actions of millions of individuals. Anderson's view was that the left should not condemn itself to irrelevance by ignoring this debate. Indeed, he stressed that it would be fatal for the left to indulge in ultra-left posturing, rather it should support any modernising forces; and in 1964 this meant that Anderson argued that the left should support Wilson. However, Wilson was not to be supported uncritically; whenever he retreated from the modernisation project, the duty of socialists was to use all means available to push him back in line.

Anderson's essay, *Critique of Wilsonism*, was offered as an 'immediate analysis and criticism of the Labour programme'. Wilsonism was made possible as Wilson stepped into the 'geo-political space' created for European Socialism by the dissolution of the Cold War. Wilsonism, moreover, had gone some way to realise the potential latent in this situation: it was not simply a programme, it was 'first and foremost a strategy' that centred on Wilson's 'acute perception' of the nature of the contemporary crisis. Specifically, Anderson believed that Wilson aimed to prise Britain's intellectuals from the conservative bloc that underpinned the existing hegemonic structure. Indeed, he saw both Wilson's attacks on the amateur aristocratic establishment, the parasitical speculators, and his stress on the need to modernize Britain, as dovetailing neatly with his own Marxist prescriptions for Britain (Anderson 1964, 4-5).

However, a danger existed. Even as the status quo had been found wanting, the old ideology and social relations remained strong enough to displace the Labourist offensive against it. Indeed, Anderson noted that Wilson himself had a tendency to wax lyrical about precisely those pre-capitalist anachronisms in British society which deflected proletarian anger away from its real source; while he 'sounds most socialist when he is talking of the indeterminate distant future' (Anderson 1964, 11). Anderson then listed the limitations of Wilson's manifesto with regard to public ownership, land and housing, education, planning and foreign policy.

In each case the vagueness of Wilson's programme was noted. Thus, even on education policy, which Anderson saw as 'the lynchpin of the whole system of hierarchical discrimination and inequality', Wilson made only general statements regarding the possibility of ending of the public school system (Anderson 1964, 15). Moreover, even these promises were softened because they were incorporated into his proposal to establish an Educational Trust, which would be limited to making policy recommendations. Similarly, with regards to foreign policy, Wilson showed no sign of opposition to US imperialism. However, while there was a disquieting silence on colonial issues, Anderson did take some heart from the aid programme promised to the Third World, and Wilson's view that trade inequalities with the South should be overcome (Anderson 1964, 17).

Given such shortcomings, it would seem only natural that Anderson should resolutely criticise Wilson. Indeed, he claimed that the responsibility of any socialist must be to 'take their distance from the Labour programme and criticise it from a fully independent perspective' (Anderson 1964, 20). However, the logic of his own analysis undermined the resolve of his critique. For his history, as we have seen, suggested that the Labour Party was the organic party of the English working class. He thus claimed, paralleling Sartre, that 'it is useless to blame Wilson or the Labour Party for their deep-rooted evasions'. Labour's failure was not Wilson's, but was the consequence of the left's inability to transform the party in the 1950s. However, if history had left us with no alternative then what was the function of Anderson's critique? His reply to this criticism was ingenious: 'The very vices of Wilsonism offer the possibility of transcending it' (Anderson 1964, 21).

By contrast with Gaitskell's ideological absolutism, Wilson offered an 'open ended' programme. So Anderson represented Wilson's rhetorical ability to appeal to all people, as a positive advance from previous labour ideologies which had blocked socialist progress: the ambiguities in Wilson's formulations opened a space for the left. Moreover, the new leader himself represented the end of 'the long reign of mediocrity': he was the first capable leader produced by the Labour Party in half a century (Anderson 1964, 21). His tempo could help him, as Prime Minister, 'achieve that self renewing momentum, which is crucial to a working-class government in a capitalist environment': Wilson 'as a leader may in the end represent a certain moment in the auto emancipation of the working-class movement in England' (Anderson 1964, 22).

This result was by no means certain; it rested on the left's ability to make concrete demands on the leadership, as and when the moments arose. Maximalist demands were therefore to be rejected in favour of a left reformist critique of Wilson from within the Party that aimed at pulling him in a leftward trajectory: 'It is useless for the left to put forward purely voluntarist demands, which have no point of insertion into the political context of Britain in 1964. Abstract maximalism of this kind is, in the current situation, wholly sterile. On the contrary, at every point the left should try to press demands which are firmly rooted in the present problems and perspectives of the labour movement, but which creatively prolong and surpass them' (Anderson 1964, 23). These demands should be aimed at confronting the power of capital, so that on every area of Labour's official programme the left was to work for the most egalitarian and 'socialist' interpretation of those policies, and push for the implementation of that interpretation. In addition the unions should demand not greater wages but 'workers' control'. At plant level this would act as a prerequisite to incomes policy, and the incorporation of unions into the state at government level. Anderson saw in incomes policies the very real danger of 'extinguishing working-class consciousness and autonomy', however, he believed that this could be outweighed by the gains made by the democratisation of the shop floor (Anderson 1964, 25). Finally, the democratisation and rationalisation of the culture industry would allow for an attack on the modes of communications through which England's hegemonic ideology was reproduced. Practically this meant that Anderson aired his support for the recommendations of the Pilkington Committee on television (Anderson 1964, 27).

NLR's enthusiasm for Wilson was further expressed in two other articles and an editorial written just as Wilson began to settle in at No 10 over the winter of 1964-5. The first published essay was an editorial written immediately after the election victory. Surprisingly, the population as a whole had accepted Wilson much less enthusiastically than had the intelligentsia. Indeed Wilson did not so much win the election – he polled fewer votes than Labour's 1959 total – than Alec Douglas Home, the leader of the Conservative Party, lost it – losing two million votes to the Liberals. In an editorial entitled *Divide and Conquer* Anderson attempted to come to terms with this problem. This article contained two points of note: first, the low Labour vote was seen as a confirmation of Anderson's analysis of the corporate character of the English working class; second, Anderson believed that the low vote could lead, disastrously, to Wilson taking a defensive stance. Fortunately, Anderson noted, Wilson understood that the defensive is the death of the revolution and the only way to break the old order would be to polarise opinion. Labour, Anderson argued, must 'divide and conquer'; that is it must take on the old to draw in and radicalise the proletariat behind it (*NLR* 28 1964, 1-3).

Anderson's orientation towards Wilson was further elaborated in the next edition of *NLR*, published in January 1965. In his essay *The Left in the Fifties* he developed his earlier suggestion that Wilson had taken up the mantle of the New Left. However, his analysis of this phenomenon was designed to facilitate the rebuilding of 'an independent, combative left', rather than to remain transfixed by the glow of Wilson's charisma. Anderson began his analysis by outlining the objective condition pertaining in 1950s Britain – a period when apologists for capitalism had managed both to negatively identify socialism with Stalinism, while positively identifying capitalism with affluence (Anderson 1965a, 3-4). However, affluence did not cure alienation; and CND's popularity was a reflection of this. 'The base of the movement was very different in character [from the leadership]. CND also marked the revolt of great numbers of working class and lower middle class youth against the whole society of which the Hydrogen bomb had become the sanction'. However, while the base of CND was made up of this milieu its leadership came from the tradition of 'authentic English liberalism [which] was fighting its last and most critical battle' (Anderson 1965a, 10). Unfortunately this battle was lost at the Labour Party conference of 1961.

Anderson argued that CND had failed to transform the Labour Party because 'it had been unable to present a coherent and comprehensive alternative to the official policies of the Labour Party'. This reflected liberalism's historic failure to comprehend society as a 'concrete universality'. Practically, CND had failed to recognise that the Cold War had four moments: 'a struggle between capitalist and socialist systems, a conflict between parliamentary and authoritarian political systems, a contest between imperialist and indigenous national systems and a confrontation between technologically equivalent and reciprocally suicidal military systems'. CND had concentrated on just one of these four moments – the last; transforming what was objectively a challenge to the whole of British capitalist society into a moral campaign. This moralism was always susceptible to a nationalist critique, against which CND refused to reply. This pertinent point was weakened because Anderson did not offer a reply himself. He argued that the four moments were not equivalent but then maintained that 'no movement, or man in the torment of the time attained a concrete universality: the truth of the Cold War' (Anderson 1965a, 11-13). The defeat of unilateralism at the 1961 Labour Party conference also reflected the corporate nature of the institutions of the English proletariat, as the medium of CND's defeat in 1961 was the trade union bloc vote (Anderson 1965a, 9). The weakness of the Labour left was that they reflected the corporatism of the class represented by this vote (Anderson 1965a, 18).

The New Left, meanwhile, had outlined a powerful cultural critique of post-war capitalism. Moreover, it did so as the inheritor of Britain's Romantic tradition. Unfortunately, this tradition had always 'remained sociologically disestablished'. Drawn from the elite, the first New Left shared many of its limitations. Most importantly, 'amateurs' ran it, and, correspondingly, as a milieu, rather than a movement, the New Left was eventually paralysed by its own confusions. Its cultural critique of capitalism, while of 'great sophistication and theoretical brilliance', was without any 'programmatic edge'. When the New Left sought to break out of its isolation, as it did in 1960-1, when it intervened in the debates on unilateralism within the Labour Party, the consequence was that it was broken as a movement by the Labour Party machine (Anderson 1965a, 15-17).

Thus, the three strands of the Left in the 1950s – the New Left, CND and the Labour left – had all failed to provide a viable alternative to the status quo. Paradoxically it was just at the point when the Conservatives went into deep crisis that the left had collapsed. The irony of history was thus that, 'the inheritor of the crisis had another name: Wilson' (Anderson 1965a, 18). Wilson had stepped into the fray just as objective circumstances favoured the left, as they had never done before. Anderson believed that Wilson could play the preliminary role of modernising the state before the transition to socialism was feasible. Once this preliminary task had been completed, the real work of socialist reconstruction could begin. Anderson did not, however, totally ignore the 'utopian goal' of socialist advance. Rather, he penned an outline of the sort of party that would be necessary to undertake this task, once Wilson had completed the role prescribed for him. This essay was entitled *Problems of Socialist Strategy* and was published in 1965.

A STRATEGY FOR SOCIALISM

Anderson began *Problems* by distancing himself from the old New Left. They had developed a moral critique of capitalism which lacked strategic focus, while, conversely, he believed, a viable socialist current must, first and foremost, develop a strategic orientation. To develop such a strategy for Western socialists Anderson drew inspiration from Gramsci's delineation between Eastern and Western European states: a difference that was the basis for the divergent political forms that socialist organisation took in the East and in the West. The dichotomy between social democracy and Communism was a false one, for they each developed separately in response to distinct problems. Leninism 'was almost perfectly adapted to the specific conditions of its time and place'. Indeed, it 'represented an immense, Promethean progress for Russia, as it does today for China' (Anderson 1965b, 227-230).

Alternatively, the existence of bourgeois democracy in the West meant that these societies constituted, Anderson argued in Gramscian tones, 'a wholly different universe' (Anderson 1965b, 230). Social democracy was the Western response to this phenomenon, which, regrettably, unlike Leninism, was far from perfectly adapted to its time and place. For where Leninism had created, in albeit distorted forms, socialist societies,[18] social democracy's historical record that was 'arrestingly poor' (Anderson 1965b, 233). The reason for this poor record was centrally rooted in a 'strategic error'. Social democracy had fetishised parliament as the seat of real power in the West, while, in fact, power is much more 'polycentric' in its distribution (Anderson 1992d, 39). Social democracy had thus trapped itself in an electoral game for which the prize was an illusion: 'the heteronomy of the state is the root cause of the failure of social democracy' (Anderson 1965b, 237).

Anderson argued that both Leninism and social democracy were limited by their reified conceptions of the state as the sole seat of power, and while in the East this was partially legitimate, in the West both schools of thought missed the crucial role of civil society in the maintenance of capitalist hegemony. Anderson thus neatly sidestepped the debate between reform and revolution: the long-term goal of socialist transformation in the West could only be achieved by rejecting these two strategies, for the alternative Gramscian project of creating a 'hegemonic party' (Anderson 1965b, 239). But where was such a party to spring from? Anderson answered that potentially the Labour Party could play such a role (Anderson 1965b, 259).

By a hegemonic party Anderson had in mind an organisation that would fight for a socialist culture across the whole range of institutions within civil society as well as the state: 'Its arc of action must embrace not only the bare institution of the state, but the whole complex landscape of civil society as well' (Anderson 1965b, 244). Such a party could not be tied to any one class, and its strategy could not be based primarily on the trade unions – 'a purely working-class party tends, by its very nature, towards either corporatism or outright subordination' (Anderson 1965b, 241). Rather, intellectuals would play a crucial role in the formation of an ideology capable of underpinning a 'new historical bloc' that would draw in wide sections of society beyond the working class (Anderson 1965b, 240-242).

The party must also be a 'prefiguration of the society it sets out to create' (Anderson 1965b, 244). The Labour Party, by contrast, was permanently 'lodged in the social structure of Britain' through its organic links to the working class. This class was corporate and, therefore, so too was the Labour Party. Moreover, those workers who voted for the Labour Party were both less of a percentage of their class, and less enthusiastic than the *haute-bourgeois* supporters of the Conservatives. Moreover, Labour Party membership was dropping, while the leadership had, historically, always suppressed the youth wings of the Party because of their susceptibility to radical influence. The party also had no daily paper, and consequently it had to react to opinion shifts rather than shape them; this was of enormous importance to Anderson given his stress on the centrality of the communications structure as reproducer of the system of hegemony. Additionally, the Labour Party's narrow electoralism was itself a major barrier to the growth of its own mass membership; ordinary folk, it seemed, were less enthusiastic about simply winning seats than were party leaders. Furthermore, these ordinary working people were in large part responsible for the decline in the youth organisations. For the 'proletarian positivity', so respected by Williams, had, as one of its effects, the stifling of the youth (Anderson 1965b, 257). To break from the malaise would take a new ideology – one capable of furnishing a national daily newspaper that sat in style somewhere between *The Guardian* and the *Daily Mirror*. Before he discussed the nature of such an ideology, Anderson examined the social forces capable of challenging the old order.

Anderson began his analysis of Britain's social structure from a perspective independent of both right-wing psephology and left-wing populism. The right understood society to be composed of four distinct groups of electors; the political task was thus to win over the middle ground. Left-wingers, by contrast, talked vaguely of 'people' whose common humanity could be used as a unifying force. In both of these perspectives 'the concrete, determinate reality in either case vanishes' (Anderson 1965b, 259). In place of these abstractions, Anderson sought to unwrap Britain's true social structure. Concretely he analysed the working class, the lower middle class, the intelligentsia and women.

According to Anderson the English working class was a corporate class. Indeed, deference was a characteristic of both Labour-voting and Conservative-voting workers. However, Labour-voting workers had broken from at least some of the worst excesses of bourgeois ideology through their realisation that they were strong only through collective action. The key difference between Labour-voting and Conservative-voting workers was unionisation rates; the higher the rate of unionisation, the higher likelihood of a vote for Labour. Anderson therefore saw in unionisation the basis for a collectivist consciousness inside the working class. 'Unionization changes the consciousness of workers, however imperfectly, and in doing so frees them from the elementary forms of mystification' (Anderson 1965b, 263). Moreover, since Conservative and Labour-voting workers had little differences in economic interest, the key factor that could explain their differential voting patterns was ideological. Workers, he argued, had been won to the unions and thus to Labour through a battle of ideas: 'the struggle to win the Conservative section of the working class can … only be won in the last analysis on the ideological plane' (Anderson 1965b, 283).

However, as the Labour Party and the trades unions were corporate institutions, simple union membership and Labour voting were not in themselves reflections of a socialist consciousness. Fortuitously, there did seem to be a developing consciousness which could hold forth the potential for a future development of socialist consciousness. Lockwood and Goldthorpe had identified the development of what they called 'instrumental collectivism' inside the working class (Goldthorpe & Lockwood 1963). Instrumental collectivism was an ambiguous term that denoted the supposed growth of a 'rational' basis for collective thinking. Previously there had existed 'solidary collectivism' – in essence an uncritical gut-reaction unionism. Instrumental collectivism, by contrast, Anderson argued, was double-edged. On the one hand, it could lead workers to perceive their rational interests to lie in the opposite direction from the development of class-consciousness. On the other hand, it could mean 'for the first time the penetration of reason, of rationality into this closed, affective universe of the workers' (Anderson 1965b, 265). Thus, instrumental collectivism could act to undermine the empiricism and traditionalism at the heart of capitalist hegemony in England. Given that Anderson saw the battle for the hearts and minds of the workers as primarily an ideological affair, this growth of reason could only help socialists win hegemony inside the working class.

Instrumental collectivism was also growing in the second group Anderson chose to analyse – white-collar workers. He began his analysis of this group by rejecting John Strachey's interpretation of their class location as merely another section of the proletariat. They had different life experiences, Anderson argued, and therefore could not be subsumed under the broader rubric of proletarian. Indeed, their shift towards 'instrumental collectivism' did not come from the direction of 'solidary collectivism' but from the opposite extreme, they were abandoning a tradition of radical individualism (Anderson 1965b, 269). Nevertheless, their ideology was converging with that of blue-collar workers, and, as bureaucratisation increased, their status too converged with that of blue-collar workers. Thus, Anderson concluded, like blue-collar workers, 'the key to the consciousness of this stratum, too, lies in the trade unions'. So while white-collar workers may not have been classical proletarians, the changes in the nature of their work and the growth of an instrumental collectivism within the stratum meant that through arguments for unionisation, the door to socialist consciousness could be opened to them.

The third social group that Anderson analysed were the intelligentsia. The groups discussed above represent those whom the Labour Party would have to win to form a permanent majority – the quantitative element in Anderson's analysis. The intelligentsia, by contrast, were, again along Gramscian lines, the ideological producers who would be the 'decisive qualitative dimension' in the formation of the unifying ideology itself. 'The problem of ideology leads directly to the problem of the British intelligentsia', he wrote, 'because of their role as sources of consciousness in society' (Anderson 1965b, 269). This was not to suggest that the British intelligentsia were a particularly sparkling lot. Indeed, he argued, there did not exist in Britain a real intelligentsia at all; surveys of their opinions reflected their 'petty, null philistinism' (Anderson 1965b, 271). Labour, however, must, if it sought to become a hegemonic party, win this group for socialism. It could only do this by working thorough their professional organisations – from the British Medical Association to the National Union of Students – 'to politicise them from within', forming, within each, separate Labour associations to battle for the leadership of these societies. To win such battles, politics must become 'not an abstract allegiance to party, but a concrete programme for the transformation and liberation of their situation'. The main activity for socialists must therefore be 'to make socialism an active, living presence in every intellectual group' (Anderson 1965b, 274 & 276).

The final group in Anderson's analysis of Britain's social structure were women. 'Feminine conservatism' was, he argued, 'one of the greatest single stumbling blocks to the Labour Party'. This problem could be overcome by Labour if, first, it recognised the existence of women's oppression, and, second, it then took up the 'elementary rights of women' in its programme. Again, Anderson saw unionisation as a crucial lever by which the door could be opened to the development of socialist consciousness by women. However, he located the basis for women's oppression primarily in the ideological structure of society, not as an epiphenomenon of material forces: 'It must be recognised that the root of the problem does not lie in the immediate economic interests of women, but in the whole ideology which suffuses their lives'. Anderson suggested that to undermine this ideology 'only a counter ideology which offers a new vision of women's social role and purpose as an integral part of a new vision of culture and society, will liberate women' (Anderson 1965b, 277-278).

Anderson concluded his discussion of England's social structure with the argument that Labour must aim to become a hegemonic party. Unlike the existing Labour Party's fetishisation of parliament, such a party would build an ideology that would be authentic because it would be linked to the real-life experiences in civil society of real people. Thus, the end would be not so much the capturing of parliament or the smashing of the state, as the formation of the party itself. It would be a mass party with a vibrant youth organisation and an imaginative press.

Finally, Anderson addressed what for him was the crucial question – the nature of socialist ideology. Somewhat paradoxically, given his own admission that 'the whole strategy discussed above depends on one immense precondition: a socialist ideology', this is the least satisfying section of the whole essay (Anderson 1965b, 282). For, at just eight pages, the culmination of Anderson's essay was highly schematic. The ideology itself would only be viable if it integrated all national cultural traditions. These he outlined, as we have seen, as a corporate but solidarity-enhancing class consciousness, classical English liberalism and the moral and aesthetic critique of the Romantics and their descendants through Leavis to Williams.

Labour, regrettably, only reflected the first two of those, and then, unfortunately, in a negative dialectic through which the vices of one were reinforced by those of the other. One strand which, however, existed within each of those traditions, was the idea of democracy. This element could be utilised to unite them and thus to transform them into a socialist critique of existing society (Anderson 1965b, 283-284). Democracy, in and of itself, would not be sufficient as a socialist ideology but would be a prerequisite for such an ideology. To go beyond this basis, he argued, the concept of democracy would have to be deepened through practice. The democratisation of the work situation would in Anderson's opinion be the key to this practice. Workers' control would be the means of creating democracy within the workplace and thus of expanding the meaning of democracy within British culture.

Beyond this a 'total theory of man', which would not only account for the 'problem of work' but also that of sexuality and all other areas of life, was necessary if a socialist ideology were to be created. Raymond Williams had made the first tentative attempt in Britain at going beyond positivism to such a social theory. It was the task of the left to continue and expand his labours: 'The ultimate goal was therefore necessarily a new model of civilisation' (Anderson 1965b, 287 & 289).

However, Anderson argued that 'the suggestions which follow are inevitably elliptical and utopian', and 'any considerations of socialist strategy in Britain today must as yet be academic' (Anderson 1965b, 223 & 282). His political position around the time of the election of the Wilson government in 1964 could thus perhaps best be described using Romain Rolland's oft-quoted phrase 'optimism of the will, pessimism of the intellect'. The weight of Anderson's historical analysis suggested that there could be no way out of the English crisis. However, this did not lead him to embrace despair. Rather, he sought to make the best of an awful situation. He believed that critical support for Wilson was necessary if socialists were to stand any chance of entering the mainstream. Thus, he offered Wilson that support, while simultaneously refusing to submerge himself completely into Wilson's cause. In particular, he argued, the left should not confine itself to the struggle in parliament, but should rather seek to develop a nationally popular counter-hegemonic strategy: a model taken from the PCI.

However, there did exist a link between his 'realistic' critique of Wilsonism, and his 'utopian' outline of a future socialist strategy: the Labour Party. For the logic of Anderson's argument was that in modernising Britain, the Labour Party would create the conditions necessary to begin a process of self-modernisation. This perspective, while a rationalisation of critical work within the Labour left, also contained the seeds of Anderson's future evolution. For if the Labour Party failed to engage in the process of national modernisation, then support for it could be quickly dropped. If Anderson ceased to support Wilson then we might posit two possible directions for his future political evolution as conceived on the basis of his existing social theory. The first would be to follow Deutscher into the watch-tower. Anderson's analysis of the state of Britain suggested that there could be no escape from an overwhelming aristocratic hegemony and thus the only possible role for socialists would be a principled distancing of themselves from the squalor of the real world; this, indeed, was the stance he took with the relaunch of NLR in 2000. The second direction – the one that Anderson took after 1964 – would be to search for a new agency to take up the challenge offered by the crisis of the British state where Wilson had failed. As we shall see, he was aided in this evolution of his Marxism through a dialogue with, above all, Nicos Poulantzas and Louis Althusser.

CHAPTER THREE

TOWARDS REVOLUTIONARY SOCIALISM

Alongside many others of his generation, Anderson experienced a deep political radicalisation in the decade after Wilson's first election victory. This evolution of his thought was facilitated by a number of forces that acted upon him at the time. First, the experience of Labour in office very quickly dampened the ardour of his support for Wilson. Second, the development of an increasingly radicalised domestic opposition to both Wilson and Heath acted as a pole of attraction that drew him towards revolutionary politics. Third, this domestic radicalisation was set in the context of an international radicalisation: in particular the Tet offensive in Vietnam, the Chinese Cultural Revolution, the May 1968 general strike in France, the Prague spring and the Portuguese Revolution all combined to give the impression that the tide of history was with the international left. Fourth, there was a shift within western Marxism from a dominant Hegelianism to an anti-Hegelianism, first associated with Althusser and Poulantzas and then with Della Volpe and Colletti, that facilitated Anderson's development of a more flexible theoretical framework with which to underpin his new politics.

AGAINST THE OLD NEW LEFT

Socialism and Pseudo-Empiricism was written as a defence of the theses of *Origins* against Edward Thompson's spirited polemical assault upon it in his essay *The Peculiarities of the English*, first published in the 1965 edition of *The Socialist Register*. The central criticism that Thompson made of *Origins* was of its normative structure: 'There is, indeed, throughout their analysis an undisclosed model of Other Countries, whose typological symmetry offers a reproach to British exceptionalism'. In contrast to this methodology, Thompson insisted that capitalist development 'happened in one way in France, in another way in England' (Thompson 1978, 247 & 257). Substantively, Thompson criticised Anderson's model of England's seventeenth-century revolution. While he agreed with Anderson that this revolution had been made by landowners, he insisted that these aristocrats were in fact a 'superbly successful and self-confident capitalist class' (Thompson 1978, 252). Moreover, these landowners had influenced the production of, in Adam Smith's political economy, a distinctive and cogent ideology (Thompson 1978, 254). Thompson argued that the English Revolution had, as one of its main effects, the settlement of 1688, which both facilitated capitalist development, and did so in a framework that was flexible enough to survive for a century and a half. Then, in 1832, those small capitalists who had been excluded from the original agreement, but who had since grown in stature, were incorporated into a new settlement that restored the original's 'flexibility' (Thompson 1978, 260). Regarding the question of the dominance of an aristocratic ideology, Thompson directed Anderson's attention to Bagehot's description of the royal family as a 'retired widow and an unemployed youth'. This 'cynicism' and 'self confidence', he argued, exemplified 'emasculated bourgeois republicanism in England' (Thompson 1978, 263). The English aristocracy were useful to the bourgeoisie because they acted as a stabilising influence within the constitution, and diverted the radicalism of the working class away from the actual source of its oppression. Thompson also suggested, contra Anderson, that Protestantism had facilitated the growth of rationalism, and in turn had nurtured a culture that had produced thinkers of the calibre of Darwin, Bacon and Smith amongst scores of others, whose care with evidence could not easily be dismissed as 'empiricism', nor could their scientific breakthroughs be dismissed as 'traditionalism' (Thompson 1978, 268 & 272 & 274).

However, it was Anderson's conceptualisation of class that more than any other element of his thesis outraged Thompson. Anderson, he wrote, tended to clothe class 'throughout in anthropomorphic imagery' (Thompson 1978, 279). Thus, he flattened the struggles that had occurred for hegemony within the proletariat into an overarching unity, within which Labourism was never seriously challenged. Class, thus perceived as a unified 'it', had two immediate consequences for Anderson's work. First, it enabled him to ignore the real struggles for hegemony that had taken place between reformists and revolutionaries within the British labour movement over the preceding century. Second, it permitted him to read off the attitudes of the mass of workers from the ideologies of their leaders in the Labour Party and trade-union movement.[19] Thus, 'history is flattened, stretched, condensed; awkward facts are not mentioned; awkward decades are simply elided', in the pursuit of an untenable argument. So, while Thompson did not deny that Labourism was hegemonic within the English working class, he did deny that this hegemony was written in stone. In particular, he took offence at Anderson's dismissal of the existence of minority socialist traditions within the English proletariat (Thompson 1978, 275-276).[20] In contrast to Anderson's schematic history, which had the effect of misrepresenting crucial periods of struggle, Thompson argued, 'we can only describe the social process ... by writing history' (Thompson 1978, 289). Anderson's schema was particularly debilitating because of his reluctance to seriously investigate any of the periods of working-class resistance that he briefly mentioned. Indeed, for Thompson, the schematic structure of Anderson's history, by focusing on overarching themes, tended to act as an objectivist apologia for the status quo. The schematic structure of his thesis was therefore not a forgivable vice, given the overall nature of his work, rather it masked a further shift towards idealism, through which the past was not simply viewed through the lens of the present, but was constructed from the ideologies of the present with scant regard for accuracy. Anderson's schematic method therefore led to 'reductionism' whereby there occurred a 'lapse in historical logic by which political or cultural events are 'explained' in terms of the class affiliation of the actors' (Thompson 1978, 275 & 290).

Anderson replied to Thompson with what was ostensibly an aggressive defence of his own model of English social development against Thompson's alternative. However, his reply was also the medium through which he began a process of theoretical and political self-criticism. There were two main areas where Anderson began to shift. First, he both acknowledged the implicit idealism to be found in *Origins* and noted that there were signs of 'a counter idealistic trend within European Marxism of a potentially comparable strength and sophistication' to the earlier tradition upon which he had drawn: 'Althusser's work has this promise'. Interestingly his criticism of this work was of its idealism. 'Its conceptual innovations are borrowed from Bachelard and Lacan, psychoanalytical thinkers both within the idealistic tradition' (Anderson 1966, 32). It thus appeared that Anderson was persuaded that his arguments needed a firmer materialist grounding, but not necessarily that Althusser's system offered this. *Socialism and Pseudo-Empiricism* thus appears as a transitional work within which Anderson began to shift from an explicitly idealistic, to a more self-consciously materialistic, outlook. Second, Anderson began to be persuaded of the possible development of a viable socialist strategy in England.

Anderson opened his response to Thompson with the admission that 'our essays are abstract, schematic and incomplete'. However, he took offence at Thompson's criticism of them for being so since 'we were well aware of this and said so ourselves from the outset'. As to the more substantive points he suggested that on each issue Thompson had made 'consistent and specific misrepresentation of the whole drift of our work' (Anderson 1966, 4-5).

Nevertheless, despite the stridency of Anderson's tone, he remained silent about Thompson's main criticism of the *NLR* thesis: that is of its normative structure.[21]

On the class character of the aristocracy Anderson wrote that 'we never denied that the landowners constituted a capitalist class ... we made it the very pivot of our whole interpretation of the transition from the distinctive 18th century to the distinctive 19th century dominant bloc' (Anderson 1966, 6). However, Anderson maintained that a capitalist class was not the same as a bourgeoisie: 'A bourgeoisie, if the word is to mean anything at all, is a class based in towns; that is what the word means. It is ludicrous to call a landowning class a bourgeoisie' (Anderson 1966, 8). By eliding over this distinction, Thompson had missed the central point to *NLR's* analysis of the present crisis, its political implications: 'Thompson nowhere ventures even the smallest comment on this' (Anderson 1966, 17).

As to Thompson's analysis of bourgeois ideology, Anderson argued that 'we did not say that the English bourgeoisie has no cultural achievements to its credit ... What we said was that it produced no major political philosophy that became hegemonic in the society' (Anderson 1966, 17). So, Anderson criticised both Darwin and Smith for producing theories that reduced human relations to natural relations and thus refused to develop 'a total theory of man' (Anderson 1966, 22). With respect to the influence of Marxist and socialist thought on the British working class, Anderson accepted Thompson's criticism, but then suggested that Thompson, 'having correctly rebuked us for the error of ignoring Communism in Britain promptly then goes overboard in the opposite direction, and wildly exaggerates its role' (Anderson 1966, 24). As to Thompson's reading of Gramsci, Anderson suggested that his interlocutor was 'illiterate' and that 'hegemonic activity can and must be exercised before the seizure of power' (Anderson 1966, 28).[22]

Anderson then argued that Thompson's criticism of *NLR's* economic reductionism was particularly ill-conceived, as *NLR's* account of English history was based upon insights of the 'idealistic' Western Marxist tradition. Ironically this idealism is given extra weight in Anderson's response to Thompson's criticism of his model of class. He argued that Thompson's discussion of class was 'impeccable', but 'superfluous' as Talcott Parsons had said it all thirty years previously (Anderson 1966, 30-31).

Finally, Anderson argued that the purpose of his thesis was to develop a total account of contemporary Britain as a guard against the impressionistic politics of the old New Left. That Thompson had failed to respond to this issue was in Anderson's eyes an astonishing failure on his part to go beyond the failed 'moralistic' politics of the old New Left (Anderson 1966, 32 ff).

A SOCIALIST PROJECT FOR BRITAIN

As we have seen, in *Origins*, Anderson rejected, as unviable, the contemporary possibility of socialist advance in England. Moreover, he repeated this claim in *Socialism and Pseudo-Empiricism*: 'the whole of our historical analysis of the labour movement was devoted to explaining why there was never any chance of there being a hegemonic strategy available to the Left in Britain' (Anderson 1966, 23). However, *Socialism and Pseudo-Empiricism* is an opaque document precisely because of its polemical structure. Reading between the lines it appears that Anderson and Thompson shared more assumptions than the tone of their argument would suggest. For Anderson agreed with an earlier assessment made by Thompson and John Saville that the Marxist tradition in England was 'weak' (Anderson 1966, 26).[23] Now, a weak tradition is very different from no tradition at all. Importantly, a weak movement suggests the possibility of future strengthening, while the formulations contained in *Origins* precluded such a possibility. The growth of a weak tradition implied that socialism could potentially become a real force in English politics: but how? In *Origins* Anderson had argued that such a development must be predicated on a modernisation of the British state. In *Socialism and Pseudo-Empiricism* he took the first steps towards rejecting this position. Interestingly he did so without fundamentally overhauling his previous analysis of the British social formation.

The first criticism of Anderson's thesis to be published in *NLR* was written by James Hinton, then a member of the *International Socialism* (*IS*) Group. This was published in *NLR* 32 in 1965. Within the *IS* group's journal Anderson's position – and more generally the whole course of *NLR* – had been strongly criticised by heavyweight old New Left figures Peter Sedgwick and Alasdair MacIntyre as a rightward deviation under the pressure of Wilsonism (Sedgwick 1965; MacIntyre quoted in Foot 1968, 317). Nevertheless Anderson accepted the general thrust of Hinton's criticisms (Anderson 1966, 30). Hinton's critique of Anderson's position was outlined via a review of Roydon Harrison's book, *Before the Socialists*. In this book Harrison had attempted to locate a material explanation for the development of bourgeois hegemony over the working class at the time of the Second Reform Act of 1867. He argued that a Labour aristocracy had developed after the defeat of Chartism, which saw itself as both the representative of the working class and, at one and the same time, better than this class (Harrison 1965, 32). Hinton argued that while this process explained the nature of British politics at the time of the Reform Bill, it did not explain later developments. Specifically, this class was 'reproletarianised' between 1910 and 1926, and therefore its development in the late nineteenth century could not account for the defeats of 1926, 1931 and 1951. Hinton explained these defeats as a function of the role of an official labour bureaucracy that had developed in the late nineteenth century, and which underpinned much of the corporatism of the Labour movement of the twentieth century. Hinton concluded that Nairn and Anderson's 'assertion of the primacy of political and ideological factors led them to reject not only those socioeconomic movements towards greater or lesser cohesion of the working class but also ... they found themselves pouring scorn over the growth of hegemonic class consciousness within the socialist revival of the 1890s and almost entirely forgetting to mention the revolutionary movements of 1910-26. This is an odd way for the Left to set about evaluating its own heritage' (Hinton 1965, 77).

If Hinton's criticism was correct, and revolutionary consciousness did develop at certain moments within the history of the English working class, then the question that required an answer was certainly not why cannot such a form of consciousness develop, but rather why did the revolutionaries not win the battle for hegemony within the working class? Anderson's answer to this problem was to suggest that while a weak Marxist movement had existed in Britain from the late nineteenth century, this movement had not created a vibrant Marxist culture and therefore had proved itself inadequate to the task of arming a generation of militants with the necessary politics to overturn the hegemony of Labourism. Thus, the fact that 'there has never been a Marxist culture in this country' meant that 'the preconditions for a real, autonomous Marxism did not exist' (Anderson 1966, 26). So Anderson prefigured the argument that he himself would later develop in *Components of a National Culture* that the left needed to create such a Marxist culture so as to underpin a viable form of Marxist politics.

A MORE FLEXIBLE FRAMEWORK: POULANTZAS' CRITIQUE

Anderson's *Socialism and Pseudo-Empiricism* was published in the January/February 1966 edition of *NLR*. Nicos Poulantzas' critique of the Anderson/Thompson debate, *Marxist Political Theory in Great Britain*, was first published in the March 1966 issue of *Les Temps Modernes*. However, while it was published too late for Anderson to incorporate a comment on it in *Socialism and Pseudo-Empiricism*, it is apparent that he had read the article prior to its publication (*NLR* 35 1966, 1). While Poulantzas was impressed by the quality of the English debate, his critique of Anderson centred on the limitations of his concept of the totality. In particular Poulantzas utilised Althusser's critique of the Hegelian conception of an expressive totality to criticise Anderson's utilisation of concepts drawn from the early Lukács.

Althusser argued that the Hegelian totality was 'not really ... articulated in spheres ... its unity is not its complexity' (Althusser 1969, 204). This he contrasted with the Marxist concept of the totality, which is characterised by its 'complexity', where 'levels' exist that are 'distinct and relatively autonomous'

(Althusser 1970, 97). The key weakness with the Hegelian concept of the totality was that it could 'never provide the basis for a *policy*' (Althusser 1969, 204). This criticism, whether or not it could be applied to Lukács' conception of the totality, did appear to strike at a real weakness with Anderson's utilisation of this concept.

Poulantzas utilised this Althusserian framework to analyse the Anderson-Nairn thesis at two levels. First, he examined their discussion of the class structure of English society; second, he looked at their examination of Labourism. Poulantzas' suggested that the analysis of the English social formation outlined by Anderson and Nairn was superior to Thompson's alternative, precisely because they 'attained a level of critical comprehension of the concepts of Marxist political science' quite alien to Thompson's 'empirical and circumstantial account'. However, the Hegelian historicism and subjectivism of Anderson and Nairn's account led them to develop a too simplistic and monist account of English social development: it did not account for 'the type of unity which characterises a social formation ... an objective complex whole with a plurality of specific levels of structure with a dominant in the last instance, the economy'. Anderson's account was monist in the sense that his totality was determined by the class consciousness of the aristocracy. Thus, an idealistic unity was developed by Anderson which resembled a type of Parsonian functionalism (Poulantzas 1967, 60-61).

Indeed, as Anderson had ignored the economic base of society in his thesis, his analysis of the political level was left stranded atop a vacuum, for he largely overlooked the problem of the transition from feudalism to capitalism (Poulantzas 1967, 63). Anderson thus tended to ignore the real, qualitative changes that had taken place over time within the economic basis of society. For it was over time that the mode of production changed from feudalism to capitalism, and it did this in an uneven way. So, at any one time, Poulantzas argued, the English social formation should best be described as a combination of modes of production. The weakness with Anderson's thesis stemmed from his inability to temporally locate the transformation of the aristocracy into a capitalist class (Poulantzas 1967, 62). Poulantzas suggested that this was a consequence of Anderson's failure to conceptualise social formations as complex combinations of modes of production.

Despite this criticism, Poulantzas maintained that Anderson's model of the British social formation was superior to Thompson's, because Anderson at least looked at the problem of which fraction of capital was hegemonic. He accepted Anderson's argument that the aristocracy remained for a long time a distinct class which set out on its own process of capitalisation and which finally became, at the level of the relations of production, a capitalist class (Poulantzas 1967, 63). However, these propositions did not solve the problem of the nature of the system of hegemony in England.

Anderson's historicism, he suggested, led to an idealistic identification of society as a product of the class-consciousness of the aristocracy. Marxism, by contrast, would allow for the feudal character of the state because of its relative autonomy (Poulantzas 1967, 65). The dominant ideology, however, attained its internal unity because it expressed the particular unity of a social formation founded upon 'a determinate mode of production' (Poulantzas 1967, 67). That this mode of production was capitalist would at first sight appear to undermine Anderson's central thesis: for if the dominant ideology reflected the dominant mode of production and was a capitalist ideology, then surely the lack of a coherent bourgeois ideology could not account for working-class corporatism? (Poulantzas 1967, 71). What did this mean for the workers?

It should have meant a lot, because Anderson's discussion of the corporate character of the English working-class was predicated on the aristocratic ideology that was supposedly hegemonic in Britain. Without this ideology, and within the terms of Anderson's thesis, the limitations of proletarian Labourism could have been overcome. Indeed Poulantzas developed a line of thought that almost led to this conclusion: 'Everybody knows that in the so called underdeveloped countries an authentic revolutionary ideology is often found without a reconstituted bourgeois ideology' (Poulantzas 1967, 71). Despite the potential implications of this line of argument, Poulantzas suggested that Anderson's analysis of the corporate nature of the English proletariat was one of the strongest points of his thesis, albeit that Anderson needed to give this analysis a firmer materialist foundation, as in his original he had reduced Gramsci's concept of hegemony 'incorrectly to the Lukácsian notion of class consciousness'. Thus, in Anderson's work, the 'properly political structuration of a class is reduced to the constitution of a global conception of the world which becomes the unifying principal over the determinate social formation' (Poulantzas 1967, 61). Anderson's anthropomorphism blinded him, according to Poulantzas, to the vitality of his own insights. For whereas Anderson had suggested that a key conduit of the system of hegemony were intellectuals, he had also implied that the hegemonic system was a self-reproducing, unmediated, reflection of the aristocratic centre. By contrast, Poulantzas argued, 'the hegemony of the proletariat denotes quite precisely the properly political constitution of the specific objective interest of the working class into the real general interest of all workers despite their particular differences' (Poulantzas 1967, 73). So Poulantzas took Anderson's appraisal of the role of intellectuals to rescue his analysis of Labourism in its generality, if not its specifics. For Poulantzas not only argued that it was in his discussion of Labourism that Anderson was at his strongest but it was here that Thompson was weakest: 'Here Thompson's objections seem ill founded' (Poulantzas 1967, 71).

Now Anderson had made no pretence at agreeing with Thompson – except in so far as Thompson added details to his admittedly schematic presentation. However, he claimed mostly to accept Hinton's criticism of the central thesis of *Origins*. What then was his position on Poulantzas? As we have seen, in *Socialism and Pseudo-Empiricism*, he simply made the point that the Althusserian turn was interesting (Anderson 1966, 31). A year later, in the anonymous introduction to the translation of Poulantzas in *NLR*, Anderson welcomed the contribution as 'a renewal of the international traditions of the classical socialist movement' and suggested that *NLR* would publish a reply in a forthcoming issue. While this reply, unfortunately, was never published there was a line in the introduction which suggested that Poulantzas' arguments were to be preferred to those of Hinton. Poulantzas' 'study is concerned with the theoretical infrastructure of the debate, [and] as such it represents an important advance over previous discussion, allowing the reader to assess the fundamental conceptual issues posed by the analysis attempted in *NLR*' (*NLR* 43 1967, 55-56).

This did not mean that Anderson simply rejected his earlier appreciation of Hinton. Rather Hinton's insight was submerged as an element in Poulantzas' general framework. For Poulantzas' model of hegemony was much more flexible than was Anderson's interpretation of the concept in *Origins*. Poulantzas suggested that competing ideologies could exist in a system of hegemony within which one was dominant (Poulantzas 1967, 68). This framework allowed for the existence of socialist currents in the Labour movement where Anderson's earlier framework did not, while recognising that a corporate, Labourist ideology was hegemonic. Thus, whereas Anderson's original thesis suggested a much more uniform totality which precluded the existence of a socialist current, Poulantzas suggested that the totality should be understood as a looser structure which would allow the existence of a viable socialist current. However, Poulantzas argued, without the key input of socialist intellectuals this current could never become hegemonic. Thus, 'the analysis of Anderson and Nairn concerning the absence of intellectuals in the Gramscian sense from the political organisation of the working class in Britain, are in this respect, much more convincing' than Thompson's arguments (Poulantzas 1967, 71).

Consistent with this criticism, Anderson maintained the internal coherence of his position while agreeing with both Hinton and Poulantzas. For while Hinton suggested that socialism was a living force within the British proletariat, he did not deny the hegemony of Labourism. Similarly, Poulantzas argued that a system of hegemony was characterised by a plurality of competing ideologies. So Poulantzas and Hinton could agree on the weak but nevertheless real influence of socialism on the British proletariat. Moreover, whereas Hinton argued that the Labour and trade-union bureaucracy guaranteed the hegemony of Labourism, Poulantzas' model could underpin this argument ideologically by suggesting that only when a socialist intelligentsia was formed could the hegemony of the Labourist bureaucrats be overturned.

WILSON AND THE WORKING CLASS

Anderson signalled *NLR's* shift away from its critical affiliation to Wilsonism with the publication, in *NLR 34*, of Bob Rowthorn's critique of Wilson's incomes policy (Rowthorn 1965, 11). Before Labour's election victory *NLR* had associated itself with John Hughes' arguments in favour of incomes policy (Hughes 1964). The experience of Wilson in office persuaded the *NLR* team of the bankruptcy of this perspective. In his introduction to Rowthorn's essay, Anderson wrote that 'Rowthorn ... shows that a precondition of the [incomes policy's] realisation is the effective destruction of the British labour movement' (*NLR* 34 1965, 1). The question therefore arose of how to defend the English working class against Wilson's government, for, as Coates argued elsewhere, 'in the early 1960s ... the representative institutions of industrial capital ... urged the state to play a more positive role in planning the future levels of costs and demand ... under the Labour government these demands became more insistent and blending with Labour's own interventionist propensities produced a full-blown attempt to make a slight but significant shift in the distribution of GNP back towards profits [from wages – PB]' (Coates 1975,123). Incomes policy was the strategy utilised by the Wilson government to accomplish this demand from industry.

However, the incomes policy did not really begin to bite under Wilson's first administration. It was only after the landslide victory of March 1966 that Wilson began to seriously test the mettle of the union movement. Anderson responded to these attacks with a defence of the union movement against the government. He did this in two ways. First, he published an essay on the unions, *The Limits and Possibilities of Trade Union Action*; second, Penguin, in their Penguin Special series, published the *NLR* collection on the trade unions, *The Incompatibles* (1967), in which Anderson's essay appeared. *The Incompatibles* operated at two levels: first, and basically, it was a defence of the unions and the working class against the government; second, it offered an attempt to formulate a strategy for trade unionism and its relationship to the struggle for socialism.

This intervention represented a decisive step to the left for Anderson. Previously his socialism had something of a detached, intellectualist quality about it. With this intervention he appeared to be responding directly to one of the key issues of the day. Moreover, since the cause of the intervention was a developing conflict between the Labour government and organised labour, Anderson's model of British society began to be fundamentally challenged.

As we have seen, Anderson had conflated the consciousness of the English working class with the ideology of Labourism in *Origins*. By contrast, in *The Limits and Possibilities of Trade Union Action*, he now posited a potential division between the Labour Party and the English working class. In responding as he did to this development, Anderson showed both that if a left opposition to Labour developed he would support it, and that given that this opposition was rooted in the labour movement he was prepared to begin to overhaul his previous framework in order to explain it. As we shall see, Anderson did not make a complete overhaul immediately, but 1967 marked the point at which he began this process.

The first duty of the left, Anderson argued, was to defend the unions against attacks from the right. However, he did not believe that this defence was the end of the socialist position on the unions: socialists must critically analyse the role of unions in the struggle for socialism. His analysis began with a résumé of the classical Marxist critique of the limits of trade-union action. Unions 'expressed' rather than 'challenged' the class divisions in society; they were a 'passive' reflection of class structure – in contrast to the revolutionary party which acted as the 'voluntarist' rupture with that structure; their strongest weapon was merely an absence: the strike; they produced only a 'sectoral, corporate consciousness'; their power, because it was sectorally based, was never on a par with that of management (Anderson 1967, 263-8).

Despite these limitations, Wilson's incomes policy was forcing trade-union struggle to become 'necessarily a political struggle' as state power became increasingly 'transparent' (Anderson 1967, 278). How then should socialists relate to this struggle? His answer to this question marked a continuation of the thesis that he had expressed in *Problems*. He argued that trade-union consciousness was a necessary element in the development of socialist consciousness and thus that trade-union struggles should be supported by the Left as a 'stage' towards the development of socialist consciousness in the proletariat. Moreover, the key strategic goal of socialists in the unions should be to foster the most democratic internal regime possible: 'it is simply not the case that there is a fatal iron law of oligarchy which inevitably produces an authoritarian trade-union bureaucracy' (Anderson 1967, 274-275).

Thus, while he supported unofficial industrial action led by shop stewards against the opposition of the right-wing leadership of various unions, he argued, by contrast with Hinton, that the two forces – bureaucracy and rank and file – should not be counterposed (Anderson 1967, 277). Rather, he understood the conflicts that did exist within the unions to be primarily shaped by ideological divisions between the left and the right. Moreover, Anderson assumed that trade-union consciousness was the necessary limit of the development of class consciousness inside the working class. Thus, he argued, 'culture in a capitalist society is in this sense a prerogative of privileged strata: only if some members of these strata go over to the cause of the working class can a revolutionary movement be born. For without a revolutionary theory, there can be no revolutionary movement. Trade unions represent too limited a sociological base for a socialist movement. By themselves they inevitably produce a corporate consciousness' (Anderson 1967, 267). This position provided the framework for both Anderson's future orientation and his present political affiliation. In the short term the divisions within the labour movement meant that he began to identify himself with the politics of the Communist Party in 1967.

The industrial strategy of the Communist Party at the time centred on the perspective of supporting left-wing candidates in the struggle for the leadership of the unions. This, in effect, became Anderson's position. However, as Willie Thompson has argued, this approach implied a fundamental strategic weakness: 'The CP was obliged by the logic of its posture and strategy to keep its public statements and analysis of the trade union affairs within the bounds of acceptability to its new or potential allies ... being the weaker partner, the Party could not avoid having to accept the terms upon which [the left union leaders] Frank Cousins, Jack Jones and Hugh Scanlon or their counterparts were willing to cooperate' (Thompson 1992, 135). The CP thus became tied to the left officials. Paralleling this development *The Incompatibles* largely accepted the left officials' perspective on industrial strategy. Indeed, while it included Paul Foot's polemical criticism of the Labour Party, the 'contemporary scene' was painted by left officials, or those close to them. Importantly, Jack Jones, then assistant executive secretary of the Transport and General Workers' Union, argued that 'today the need is not to pose some sort of necessary ideological division between the active members and the trade union officials or structure. The real need is to provide the policy and the means ... for even wider social and economic advance' (Jones 1967, 129).

Anderson's analysis of trade union action suggested an unbridgeable gulf between trade union action and socialist consciousness, and while he argued that the former was a 'stage' towards the latter, he did not mean to suggest that contemporary trade unionism could break the bonds of corporatism. Rather, contemporary developments in trade unionism had created an environment conducive to the creation of a socialist alternative to Labour: 'the great majority of British trade unionists were affiliated to the Labour Party', and this 'very party is now intent on blocking their action and shattering their autonomy'. His concluding rhetorical question was thus, 'can this immense contradiction continue indefinitely?' (Anderson 1967, 179) The implication was that it could not. However, Anderson believed that trade unions were merely 'the most elementary form' of the 'collective institutions' through which the proletariat 'experiences itself'. They did not yet represent a 'fused group capable of any social action' (Anderson 1967, 274). His next move was to examine the conditions under which a socialist 'political party' could develop from a 'rupture with the natural environment of civil society' to form a 'voluntarist contractual collectivity' (Anderson 1967,265).

DEBRAY'S INFLUENCE

We have already noted the inspiration that Anderson had taken from the Cuban Revolution. In 1967 he returned to this theme as part of his leftward evolution. However, where he had previously based his analysis of this revolution on Sartre's framework, in 1967 it was to Régis Debray, a French student of Althusser, that he looked to aid in his understanding of it. Debray, who had travelled to Bolivia to interview Che Guevara, had been captured and tortured by the military authorities there. An international campaign was subsequently launched with the aim of securing his life. Anderson and Blackburn not only wrote their essay on Debray to address the audience thus created for his ideas, they also travelled to Bolivia to help ensure his survival (Ali 1987, chapter six). The essay on Debray was not an appeal for his life; Anderson and Blackburn set out to critically appraise his ideas. In particular they learnt from Castro, via Debray, that all capitalist states were at their heart instruments of violence that needed to be smashed in the Leninist sense. This encounter set Anderson on course for an engagement with the ideas of Leon Trotsky.

The main thrust of Anderson and Blackburn's brief study, *The Marxism of Régis Debray*,[24] was the equation of Debray's Marxism with Lenin's. Debray's strength, they argued, was built upon his 'relentlessly Leninist focus on making the revolution' (Anderson and Blackburn 1968, 63). This, he perceived to be both a moral duty and 'a practical need'. Debray was not concerned with sectarianism, but rather with action, more precisely with guerrilla action. This concern with the technique of revolution, along with its ethics, 'may be initially disconcerting' to the European reader, who is used to a primary place being given to politics. However, politics was not ignored in Debray's framework, rather it underpinned his call to action (Anderson and Blackburn 1968, 65). Moreover, in his politics Debray had 'cut right through' the debate over the nature of the coming Latin American revolutions. So, where some Marxists had argued that the revolution would be bourgeois-democratic in character, while others had argued that it would be socialist, Debray turned away from what, he argued, was abstract phrase mongering, towards a solution to the problem that was based in action. It was in this sense, according to Anderson and Blackburn, that he could be compared to Lenin. For where Lenin had solved the problem of the class character of the Russian Revolution through the experience of the revolution itself, Debray was attempting to repeat this success in the 1960s. This was evidence of the 'authentically Leninist character of Debray's thought' (Anderson and Blackburn 1968, 65).

Anderson and Blackburn then defended Debray against those who criticised his account of guerrilla warfare as the key determinant of any revolution by quoting Mao as an authority: in any given historical conjuncture there was 'a principal aspect of the principal contradiction'. Guerrilla struggle was just this principal aspect in Latin America. Moreover, Debray himself had argued that 'students, trade unions, peasant leagues, and so on, would also undoubtedly be necessary if a revolutionary situation was to be successfully carried to its conclusion'. The effect of this argument was to legitimate the suggestion that outside Latin America the principal aspect of the principal contradiction could possibly include forces other than a guerrilla movement. However, Anderson and Blackburn did not develop this line of thought in their essay on Debray. Rather the *NLR* editors concluded simply, with Debray, that 'the duty of every revolutionary is to make the revolution' (Anderson and Blackburn 1968, 68). Similarly, the unnamed author of a eulogy to Che Guevara published in the next issue of the *NLR* argued that, 'our duty in the metropoles of imperialism itself is to undermine from within the atrocious and oppressive system which Che fought to destroy from without' (*NLR* 46 1967, 16).

One key strategic development that was new to *NLR* was first aired in the essay on Debray. Anderson and Blackburn argued that there was one 'fundamentally similar' feature that all capitalist societies shared, a repressive state. Thus, from Fidel Castro they learnt that while the 'armed insurrection is not the only form of revolutionary struggle, ... it is the fundamental form – to which all others will eventually lead'. Therefore, there 'is no place for reformist illusions about the nature of the state in a capitalist society' (Anderson and Blackburn 1968, 69). Anderson suggested that he had previously underestimated the repressive powers of the state. This essay thus marked his dramatic shift to the left. It also meant that his brief flirtation with the ideas of the British Communist Party had to come to an end, for the CPGB had formulated into its programme since 1951 the position that the conquest of power in Britain would come through parliament (Thompson 1992, 10).[25]

This did not mean that Anderson had broken all ties with international Communism. As we have seen, he had always been more impressed by the continental Communist Parties than he had been with their British cousin. Thus, in contrast to his positive impression of the PCI, in 1966 he had argued that the British 'Communist Party behaves in practice as a left-wing section of Labour' (Anderson 1966, 25). This opposition remained in 1967, when, as Tariq Ali reports, Anderson was 'sympathetic to the positions of the pro-Moscow CPs in Western Europe' and 'dismissed Maoist pretensions' (Ali 1987, 151). Therefore, while in 1967 Anderson was moving to the Left, this shift had not yet witnessed his break from a broad affiliation to the Communist tradition.

This Communist colouration to his thought influenced his solution to the problem of how revolutionaries were 'to make the revolution' in England. The whole thrust of Debray's position, repeated by Anderson and Blackburn, was that the small motor of the guerrilla army could not wait for the masses. Indeed, Debray strongly argued against any organic link with the masses as a recipe for Trotskyist passivity. The Trotskyists, he argued, had made two mistakes. The first was grounded in their abstract and 'utopian' understanding of revolutions. Their belief that any socialist revolution should be the act of the masses resulted in them refusing to support minorities who fought against capitalism. Thus, in effect, the revolutionary rhetoric of the Trotskyists led to their inaction. Second, this inaction was reflected organisationally through their 'liquidation of existing popular movements'. So, where minorities had organised to fight against their oppressors, the Trotskyists argued that they should liquidate their organisations into larger more moderate bodies (Debray 1967 35-41).

Trotsky, in *Our Political Tasks*, had famously argued against small groups substituting their actions for those of the masses (Trotsky 1904). By contrast, Debray argued that the guerrilla force could, through successful military action, act as an alternative to the old order. A successful guerrilla force would thus act as a moving foco[26] of the struggle. This moving foco was compared, by Debray, to Mao's liberated areas in the 1930s and 1940s. While these stationary areas were necessary in China, mobility was essential in Latin America. Indeed, it was Fidel's good fortune not to have read Mao before the revolution (Debray 1968, 20). For a dogmatic incorporation of Mao's strategy would have probably proved disastrous in Cuba. The key to a successful revolutionary struggle was not to move from strategy to tactics but from tactics to strategy: to learn from an engagement with actual struggles (Debray 1973, 187 ff). Anderson and Blackburn learnt from this and sought to develop a model of revolutionary politics in England that was based upon their experience. So, at the beginning of their essay on Debray, they argued that Marxism was 'a theory of social structures and of the contradictions within it which objectively found the revolutionary movement' (Anderson and Blackburn 1968, 64). Anderson thus moved on from Debray's call for revolutionary action to outline a revolutionary strategy for England.

Before he did this, however, he sought to come to terms with the legacy of Trotsky. The Trotskyists had both maintained an affiliation to the orthodox Marxist case for revolution in the West, and had argued that in the Third World the completion of the bourgeois-democratic revolution would involve the overthrow of the bourgeois state by the proletariat. Given that, in the essay on Debray, Anderson had signalled his general agreement with both of these positions, it seemed only natural that he should set out to engage with Trotsky's Marxism.

TROTSKY'S MARXISM

Debray had dismissed Trotskyist passivity. Yet Trotsky had not only organised the October Revolution but also he had led the Red Army to successfully defend the Russian Revolution and then had almost alone defended a non-Stalinist interpretation of Marxism throughout the 1930s. In addition to this he was, in Isaac Deutscher, served with one of the greatest biographers of the twentieth century. It was thus only a matter of time before the leftwards-moving *NLR* was forced to come to terms with his legacy. It did so, initially, through an essay by Nicolas Krasso.

Krasso, a member of the editorial committee of *NLR*, was a refugee from the Hungarian Revolution, and former pupil of Lukács. In 1967 he wrote an article, *Trotsky's Marxism*, which was an attempt at a serious political assessment of the organiser of the October Revolution. In this essay, Krasso attempted to go beyond what he saw as the one-dimensional oppositions of Stalinist slanders and orthodox Trotskyist eulogies. This essay is of interest to us not simply because of its appearance in *NLR*, in fact, according to Anderson, there were two strands to Krasso's essay. First, a Lukácsian theme that came from Krasso himself; second, an Althusserian theme that came via Anderson's own heavy editorial intervention.[27] Krasso claimed that Trotsky's Marxism was marred by what he called its sociologism, by which he meant that Trotsky tended to hypostatize social class, thus losing the specificity of any particular moment in the struggle for socialism (Krasso 1967, 72). To substantiate this claim Krasso compared Trotsky's theory of permanent revolution with Stalin's theory of socialism in one country, and then both of these with Lenin's analysis of the dynamics of the Russian Revolution as applied at Brest-Litovsk.

Lenin, Krasso argued, held a dialectical approach to politics which contained and transcended both Stalin's and Trotsky's positions. Lenin, like Trotsky, had indeed wanted to see a European revolution but presumed it naive to speculate on the likelihood of this. He was thus able to formulate a retreat at Brest-Litovsk without losing sight of the ultimate goal of world revolution. Trotsky, by contrast, allowed his belief in world revolution to prevent him from theorising a temporary political retreat. Stalin, meanwhile, ever the pragmatist, could easily come to terms with retreat but then forgot the ultimate aim of world revolution through his theory of socialism in one country. Stalin's position was, despite its crudities, 'superior' to Trotsky's because it was based on real practice (Krasso 1967, 78-79). Trotsky, Krasso concluded, simplified the struggle for socialism into a struggle of the world bourgeoisie versus the world proletariat. He thus 'abolished the concrete international differences between the various European countries. He failed to understand the fundamental difference between Russian and Western European social structures'; specifically, he refused 'to respect the autonomy of the political level' (Krasso 1967, 81 & 80). Politically, this meant that Trotskyists were compelled to follow their founder into crude and idealistic theories of socialist politics. In particular Trotsky's 'pre-Leninist' theory of the role of the intellectuals undermined his theory of the party. For, while Lenin understood that the intelligentsia were 'indispensable to the construction of a revolutionary party', Trotsky had never comprehended that socialism must come to the proletariat from without (Krasso 1967, 70).

Ernest Mandel subjected Krasso's assessment of Trotsky's Marxism to a severe criticism in both an anti-critique of Krasso's original essay and a rejoinder to Krasso's reply. Anderson, in *A Decennial Report*, wrote that his evolution towards Trotskyism after 1968 was in large part aided by the strength of Mandel's rejoinder (*A Decennial Report*, 31). I shall discuss Mandel's reply below. The debate began, however, in 1967 when the Trotskyist belief in the revolutionary role of the Western proletariat seemed quite utopian. If it was to be the May 1968 events in France that laid the basis for Anderson's broad acceptance of Mandel's arguments, this was for the future. In the short term Anderson reacted to the growing student struggles at home and abroad with an attempt to understand their place in a revolutionary strategy for England.

COMPONENTS OF A NATIONAL CULTURE

From at least as early as 1965 Anderson had explicitly stressed that socialist practice, if it was to be successful, must be underpinned by a socialist culture. In 1968 he developed this position into an explicit thesis. The result was an essay that set the tone of intellectual debate on the left for decades to come. For *Components of a National Culture* was not simply this thesis writ large but was also a *tour de force* survey of the 'reactionary culture' of the English higher education system. The context within which this essay was written was a growing international student movement, which Anderson correctly predicted would soon spread to Britain. Moreover, while the thesis of the essay did not obviously contradict the political perspectives that Anderson had held since the publication of *Origins*, the radicalising influence of Althusserian Marxism can be felt throughout the text (Anderson 1992e, 48).

At the beginning of 1968 Anderson was a convinced revolutionary socialist. However, as we have seen, he rejected the idea that the proletariat was a potentially sufficient agency for socialist advance. He believed that intellectuals were the necessary element that would provide the socialist culture which would underpin socialist practice. Moreover, following Althusser, he believed that the foundations upon which the contemporary, reactionary culture had been built had been laid in the universities. Thus, while he recognised that two struts upon which the 'student revolt' would stand would be 'challenges to authoritarianism at home, and solidarities against imperialism abroad', he also argued that a third strut would be necessary: a struggle 'against the reactionary culture inculcated in universities and colleges' (Anderson 1992e, 48). *Components* was his attempt to locate the main threads of England's reactionary culture and to begin the task of developing a total socialist critique of it.

Components was published in the summer issue of *NLR* in 1968, just a couple of months before the October anti-Vietnam war demonstrations at Grosvenor Square, and as a direct political intervention within the student movement (Ali 1987, 181). Anderson premised the essay with the claim that 'without a revolutionary culture there will be no revolutionary theory', which he took to be the Gramscian underpinning of Lenin's aphorism, 'without a revolutionary theory there can be no revolutionary movement' (Anderson 1992e, 49).

Anderson examined this culture utilising a method borrowed from Lévi-Strauss: he sought not to examine the terms of the system, 'but the relationship between the terms' (Anderson 1992e, 51). He characterised British cultural specificity through two key anomalies. First, it had developed no indigenous sociology. Second, in just about all other subject areas reactionary foreigners filled the key academic positions. These two points were interrelated. The first was a product of the lack of a Marxist challenge to domestic politics. For whereas Weber, Pareto and Durkheim etc. had developed their ideas in 'reaction' to Marxism, where this latter element did not exist, then an indigenous sociology would not grow to counter it (Anderson 1992e, 53). The second was a product of the obverse of this. Social instability on the continent had led to a 'white emigration' of key intellectuals to stable Britain, who then helped to shape Britain's reactionary national culture.

Anderson argued that the void left by the absence of either a Marxism or a developed sociology at the centre of British culture was filled by the 'pseudo centre of the timeless ego' (Anderson 1992e, 103). This timeless ego acted to legitimate the status quo, and 'quite literally deprives the Left of any source of concepts and categories with which to analyse its own society and thereby attain the fundamental preconditions for changing it' (Anderson 1969, 277).[28] While in 1964 his utilisation of a Hegelian expressive totality meant that such conclusions precluded a viable socialist practice, in 1968 his deployment of the Althusserian 'complex' totality left room for a non-utopian socialist practice because of the relative autonomy of the various levels within that totality. Thus with the last sentence of the essay he argued that, whilst a 'revolutionary culture is not for tomorrow ... a revolutionary[29] practice within culture is possible and necessary today, the student struggle is its initial form' (Anderson 1992e,

104).

So, Anderson's answer to both Che's and Debray's calls for action was a theoretical intervention within culture coupled to solidarity with anti-imperialist struggles abroad and challenges to domestic authoritarianism. These three elements seemed to combine in the student movement that escalated shortly after the publication of *Components*. For not only did this movement challenge academic authority, it was also closely associated with the anti-Vietnam war movement, whose demonstrations were witness to government use of repression. Consequently, activity within student politics fulfilled Anderson's three criteria for socialist practice noted above. The effect of this was that *NLR* threw itself into (student) politics to an extent that it has never since repeated (Birchall 1981, 70). While Anderson provided the theoretical ammunition for this activity, other editors developed the strategic rationale for the *Review's* increasingly activist posture.

The nature of this activity is best expressed in the title of the *NLR* edited collection within which *Components* was republished in 1969: *Student Power*. Meanwhile, the *Review* itself published a series of essays in the January/February 1969 issue on the student struggles. While these were not the first articles to be published by the *Review* on student power, the tone of these later essays was much more strident than the earlier ones had been. Thus, where twenty months previously *NLR's* demands had been essentially reformist – for high grants against loans and a demand for student control over education – now the tone of the essays was quite different.

This is most apparent in the essay written by Blackburn under the pseudonym of James Wilcox.[30] In this essay, he argued, applying Debray's politics to English academic conditions, that red bases should be set up in the universities. These he compared to the soviets of 1917 and the Chinese liberated zones of the 1930s (Wilcox 1969, 23). A mixture of Althusserianism and Leninism theoretically underpinned this thesis. Following Althusser, Blackburn suggested that society, being a complex totality, could be broken at various junctures. Meanwhile, he followed Lenin's theory of attacking the enemy at the weakest link in the chain. The university, Blackburn argued, was the weak link that could be won over by Marxist intellectuals. Thus, from an absolute rejection, as utopian, of the possibility of socialist advance in 1964, *NLR* had, by 1968, dramatically moved to the left. Anderson suggested that revolutionary politics within the culture was possible, while Blackburn argued that red bases in the colleges could spearhead this struggle.

MAY 1968

Anderson's political evolution to the left was given a further fillip under the influence of the French general strike of 1968. Detonated by clashes between students and police in Paris, a general strike involving some 10 million French workers evolved quickly into a pre-revolutionary situation in France (Harman 1988, 84-120). Previously, Anderson believed that spontaneous outbursts of proletarian militancy could only lead to the development within the working class of trade union consciousness. The events in France put this assumption under severe stress. However, Anderson remained convinced that the existence of a prior socialist culture was a necessary prerequisite to the development of a mass socialist movement. Anderson published two important articles in 1968 expressing this new position: the first, in *NLR 51*, was an introduction to a collection of essays written by Gramsci at the height of the proletarian militancy in post-1918 Italy; the second, in *NLR 52*, was a general introduction to an *NLR* special issue on the French events.[31]

The events of May 1968, Anderson argued, had 'vindicated the fundamental socialist belief that the industrial proletariat is the revolutionary class of advanced capitalism' (*NLR* 52 1968, 7). For the struggle of this class 'tended to overflow the limits of trade union demands and to pose the question of revolution' (*NLR* 51 1968, 24). Moreover, the French Communist Party had acted as a bureaucratic fetter against the revolutionary development of the French working class (*NLR* 52 1968, 4). Thus, where Anderson had previously suggested that the spontaneous struggles of workers could not lead to the creation of 'fused groups' (Anderson 1967, 274), in 1968, he argued, 'the voter in the polling booth is pre-eminently private, atomised, serialised, as Sartre has put it. In the occupied factory, in the Soviet-style assembly, political life is public, collective; individuals may form a fused group'. That this movement was 'detonated' from outside the working class by student struggles did not in the least take away from the fact that 'the forms which the Revolution took were classical'. Moreover, this classical structure occurred as a rebirth of the true Bolshevik spirit against the institutions which were that organisations 'formal heirs' (*NLR* 52 1968, 4-6).

These points, when taken together, would seem to suggest a full rejection, by Anderson, of the political pessimism constitutive of the Western Marxist tradition (Anderson 1976a). It would also suggest that Anderson was generalising his earlier rejection of British Communism to other Western European communist parties. Thus, the French CP's adherence to parliament would apparently indicate that it was as tied to reformist politics as were the British CP and Labour Party. Indeed, Anderson's critique of the PCF was made in general terms that suggested that the PCI too might have been losing its appeal.[32] However, while Anderson may have rejected the pessimism of the

Western Marxists, he did not reject their stress on the importance of intellectuals to the socialist project. This is evident in his continued utilisation of Gramscian themes. For, while Anderson moved from an overtly reformist to a revolutionary interpretation of Gramsci, he did so in such a way as to reinforce the predominant place given to the intelligentsia within the socialist strategic project. Thus, while Gramsci's writings from the *L'Ordine Nuovo* period were reprinted in *NLR 51*, rather than extracts from his *Prison Notebooks*, they were reprinted precisely because Anderson believed that the Turin movement represented a rare occasion 'in socialist history when a theoretical initiative by an intellectual worker had been so massively and instantaneously adopted by industrial workers' (*NLR* 51 1968, 22). Consequentially, while he suggested that 'imperialism is vulnerable everywhere', he went on, ambivalently, to write that revolution was on the agenda 'in an advanced capitalist country' (*NLR* 52 1968, 1). Formally this was true, for only in France did a pre-revolutionary situation exist. However, in his argument he meant more than this, for he also suggested that one of the lessons for Britain was that one of the reasons for the French revolt was that in France a revolutionary culture existed, while in Britain it was yet to be created (*NLR* 52 1968, 7). So a formula taken over from Debray was used to underpin an argument that the culture of the French intellectual left had helped precipitate the revolution. Where Debray had argued that 'the small motor' or foco could set the 'large motor' – the masses – into action, Anderson suggested that in France the student revolt had been able to act in such a manner vis-à-vis the French proletariat because 'every French student is a natural heir of this cumulative development' of an advanced Marxist culture. So, Sartre and Althusser had acted as necessary, if not sufficient, causes of the events of May 1968. Anderson suggested that the revolutionary groups that acted as conduits for this revolutionary culture 'had helped to unleash a class storm that shook society to its foundations'. So, while the revolutionary potential of the proletariat had been revealed, 'at the same stroke the indisputable vital revolutionary role of the intellectuals' had been made apparent: 'united revolutionary action is the priority today: united revolutionary organisation is on the horizon tomorrow'. Moreover, he argued that revolutionary socialists in Britain should aim to link the student revolt to the growing alienation of the proletariat from the Labour Party: 'In Britain, the working class has visibly begun to secede from its traditional reformist party, but it has not gained any decisive new orientation. Meanwhile, a student revolt is emerging for the first time in our history. The immediate future may depend on a convergence of the two, the link between them can only be provided by revolutionary socialists' (*NLR* 52 1968, 7).

How could such an organisation be built? Over the next two years Anderson moved to attempt to answer this problem. The beginning of an answer was expressed in his introduction to Gramsci in *NLR 51*. Here, he argued, the weakness of Gramsci's early Marxism lay in his relegation of the importance to the development of a realistic socialist strategy of the revolutionary party in contrast with the soviet movement (*NLR* 51 1968, 26). Centrally, Gramsci's early works lacked a 'theory of insurrection', which was only overcome after 1921, when he put 'politics ... in command'. Moreover, the strength of Gramsci's later position lay in his argument that politics 'always has a military substratum'. Anderson concluded, 'the lessons of this experience have yet to be invalidated' (*NLR* 51 1968, 27).

Anderson initially, for instance in the essay *Introduction to Tukhachevsky*, looked to Mao to explain the nature of the military substratum to politics (*NLR* 55 1969). However, Mao's strategy for a peasant revolution was obviously of limited relevance to Western European socialists. Anderson therefore still required a political analysis of the 'military substratum' of the Western capitalist states. Mandel's defence of Trotsky's Marxism appeared in the next issue of the *Review*, and Anderson was persuaded by it of the importance of Trotsky's thought to the development of a revolutionary politics for Western Europe (Elliott 1998, 58). However, Trotsky was a Hegelian Marxist and Mandel defended him as such (Mandel 1969, 70). The problem for Anderson was that while he had shifted towards Trotskyism politically he had been facilitated in this evolution precisely by his break with Hegelian Marxism. Althusser's Marxism had opened a door to revolutionary politics for Anderson. However, Althusser famously had great difficulties in explaining the May events (Descombes 1980, 129; Elliott 1987, 235). Anderson thus required a non-Hegelian revolutionary theory that could both explain May as Trotsky and Sartre had done, in their different ways, and, simultaneously, avoid the conflation of the 'individual and history' that was a trait of Hegelian Marxism (Sartre 1974, 51).

Towards Revolutionary Socialism: Mandel and Colletti

Ernest Mandel took up Trotsky's defence against Krasso's critique of his Marxism in *NLR* 47 in 1968. Mandel's basic critique of Krasso centred on what he claimed to be the latter's idealism. Krasso tended not only to treat life processes as essentially governed by ideas but also he understood these ideas to be immutable. Thus, he shifted philosophically back from Marx through Hegel into Kantianism (Mandel 1969, 70). In contrast to this philosophical evolution Mandel argued that only a Hegelian Marxism could provide an understanding of the dynamic nature of the modern world. More specifically, Mandel used his knowledge of Trotsky to rebut Krasso's substantive criticisms; demolishing Krasso's charge that Trotsky had no developed understanding of politics (Mandel 1968, 37). Moreover, Mandel stressed, in general Lenin and Trotsky shared both revolutionary perspectives and an understanding of the nature of the party after 1917. Thus, 'it is hard to challenge Trotsky consistently without challenging Lenin' (Mandel 1969, 87). Furthermore, as the Stalinists had been responsible for a whole series of working class defeats from 1923 onwards, it could not be seriously maintained, as Krasso suggested, that Stalin had developed a superior analysis of the European perspectives for socialism after 1923. Mandel argued that by its actions Stalinism had proved itself to be an actively counter-revolutionary ideology. Finally, Mandel argued that Trotsky's oppositional programme of 1923 was realistic. I can't be sure how far Anderson came to agree with the detail of this analysis. However, we do know that by 1971 the Board of *NLR* split over the Chinese support for government suppression of revolutionary forces in Ceylon. The majority denounced the Chinese government's actions, and thus those Maoists who had previously felt at home on the editorial committee of *NLR* left the magazine (Birchall 1981, 71). Politically it therefore appears that Anderson had shifted beyond Maoism towards Trotskyism by 1970-71. Anderson's acceptance of Mandel's arguments was not, however, unconditional. In particular he remained convinced of the idealism of any Hegelian Marxism. Moreover, while he had become convinced of the fundamental contribution Trotsky had made to the Marxist tradition, he remained sceptical of Trotsky's actual political analyses of Western social formations. These, he continued to believe, suffered from an over reliance on the Russian model (Anderson 1976a, 119 & 1976b, 52). Both of these points were, of course, connected through Anderson's insistence that the world system was more complex than the Hegelian totality would allow. How then did his non-Hegelian Marxism develop? Of especial importance in this respect was the influence on Anderson of the ideas of Lucio Colletti.

There were two strands to Anderson's utilisation of aspects of Colletti's Marxism in the 1970s. First, he was attracted to Colletti's revolutionary politics. Second, while Anderson had become convinced by Althusser's critique of the idealism of Hegelian Marxism, he remained unconvinced of Althusser's alternative. So Anderson was looking for a non-Hegelian materialist epistemology upon which to base his revolutionary politics. As Colletti based his politics on just such an epistemology, he therefore attracted Anderson both philosophically and politically.

However, while Althusser's system could be condemned for its lack of a purchase on the concrete, Colletti's was marred by the opposite weakness, it tended to collapse analysis into description. As we shall see this weakness was transposed by Anderson onto his analysis of modes of production in his history of the European state system.

Anderson was convinced of Althusser's idealism by, amongst others, Norman Geras and Andre Glucksmann (Glucksmann 1977; Geras 1977). In an anonymous introduction to the Glucksmann essay, originally published in *NLR 72* in 1972, Anderson argued that Glucksmann's analysis of Balibar's conceptualisation of mode of production 'reveals insurmountable gaps and contradictions within it' (*NLR* ed. 1977, 275). Moreover, Glucksmann had shown that Althusser's method was an 'amphibology: a terminological round trip that never leaves its conceptual starting point except in its own imagination'. However, 'if it is the case that Althusser's epistemology is a variant of metaphysical transcendentalism, this does not mean that the alternative epistemologies which he attacks are in any way adequate or scientific either ... no Marxist epistemology as such yet exists' (*NLR* ed. 1977, 279-280). So, while Anderson rejected Althusser, he also rejected Hegelian Marxism. It would also appear that he rejected Colletti's Kantian alternative. However, by at the latest 1980 he was to accept Colletti's argument that a materialist epistemology must start from Kant (Anderson 1980, 6). Moreover, in the shorter term Colletti's approach, as we shall see, greatly appealed to him. This did not mean that Anderson believed that Althusser's contribution to Marxism was simply negative. On the contrary, neither Glucksmann's nor Geras's critiques affected the Althusserian concepts of overdetermination and differential temporality; these concepts were Althusser's 'most lasting accomplishments' (*NLR* ed. 1977, 281).

Like Althusser, Colletti argued that Hegel's thought fundamentally and inescapably combined religion and logic in a system within which the former undermined the latter. Colletti also argued that Marx was a scientist and had thus broken with Hegel's legacy. However, unlike Althusser, Colletti maintained that the concept of alienation was a scientific and not a Hegelian concept. So, with Althusser, he rejected Hegel and yet, by contrast with Althusser, he embraced the young Marx. So, while he argued that Marxism was scientific because it 'consists in the discovery of objective causal relationships', he hoped not fall into the trap of embracing a mechanical model of social change (Colletti 1972, 229).

This is evident in his discussion of the Marxist method. Here he aimed his fire at those vulgar Marxists - Second International and Stalinist - who had transformed Marxism into a mechanical system. He argued that in these versions of Marxism, the Marxist concept of production tended to be confused with its bourgeois cousin. The key fault with the bourgeois model of production is that it is anachronistic. Production is seen in generic terms, as encompassing all forms of productive activity throughout history, such that it is incapable of explaining change in history (Colletti 1972, 65). This fact explains the dualism in bourgeois thought between economics and politics: politics is perceived as active and independent of passive economics. The concept of production in Marx is very different; production is a social act which changes through history. Thus, transformations in the forces of production lead to complementary changes in the social relations between people. These social relations of production in turn shape the nature of politics and ideology and other superstructural elements. Moreover, these superstructural elements in turn react back upon production in a dialectical interplay where effect became cause.

Colletti argued that vulgar Marxism, in accepting the bourgeois model of production, bought into a dualistic model of history, which in effect mirrored the bourgeois model. For, whereas in traditional bourgeois history, change is explained politically with little reference to economic contexts, the vulgar Marxist merely reversed the ordering of causality. Economic development, in this system, caused political changes without conscious human intervention. The activist element of Marxism was therefore lost in the crude Marxist model. Colletti argued that the vulgar Marxists had used generic abstractions to explain social evolution and therefore mirrored the reification of history constitutive of bourgeois thought. Colletti's understanding of generic abstractions was similar to Althusser's critique of what he termed expressive totalities. Colletti saw in generic abstractions the residue of a Hegelian idealism creeping into Marxism that led to the examination of the ideal rather than the real (Colletti 1974a, 8). However, whereas Althusser had failed to develop a materialist alternative that could viably replace the expressive totality, Colletti replaced the generic with the determinate abstraction.

As with Althusser's complex totality Colletti's determinate abstraction was an attempt to break free of crude economism. 'This whole is a totality but it is a determinate totality; it is a synthesis of distinct elements, it is a unity but a unity of heterogeneous parts' (Colletti 1974a, 14). Moreover, Colletti argued that everything is material. So the scientific method is that method 'of investigating society at its material level' which 'to be truly scientific must be a study of all aspects of the social' (Colletti 1974a, 5). The difference between Colletti's determinate scientific abstraction and Althusser's complex totality can perhaps best be understood through the way in which Colletti's model sought to achieve a more secure purchase on the concrete; something that both Glucksmann's and Geras's critiques had shown that Althusser's system had failed to accomplish.

Colletti argued that nowhere in Marx could we find 'purely economic categories, all of his concepts are both economic and sociological' (Colletti 1974a, 13). He then argued that the forces of production could not be analysed in isolation from the social relations of production. Moreover, ideology could not be abstracted out from production. Consequentially, he rejected monism for a more dialectical account of social transformation. The concept that should underpin the scientific method was that of determinate scientific abstraction.

This was that abstraction through which one mode of production could be differentiated from another without collapsing into what he called 'generic idealistic notion of society in general' (Colletti 1974a, 7-8). Thus, capitalism and feudalism could be differentiated without merging all capitalisms into one generic type. Any society could share general features with other societies and yet still be understood in its singularity.

Anderson's generally positive assessment of this approach was outlined in his *Introduction to Colletti* published in *NLR 56* in 1969. Here he argued that the main strength of Colletti's approach lay in his 'critique of the bourgeois state as a hypostatization' (*NLR* 56 1969, 18). Colletti's method of determinate scientific abstraction was able to facilitate the retrieval of the Marxist theory of the state from the hypostatization to which Stalinism had condemned it, without losing sight of the fact that the state remained a capitalist state. Anderson believed that such a methodology was necessary if socialists were to succeed, scientifically, in underpinning revolutionary politics for the West. He then took it upon himself to answer the question of what was specific and what was general in the modern Western states. To answer this question he sought to trace the genealogy of the European state system in a panoramic survey. We shall discuss this project in the next chapter. He also sought to formulate his own transformed relationship to western Marxism and Trotskyism. He did this through his essay *Considerations on Western Marxism*.

Considerations on Western Marxism

The central thesis of *Considerations* can be stated briefly. Anderson argued that the revolutionary wave that marked the end of the First World War was eventually contained in the West. Containment led swiftly to counter-revolution, and under the twin prongs of Stalinism and fascism an authentic mass-based Marxism was defeated in the West. Those intellectuals who maintained an allegiance to Marxism in this zone were thus left isolated, and quickly migrated into the academy. Western Marxism was thus characterised by its 'structural divorce ... from political practice'. In the context of the long post-war boom and the stabilisation of bourgeois democracy these academic Marxists became increasingly pessimistic as to the prospects for socialism in the West (Anderson 1976a, 42, 29 & 24). Contemporaneously, Marx's *1844 Manuscripts* were first published, and provided a safe arena for study that did not impinge upon the hallowed grounds of Comintern strategy. Western Marxism then grew as, not simply an academic Marxism, but more particularly as a philosophical Marxism. This is not to say that it bore no fruit: in the cultural and aesthetic arenas much of interest was produced. However, of necessity it said nothing about strategy. Indeed, as they were divorced from the workers' movement, the Western Marxists very quickly found that they had nothing to say to them.

1968, however, changed everything. Once more a revolutionary workers' movement was on the agenda in Western Europe. Such a movement could be best served not by Western Marxism but by that tradition represented by the works of Leon Trotsky and some of his followers. However, while Trotsky's ideas were important, the groups that had maintained an allegiance to them were not. Anderson suggested that Trotskyism was inconceivable between the 1920s and 1968. Moreover, he presumed that Trotskyism – or revolutionary Marxism – would spontaneously grow out of the mass struggles of 1968 without the help of the small groups that bore his name: 'May 1968 marked in this respect a profound turning point' (Anderson 1976a, 95). This was as true for Western Marxism as it was for Trotskyism. For while it meant rebirth for the latter, it signalled the end of the former: 'As a historical form' Western Marxism 'will fall into extinction'. Moreover, 'among the younger generation', there were signs of a shift towards 'economic and political theory', and Anderson also expressed hope that an Anglo-Saxon Marxism would develop and that this would, as part of an international debate, examine and overcome the limitations of classical Marxism through the application Marxist historiography (Anderson 1976a, 101-3 and 110). To understand how he came to such conclusions we must first examine his analysis of the classical Marxist tradition.

Anderson took his analysis of the classical tradition from Deutscher, who had characterised it as that body of work associated with Marx, Engels, Kautsky, Plekhanov, Lenin, Trotsky and Luxemburg (Deutscher 1984, 245). Importantly, in order to maintain that Stalinism was in some degenerate sense still a version of Marxism, Deutscher was compelled to redefine the Marxist analysis of the relationship between theory and practice. The classical Marxists, he argued, had maintained a close relationship between theory and practice. However, Marxism had since then degenerated into two strands; one in the West was divorced from practice, while there developed in the East a vulgar Marxism that was closely related to practice. Unfortunately, as this was the practice of the relatively backward Eastern European states, vulgar Marxism, 'reflected the requirements of the labour movement' of these countries (Deutscher 1984, 246). Practice in these countries was the bane of healthy Marxism: 'practice is sometimes the enemy of thought, thought sometimes suffers from contact with practice'.

The vulgar Marxists, he argued, were satisfied with the small fraction of the profound riches of classical Marxism. Implicit in this proposition was the position that Stalinism – vulgar Marxism – was a genuine, if corrupt, version of Marxism. Explicitly, Deutscher also maintained that Marx had developed a system far in advance of the practical needs of the working class. Thus, while

Marx's work was infused with a deep sense of proletarian practice it was not constrained by it. Stalinism was, conversely, constrained by the backwardness of the Russian workers' movement.

Deutscher's view of the classical tradition is thus of a tradition that produced superior theory and did so in relation to the mass workers' movement. This model profoundly influenced Anderson's understanding of classical Marxism. Anderson's classical tradition was slightly broader than Deutscher's – he included Preobrazhensky, Bauer, Bukharin, Mehring and Labriola in his inventory. However, this amounted to nothing more than filling the gaps in Deutscher's list. Moreover, as with Deutscher, he insisted that each Marxist reflected the objective limitations of his or her national social formation. So in just the same sense that Stalinism remained a legitimate interpretation of Marxism, albeit vulgar on account of Russia's backwardness, then, despite their split, Kautsky and Lenin could both be regarded as Marxists, albeit rooted in different national contexts.

Anderson was not unaware of the split within the Second International: 'The First World War was to part the ranks of the Marxist theory in Europe as radically as it split the working class movement itself'. Moreover, he was aware of the fact that this split was not down to a simple question of geography: it 'ran through rather than between various national contingents'. However, he attempted to maintain a geographical delineation. Thus, Rosa Luxemburg, in her polemics with Bernstein at the turn of the century and with Kautsky a decade later, 'in which the basic dividing lines of future working-class politics were finally drawn', was informed more by her Polish rather than German experiences, for the Polish working class was much more 'insurgent' than the German (Anderson 1976a, 12-14). Thus, Anderson implied that Luxemburg was correct with regard to Poland and Russia, but unrealistic regarding German politics.

This prognosis is strengthened if we look at Anderson's discussion of the German Revolution itself. For this revolutionary process of peaks and troughs between 1918 and 1923 was reduced by Anderson to 'a confused semi spontaneous rising' (Anderson 1976a, 16; cf Harman 1982). Moreover, in place of even a footnote as a pointer towards a discussion of the actual dynamics of the revolutionary wave, Anderson suggested that 'capital proved decisively stronger everywhere outside Russia' (Anderson 1976a, 15). This point is of incredible importance. For while, reading between the lines, it is clear that Anderson's heart is with Luxemburg, his head, in Germany at least, seems to be with Kautsky. Revolution simply was not on the agenda in the West.

Given that Anderson's whole thesis rests upon the argument that Western Marxism was a product of the defeat in the West, and that both subjectively and objectively Germany was the key to the international revolution in the post-war years (Carr 1969), any diagnosis of defeat must at least ask the question, could the German revolutionaries have won? Anderson's answer appears to be no. Moreover, he places no blame on the Russians for this defeat; it was purely a predetermined German matter. To substantiate this position he was forced not only to distort history but also, ironically, to ignore Trotsky's analysis of that history.

Trotsky had argued that there had existed a revolutionary situation in Germany in 1923 which was wasted by the leadership of the KPD. This tragedy was itself a product of the weaknesses of the German leadership, which, at most, had served for four or five years in an independent revolutionary movement. A strong leadership had not, therefore, had enough time to coalesce in the young party. Moreover, the party had made serious mistakes in its early years which had predisposed its leaders, understandably, to look to Moscow for leadership. The unfortunate corollary of this was that in 1923 the German leadership was constantly looking over its shoulders to Moscow. Moscow meanwhile failed to act decisively (Trotsky 1987).

Trotsky thus analysed the events of 1923 in Germany as a missed revolutionary opportunity. Moreover, he argued that amongst the political fallout from this defeat was the growth in consciousness of the Soviet bureaucracy as a social layer with interests distinct from the rest of Russian society. For as the hope of world revolution faded the bureaucracy, given the dramatic collapse of the Soviet working class, grew as an independent force in society. Anderson, however, not only failed to hint at this debate but also distorted history to make it irrelevant; for him the revolutionary crisis was over by 1920: 'The German Revolution born of the workers' and soldiers' councils of November 1918 had been decisively defeated by 1920'. This allowed him to maintain that the Russians had played no part in the defeat: 'The fateful setback in Germany occurred before the Bolshevik Revolution was itself sufficiently disengaged from imperialist intervention to be able to exercise a direct organisational or theoretical influence'. Thus, the German Revolution ends as simply a 'confused semi spontaneous rising'. Its defeat was not 'primarily due to subjective mistakes or failure' but was rather a product of 'the objectively superior strength of capitalism in central and western Europe' (Anderson 1976a, 16-18). In as far as this model is an implicit rejection of Trotsky's perspectives at the time, it did again dovetail with Deutscher's argument that Trotsky had been mistaken about the prospects for revolution in the West after the First World War (Deutscher 1987c, 513).

The corollary of Anderson's belief that the West was not ripe for revolution – that 'the bourgeois order in the West had not exhausted its historical lifespan' – was his view that the bourgeois order 'still commanded the loyalty of the largest and best trained intellectual strata in the world, whose creative performance continued to be substantial in field after field' (Anderson 1976a, 55): Thus, 'after 1920 Marxism as a whole advanced less rapidly in a large number of disciplines than non-Marxist cultures'. The logical conclusion of such a proposition would surely have been for Anderson to develop a political programme that paralleled his 1960s intervention. If then he had hoped to enrich a parochial English Marxism with Western Marxism, now it would appear that he should add to this old mix the new ingredient of bourgeois thought proper. As we shall see in his history, he had no qualms about using insights from the academy to improve his Marxist model (Anderson 1974a, 9). However, just as this perspective was formulated, it was to be rejected, for May 1968 had deeply altered the geography of international politics. It marked 'a profound historical turning point' which 'rendered potentially conceivable the unification of Marxist theory and working-class practice' (Anderson 1976a, 95). But which theory would be united with practice? Anderson decided that Trotsky's Marxism was free of the taints associated with either Stalinism or Western Marxism. Moreover, Trotskyism could trace a link from the classical tradition to the contemporary world through Deutscher, Rosdolsky and Mandel.

However, these three contemporaries were not equivalent. In particular Mandel was the leading theoretician of the Trotskyist Fourth International, whilst Deutscher had broken with Trotsky over the formation of just that organisation. Moreover, while Anderson noted the importance of Mandel's *Late Capitalism*, it was to Deutscher that he looked as Trotsky's genuine heir: 'despite his divergences from Trotsky the continuity of focus between them could hardly have been closer'. Moreover, like Deutscher but unlike Mandel, Anderson downplayed the applicability of Trotsky's theory of permanent revolution to the underdeveloped world, and argued that Trotsky was weakest when engaged in analysis of Western Europe, with the important exception of Weimar Germany (Anderson 1976a, 98-100). However, the area of greatest divergence between Mandel's and Deutscher's Trotskyisms lay in the fact that while Mandel was the consummate activist, Deutscher had explicitly retreated from political activity.

Anderson was aware that, in contrast to this position, activity was the life-blood of Trotsky's thought: 'Trotsky's life from the death of Lenin onwards was devoted to a practical and theoretical struggle to free the international workers' movement from bureaucratic domination so that it could resume a successful overthrow of capitalism on a world scale' (Anderson 1976a, 96). However, the essay ended with the dismissal of 'small revolutionary group' politics. The reason for this was that 'it is only when the masses themselves are revolutionary that theory can complete its eminent vocation' (Anderson 1976a, 105-106). Moreover, he suggested that as the Western masses had not been revolutionary before 1968, 'Trotskyism was a delayed birth' (Anderson 1976a, 96). Trotsky's own opinion of those who refused to build the party in periods of quiescence as well as upheavals, and instead argued that the masses are not ready, was that they condemn themselves to irrelevance in periods of crisis. They 'publish their little journals and their theoretical studies in a corner, on the side lines, away from the actual developments of revolutionary thought, let alone the movement of the masses' (Trotsky 1973, 365).

Anderson's understanding of the nature of the revolutionary movement is diametrically opposed to this. His view was that socialists in Britain should join neither one of the competing revolutionary groups nor the Labour Party. Rather, socialists should merely wait for the masses to speak. Moreover, the Marxist concept of proletarian 'self emancipation' could only be achieved if a new type of 'organic intellectual' stratum spontaneously developed inside the working class in the new revolutionary epoch, that could truly lead a self-emancipatory movement. The precondition for the development of such a movement, he argued, was that it would be 'free of organisational constraint' (Anderson 1976a, 104-106). Ironically, given Anderson's anti-Hegelian framework, it appeared that his conclusions mirrored those of the ultra-Hegelian and spontaneist ex-Trotskyist CLR James.[33] Indeed, Anderson's conclusion seems nonsensical given his philosophical position, and he himself later recognised that this position was 'reductionist' and rejected it. However, this rejection did not lead him to re-embrace activity, but rather led him to suggest that Marxism's proper arena of interest should be the study of history (Anderson 1976a, 109-110). Thus while *Considerations* may have been a repudiation of the Western Marxist tradition it was not a call to arms. Instead, Anderson suggested that Western Marxism had fitted with the period from the 1920s to 1968 but did not fit any longer. As such, struggles for or against it would be worthless; it was simply to be hoped that a new generation of Marxist strategists would spontaneously take the place of the philosophers.

However, a less diligent Trotskyist could have read *Considerations* in an activist manner. This Anderson aimed to put right in an afterword written two years after the main body of the text:[34] 'The conclusions of the essay invite an activist reading of its thesis that could be scientifically untenable and politically irresponsible'. Against such a reading, Anderson maintained that Marxism must above all be 'a theory of history'. As such it is primarily 'knowledge of the realm of the dead'. Moreover, such knowledge would be more certain than knowledge of the present. Therefore, 'there will always remain an inherent scissiparity between knowledge and action, theory and practice for any possible science of history' (Anderson 1976a, 109-110). Specifically, Anderson argued, Marxists should examine their models of bourgeois democracy, the state, nationalism, economics, the party, socialist strategy East and

West, the nature of the socialist camp, and the theory of permanent revolution (Anderson 1976a, 114 ff).

With regard to political-economy, Anderson intervened in an important revisionist debate in the 1970s. In *Considerations* he argued that contemporary research had placed 'doubts' over the viability of the labour theory of value. Given that this related, as Anderson noted, to the cornerstone of Marx's politics, this debate was of more than academic interest.

'The most hazardous conclusions that the system of *Capital* yielded were the general theorems of the falling rate of profit, and the tenet of an ever increasing class polarisation between bourgeoisie and proletariat. Neither has yet been adequately substantiated. The first implied an economic breakdown of capitalism by its inner mechanisms; the second a social breakdown by way ... of an ultimate absolute preponderance of a vast industrial working class of productive labourers over a tiny bourgeoisie, with few or no intermediary groups. The very absence of any political theory proper in the late Marx may thus be logically related to a latent catastrophism in his economic theory, which rendered the development of the former redundant' (Anderson 1976a, 115).

Whether or not these ascribed views were true of Marx's thought, Anderson's acceptance of their validity caused him to doubt Marx's theory of value and thus to doubt his account of the dynamics of bourgeois society. These doubts were highlighted in the mid 1970s when a number of radical economists began to debate methodological issues in Marxist economics. Anderson opened the pages of *NLR* to this debate where Bob Rowthorn defended classical Marxism, Ian Steedman and Geoff Hodgson developed neo-Ricardian critiques of Marxism, while Erik Olin Wright attempted a synthesis of the two schools (Rowthorn 1974, Hodgson 1974, Steedman 1975, Wright 1979). Anderson himself did not publish a clear indication of his position within the debate. However, *NLR* did co-sponsor a conference entitled *The Value Controversy* in November 1978 and published the main papers delivered at the conference in a book of that title in 1981. Moreover, between the conference and the publication of the book, *NLR* published only one paper from the conference, Erik Olin Wright's attempted synthesis of neo-Ricardianism and Marxism, described in *Themes* as one of the 'central contributions' to the conference (*NLR* 116 1979, 1). Furthermore, the only sign of *NLR*'s editorial intervention in *The Value Controversy* was the publication of a new essay by Wright, whose attempt to synthesis classical Marxism and neo-Ricardianism saw him reduce the labour theory of value to a 'compelling way of understanding exploitation' (Steedman et al 1981, 161).

As we shall see in chapter five, the debate on value theory occurred at around the time that Anderson became convinced of the 'fundamental' importance of G.A. Cohen's reinterpretation of orthodox Marxism (Anderson

1980, 40). Interestingly, Cohen was convinced that the labour theory of value was 'irrelevant' to the development of Marxist politics (Cohen 1981, 202 and Cohen 1978, 116 and 196). In its place Cohen argued that exploitation could be understood to be an 'injustice' irrespective of affiliation to the precepts of the labour theory of value. Thus, he argued that the existence of this injustice was a good reason for overthrowing capitalism (Cohen 1981, 206). However, that there was a moral reason for overthrowing capitalism was not central to Marx's value theory. Rather, value theory underpinned Marx's account of the laws of motion of the capitalist mode of production. Once this element was excluded from his thought then only a moral condemnation of inequality remained. This insistence on the moral aspect of socialist politics was, as Ben Fine and Lawrence Harris have argued, the general conclusion to which socialists who rejected the labour theory of value gravitated: they 'reduce Marxism to a moral polemic rather than a science' (Fine and Harris 1979, 30).

Summary

In 1964 Anderson was a critical supporter of Harold Wilson's new government. Six years later he was a convinced revolutionary Marxist. This dramatic radicalisation must be understood as a consequence of the interplay of extrinsic and intrinsic histories. Extrinsically, Anderson was just one of millions who found themselves radicalised by the events of the late 1960s. Intrinsically, his understanding of Marxism had been given a more flexible twist by his shift from an acceptance of a Hegelian to an Althusserian perception of totality. His earlier interpretation of Hegel's system had led him to reject the possibility of revolutionary socialist practice in Britain. His reading of Althusser, by contrast, opened the door to his embrace of revolutionary Marxism. However, it did this without forcing him to question the fundamentals of his analysis of British society. This evolution took him into the orbit of Trotskyism. However, this trajectory did not lead him fully to embrace Trotsky's politics. Rather, he predicated the development of correct political practice on the solution to the problem of the specificity of the structure of the Western European states. Thus, Anderson silently displayed the marks that Western Marxism had left on him. For whereas the classical Marxists had developed their ideas in close connection to the working-class movement, Anderson appears to have accepted the Althusserian notion of 'theoretical practice'. The theoretical task at hand, as Anderson saw it, was to develop a socialist strategy that could confront the modern Western states in the way that Leninism had confronted Tsarism. Anderson took this problematic and attempted to solve it by writing a history of the European system of states from antiquity to the present day, thus mapping the contours of its complex social structure.

CHAPTER FOUR

A REVOLUTIONARY STRATEGY FOR THE WEST

1968 marked a watershed in post-war history as, for the first time since the 1920s, socialist advance appeared to be on the horizon almost everywhere (Harman 1988). Unfortunately, Anderson believed that the subjective forces on the left did not match the objective potential for social transformation in this period. In particular, all of the various strands of Marxism had at their heart a lacuna; they contained no satisfactory theory of the modern bourgeois state as it had evolved in the West. Anderson believed that it was imperative that the Marxist left addressed this lacuna in their theory, and he therefore turned to this task in the early 1970s, doing so with an increased sense of urgency after the derailment of the Portuguese Revolution in the mid 1970s.

As we have seen, while from around 1970 Anderson had come to identify himself politically with Trotskyism, he had not been convinced that Trotsky's analyses of particular West European social formations were of direct strategic relevance to the modern world. In particular, while he believed that Trotsky's analysis of the victory of Nazism in Weimar Germany was of exemplary clarity, as Weimar was 'an atypical form of bourgeois state', Trotsky's discussion of its structure was of limited general value to those socialists who were attempting to analyse modern Western states. Moreover, Trotsky's other attempts to analyse Western states were much less satisfactory: despite his insights, he had failed to develop a 'systematic account' of the nature of bourgeois democracy. This was most evident in his analyses of Popular Front regimes in France and Spain and in his characterisation of the Second World War as an inter-imperialist conflict. In all of these cases, Trotsky had failed to do what he had done so well in his writings on Germany: to distinguish clearly between bourgeois democratic and fascist regimes (Anderson 1976a, 119). Anderson saw it as a political priority to remedy this failing in Trotskyist theory.

Anderson's attempt to locate the *differentia specifica* of the West was planned to cover four volumes. The first two would draw a history of Europe up to the epoch of the bourgeois revolutions, the third would analyse these revolutions, while the fourth would detail a sociological outline of the modern Western world. In this sense the project was structured as an extension on a grand scale of the methodology of *Portugal and the End of Ultra-Colonialism* and *Origins* – albeit utilising a different concept of the totality. Unfortunately, only the first two volumes, *Passages From Antiquity to Feudalism* and *Lineages of the Absolutist State*, were ever published. This does not mean that we have no clue as to Anderson's political conclusions. On the contrary, he published two essays that supply us with a schematic impression of the probable content of these volumes: *The Notion of a Bourgeois Revolution* and *The Antinomies of Antonio Gramsci*. I shall discuss these essays as surrogates for the unpublished manuscripts.[35]

THE *DIFFERENTIA SPECIFICA* OF THE WEST

Anderson's prime objective in his historical and theoretical works of the early 1970s was to 'situate the specificity of the European experience' (Anderson 1974a, 8).[36] From Machiavelli in the sixteenth century, he argued, European thinkers had understood the 'Ottoman State as the antithesis of a European monarchy'. Moreover, from the seventeenth century onwards, this comparison had begun to universally favour the Europeans (Anderson 1974b, 397 & 399). By contrast with this pattern, Marxist scholars in the twentieth century had downplayed the difference between Europe and the rest of the world. Specifically they had 'generally asserted that feudalism was a worldwide phenomenon'. This position implied that for these Marxists 'all privilege to Western European development is thereby held to disappear'. Thus, through their definition of feudalism as, in effect, 'landlordism', twentieth century Marxists had undermined their own attempts to develop realistic models of the 'unique dynamism of the European theatre of international feudalism' (Anderson 1974b, 401-2). Anderson sought to overcome this methodological weakness, and thus his history was positioned in opposition to this dominant Marxist paradigm of the day.

Anderson looked to Marx to aid this project. In the *Grundrisse* Marx had argued that pre-capitalist societies could be differentiated through comparative examinations of their 'laws and states'. Following this insight, and in line with the Collettian methodology noted in the last chapter, Anderson concluded that 'pre-capitalist modes of production cannot be defined except via their political, legal and ideological superstructures, since these are what determine the type of extra-economic coercion that specifies them' (Anderson 1974b,

403-404). Since the key institution of extra-economic coercion was the state, Anderson delineated pre-capitalist modes of production along lines set by their differential state structures.

In his comparative analysis of a series of European and non-European states, Anderson came to the conclusion that, while feudalism was more restricted in its geographical spread than previous Marxists had believed, it was not coterminous with medieval Europe. Specifically, pre-Meiji Japan bore all the hallmarks of the feudal mode of production (Anderson 1974b, 413). Given that Japan had neither witnessed an endogenous transition to capitalism, nor begun a spontaneous movement towards absolutism, this implied that the structure of feudalism *per se* could not explain the emergence of the capitalist mode of production (Anderson 1974b, 416).[37] Something else beyond this structure was necessary for capitalism to take hold in Europe. Anderson looked for this key to Europe's specificity in its genealogy. For 'the whole genealogy of Japan … presents an unequivocal contrast with the descent of feudalism in Europe' (Anderson 1974b, 418).

Anderson argued that the specificity of Western European feudalism lay in the nature of its foundation.[38] Born of a fusion between Rome and the Germanic tribes, the uniqueness of the West was rooted in its Roman heritage. In particular, Roman law supplied a legal framework which both underpinned 'Absolutist public authority' and 'absolute private property'. This dual role of Roman law provided Western Europe with its *differentia specifica*. Moreover, Roman law facilitated both the development, after the Renaissance, of absolutism, and, co-temporally but distinctly, facilitated the development of capitalism (Anderson 1974b, 428-429).[39]

Anderson defined feudalism as a mode of production characterised by a combination of a 'natural economy, dominated by the land', where 'neither labour nor the products of labour were commodities'. Legally defined as serfdom, the peasant was bound to the earth, which was 'owned' by the lord but in 'degree only'. The corollary of this was that the lord was required to use extra economic means to extract surplus. These forces of extra economic coercion ensured that sovereignty was devolved downwards from the state proper to the lords. However, nowhere did the lords exercise absolute property rights. Thus, while sovereignty was in effect parcellized, it was combined with 'scalar private property in land' (Anderson 1974a, 147-8 & Anderson 1974b, 414). How then did the absolutist states of the early modern period relate to these medieval machines?

The central claim of Anderson's thesis in *Lineages* was that absolutist states were 'redeployed and recharged apparatus of feudal domination' (Anderson 1974b, 18). Moreover, the nature of the demise of each specific absolutist state was predicated upon the level of the development of capitalism within each one, which, in each case, turned on their genealogy. Anderson argued that there was a fundamental difference between Eastern and Western absolutisms. Absolutism in the West had evolved spontaneously from Western feudalism, while absolutism in the East was a product of the military competition between the Eastern states and the Western absolutist monarchies (Anderson 1974b, 15 & 197). Moreover, while the development of Western absolutism coincided with the end of serfdom in the West, the development of Eastern absolutism coincided with the reintroduction of serfdom in the East (Anderson 1974b, 195). This distinction meant that, while Eastern and Western states shared many formal similarities, the development of the Eastern states was not, unlike those in the West, 'overdetermined' by the development of a capitalist civil society (Anderson 1974b, 22). This explained the differential experiences of all the European states in the epoch of bourgeois revolutions.

In the West there had developed a capitalist civil society which could pose as an alternative to absolutism once that system went into crisis. In the East, by contrast, no well-developed bourgeoisie existed. Prussia's specificity lay in its annexation of West German provinces. These provided the new Germany with the critical bourgeois mass to facilitate the development of a capitalist solution to the crisis of the *ancien regime*. As a consequence of their divergent structures each manifestation of absolutism gave birth to distinct offspring. In the West – England, Spain and France – bourgeois revolutions from below broke the absolutist monarchies, while in the East – Russia – absolutism was overthrown by a socialist revolution. Germany and Italy were transitional cases that encompassed elements of both Eastern and Western patterns. Their distinct fate was thus to be overthrown by bourgeois revolutions from above (Anderson 1974b, 431).

This conclusion had a direct political corollary. Anderson ended his chapter on Russia with the suggestion that the Tsarist autocracy in 1917 was a feudal state, and thus that the experience of the Bolshevik revolution was of limited value to socialists facing modern capitalist states in the West.[40] 'The Russian Revolution was not made against a capitalist state at all. The Tsarism which fell in 1917 was a feudal apparatus: the Provisional government never had time to replace it with a new or stable bourgeois apparatus. The Bolsheviks made a socialist revolution but from beginning to end they never confronted the central enemy of the workers' movement in the West. Gramsci's deepest intuition was in this sense correct: the modern capitalist state in the West remained – after the October Revolution – a new political object for Marxist theory and revolutionary practice'. Conversely, the 'transmutation' of the Prussian state into a capitalist state under Bismarck 'assured the integral survival of the old state apparatus into the Versailles epoch ... the failure of the November Revolution in Germany ... was grounded in the differential nature of the state machine' vis-à-vis its Russian counterpart (Anderson 1974b, 359).

So, Anderson, in a wonderful panoramic study, outlined a genealogical underpinning of the differential reactions of the European states to the crisis of absolutism. However, this was in a sense a purely negative feat, for, while this thesis implied that Leninism was of a limited strategic significance to modern Western socialists, Anderson did not outline an alternative strategy. Moreover, his analysis of the fundamental distinction between Eastern and Western absolutism was incoherent.[41]

Absolutism, Anderson argued, 'represented a decisive rupture with the pyramidal, parcellized sovereignty of the medieval social formation' (Anderson 1974b, 15). Despite this claim, he maintained that the absolutist states were feudal structures as 'throughout the early modern epoch, the dominant class – economically and politically – was the same as in the medieval epoch itself: the feudal aristocracy'. So while the aristocracy had, during this period, undergone a 'profound metamorphoses', it was 'never dislodged from command over political power'. Thus, all that had changed in the transition to absolutism were 'the forms of feudal exploitation' (Anderson 1974b, 18).

Fulbrook and Skocpol have argued that through these formulations Anderson is compelled to retreat from his definition of feudalism as a system characterised by the parcellization of sovereignty and the existence of scaler property in land. Ironically, to characterise the absolutist states as feudal, Anderson 'ends up equating feudalism with a type of landlordism, just like the Marxists of whom he is critical' (Fulbrook and Skocpol 1984, 186). So, while he is keen to deny that the absolutist states were capitalist states, absolutism does not easily fit with his own model of feudalism.[42] There is therefore a degree of arbitrariness in his classification of the absolutist states generally, and thus Russia in 1917 specifically, as feudal states. One solution to this problem, which evidently did not appeal to Anderson, would have been for him to characterise absolutism as a distinct mode of production. A second solution would have been to classify absolutism as a transitional form between feudal and capitalist states. However, drawing on ideas from Althusser, while Anderson was keen to argue that absolutism in the West nourished an independent capitalist class, he was convinced that this class was separate from the absolutist bureaucracy, which remained feudal.

Anderson's thesis that the absolutist states were feudal structures related as much to his definition of capitalism as it did to his definition of feudalism. He argued that the policy of the absolutist states was mercantilist; moreover, this policy 'undoubtedly demanded the suppression of particularistic barriers to trade within the national realm, and strove to create a unified domestic market for commodity production'. However, mercantilism was not a proto-capitalist policy, rather it 'represented the conceptions of a feudal ruling class that had adopted to an integrated market'. Indeed, mercantilism was the 'antipode' of the 'classical bourgeois doctrine of laissez-faire' (Anderson 1974b, 35-36). 'Absolutist monarchies introduced standing armies, a permanent bureaucracy, national taxation, a codified law, and the beginnings of a unified market ... all these characteristics appear to be predominantly capitalist' (Anderson 1974b, 17). However, this was not so, not only were these states feudal, they were also 'archaic'. The absolutist state was a 'machine built for the battle field', and its aggressive nature was a product of a 'swollen memory of the medieval functions of war'. Thus, the wars and diplomacy that concluded with the Treaty of Westphalia were not characteristically modern phenomena. Anderson suggested that the 75 years of war in sixteenth century Europe, and the 93 years of war in the following century, were products of the feudal nature of these states: 'such calendars are foreign to capital' (Anderson 1974b, 32-33).[43] For, while mercantilism was a 'bellicist' policy, the policy of laissez-faire was 'pacifist' (Anderson 1974b, 36).

Anderson argued that the 'apparent paradox of Absolutism in Western Europe was that it fundamentally represented an apparatus for the protection of aristocratic property and privileges, yet at the same time the means whereby this protection was promoted could *simultaneously* ensure the basic interests of the nascent mercantile and manufacturing classes'. However, the capitalist aspect to mercantilism was simply a fortuitous accident. Thus, the state remained feudal while 'hybrid capitalisations of feudal forms abounded' (Anderson 1974b, 40). He came to this conclusion via the distinction he drew between capitalism and mercantilism. Mercantilism, he argued, was a system characterised by the 'indistinction' of the economy and polity, while the 'classical bourgeois doctrines of laissez-faire, with their rigorous formal separation of the political and economic systems, were to be its antipode'. Therefore, as the absolutist states were mercantilist they could not be capitalist, and indeed they remained feudal because of the 'indistinction of economy and polity in the transitional epoch' (Anderson 1974b, 36). However, Anderson defined all pre-capitalist societies by the indistinction of their economic and political systems, and understood differences between their modes of production to be constituted through their superstructures. Unfortunately, according to such criteria it is plain that the absolutist state structure of early modern Europe were distinct from those of earlier feudal states, and therefore the absolutist states could not be coherently described as feudal in his own terms.

Anderson's problem here lies in the contradiction between his use of a generic abstraction to define capitalism, and his descriptive model of feudalism. There is therefore a constant elision in the meaning that he ascribes to feudalism in his work, while capitalism is defined to be rigidly distinct from its parent. Marxism, by contrast, demands a realist model of modes of production.

In particular it demands, in Marx's words, that, capitalism be understood as a 'process, in whose various moments it is always capital' (Marx 1973a, 258). Bukharin, for instance, argued that capitalism has evolved through commercial, industrial and finance phases towards its modern (1925) phase of state capitalism (Bukharin 1982, 15-16). In a similar vein Holton criticises Anderson's undynamic model of capitalism and his associated refusal to confront the 'proto-capitalist' policies of the mercantilist absolutist state (Holton 1985, 97). Through these policies absolutist monarchs could facilitate capitalist accumulation, for their own ends, while remaining in essence a feudal class.

The monarch could act in this way because, as Miliband points out, he was not identical with the aristocracy as a whole. Miliband suggests, echoing Thompson's critique of *Origins*, that Anderson's use of an anthropomorphic model of class mediated against his acknowledgement of this, and thus undermined his analysis of the absolutist state. For when Anderson, correctly in Miliband's view, argued that the absolutist state represented the aristocracy, he underestimated the extent to which this class was divided into strata, and consequently he underestimated the extent to which the absolutist state could act with relative autonomy, which could in turn explain the contradictory nature of the state's relation to capitalism. Because Anderson stressed the feudal nature of the state, at the expense of this autonomy, he was thus ill equipped to explain the novel structure of the absolutist state (Miliband 1983, 56 ff).

These problems suggest that Anderson's characterisation of the absolutist states as feudal obscured as much as it revealed. This had a direct political influence on his Marxism. For he believed that he had proved that the Western states were qualitatively distinct from their Eastern cousins. However, if the Russian state in 1917 was something other than a feudal state, then the exact degree of its divergence from the West remained to be established. Thus, his critique of the transferability of the Trotskyist revolutionary paradigm to the West was built upon weak foundations; indeed, the whole thrust of Anderson's discussion of this issue seems to miss the point. February was not October; the state that the Bolsheviks faced had changed after Lenin had characterised the Tsarist state as feudal in the late nineteenth century. Anderson notes Lenin's earlier analysis of late Russian feudalism, but does not mention the transformation in Lenin's own perspective (Anderson 1974b, 355). In fact, Lenin maintained that the state that the Bolsheviks faced between February and October 1917 was a weak capitalist state: 'state power had passed to the bourgeoisie' (Lenin 1970, 14). Moreover, he maintained that the bourgeois democratic revolution was to this extent 'completed' (Lenin 1970, 15). Similarly, Trotsky argued that the February Revolution had placed the state apparatus in the hands of the bourgeoisie (Trotsky 1977, 172 & 329). So, according to the two leaders of the Revolution, the Russian State, over the summer of 1917, was a bourgeois state. Commenting on a similar point Paul Hirst has argued that 'because the provisional government did not and could not turn itself into a stable bourgeois republic, does not mean that the October Revolution was not made against a state representing the bourgeoisie and its political allies' (Hirst 1985, 120).

Be this as it may, in his 1976 essay *The Notion of a Bourgeois Revolution* Anderson developed his thesis that the modern Western state was a qualitatively different structure to that faced by the Bolsheviks in 1917. In this essay he divided bourgeois revolutions along 'two temporalities'. The first, in the West, 'belongs to an epoch prior to the industrial revolution'; these were revolutions 'from below'. The second encompassed events in 'Germany, Italy and Japan' which were revolutions from above; these came after industrialisation (Anderson 1992f, 116). The most notable divergence of this summary from that given in *Lineages* is that in *The Notion of a Bourgeois Revolution* the analytical significance of industrialisation replaces that of genealogy as the explanation of the differential trajectories taken by various states.[44] A second difference is that in this latter summary the Russian Revolution no longer inhabited the same conceptual framework as those other revolutions.

Anderson argued that a theoretical framework could be demonstrated to 'delimit the space of any imaginable bourgeois revolutions'. They could be overdetermined from above, by the potentiality of a compromise developing between feudalism and capitalism, two modes of production based upon private property; from below, by the actions of the masses beneath the bourgeoisie; from within, by the necessarily heterogeneous nature of the bourgeoisie; and from without by the competitive relationship between the revolutionary state and its 'external environment'. Anderson rejected the 'crude' Marxist model of bourgeois revolutions which saw these revolutions as conflicts between rising industrial bourgeoisies and declining feudal nobilities. Indeed, in contrast to his earlier normative methodology, he argued that 'it was in the nature of bourgeois revolutions to be denatured: every one was a bastard birth'. In none of the upheavals – including France – 'did there ever occur an expropriation of the noble lands by the bourgeoisie'. They were all thus 'strikingly incomplete... and nowhere was a characteristically modern state generated' (Anderson 1992f, 110-115).

Whatever the basis for his new argument its consequences are striking. First, Russia, it implied, no longer inhabited the same conceptual framework as the West, while, second, modern bourgeois states, while built upon the foundations laid by the bourgeois revolutions, were, in fact, products of later processes. Anderson made the political consequences of this position explicit in his essay on Gramsci; an 'enormous gulf separated the Russian State from those in the West' (Anderson 1976b, 51). The problem remained then of uncovering the structure of bourgeois power in the West.

THE STRUCTURE OF BOURGEOIS DEMOCRACY

That the nature of bourgeois democracy was at the forefront of Anderson's thought throughout the 1970s is evident both in his work of the period, and in a series of essays that he published in *NLR* over the decade. In these essays, Anderson and his colleagues attempted to excavate the structure of bourgeois democracy so as to be better placed to aid its overthrow. These attempts to comprehend the structure of bourgeois democracy were, moreover, written in the context of a wider debate across the revolutionary left on this question.

At the end of 1971 *NLR* carried an essay by Robin Blackburn on the Heath government. In this essay, Blackburn foresaw the coming clashes between Heath and the labour movement. He argued that Heath 'shows none of his predecessors' inclination to overestimate the political strength of the trade unions'. Heath knew that nothing remotely like a real general strike 'was possible in the present state of the British labour movement'. He was determined to wage class war to solve Britain's economic crisis at the expense of the working class. Moreover, given the weak traditions of radicalism in the British labour movement this was a less risky strategy than it would have been in France, Japan or Italy. Therefore, while Heath's project would lead to an increased economic militancy on the part of the working class this would not cross over into an increased political militancy. Paradoxically, while the entrenched parliamentarianism of the British working class would thus act as a brake on their political radicalisation, Heath's switch from a predominantly Atlanticist orientation for British capital, to a predominantly European orientation, would bring him into conflict with this parliamentarist tradition, opening a door to revolutionary politics. Heath's new orientation would, Blackburn believed, 'undermine traditional fetishes and ideologies: above all it will weaken the already waning power of parliament' (Blackburn 1971, 19-22). Anderson's general assent to this diagnosis was signalled in the introductory *Themes* section to Blackburn's essay, in which he argued that 'in spite of the economic rationality of Heath's new course, it will disrupt political patterns that have long been an obstacle to the spread of revolutionary politics in Britain' (*NLR* 70 1971, 1). Therefore, while *NLR* fundamentally underestimated the prospects for radicalisation in the coming months (Kelly 1988, 104-15), they did have an optimistic perspective for liberating revolutionary socialism from its British political ghetto.

In early 1973 *NLR* returned to the subject of the Heath government, this time after the upsurge of economic and political militancy of 1972. Anthony Barnett, another member of the editorial committee, argued, in contrast to Blackburn, that it was Wilson, not Heath, who had best understood the unions (Barnett 1973, 36). Heath had misjudged the TUC, assuming that its resistance would simply collapse. To explain this miscalculation Barnett referred to the structure of bourgeois democracy. Capitalism, he argued, operates through the separation of economics from politics. This separation helped legitimise economic exploitation by removing it from the arena of political debate. Heath, by intervening politically into the workings of the economy, especially through the Industrial Relations Act, destroyed this mystification. He thus caused a growth in the politicisation of economic issues inside the working class and earned himself the hatred of many members of his own class. Moreover, his actions led to the politicisation of the law and hence to the further undermining of the structures of bourgeois legitimation (Barnett 1973, 38). Anderson again appears to have agreed with this prognosis: 'Heath's strategy failed to mobilize bourgeois power effectively against the working class, in part because of the structural constraints within the framework of capitalist democracy' (*NLR* 77 1973, 1). Thus, for Barnett and Anderson, while bourgeois democracy was structurally functional to the free workings of capitalism, it also provided constraints upon the actions of the bourgeoisie itself (Barnett 1973, 37).

The obvious question for socialists was how flexible were these constraints. In Britain the state had been pushed, but not anywhere close to its limits. But if the British system could be brought into question what then of much weaker Western states? An obvious case study presented itself in the form of the collapse of fascism and subsequent attempts to institutionalise bourgeois democracy in Portugal and Spain. In a substantial essay, Blackburn argued, and Anderson appeared to agree, (*NLR* 87-8 1974, 1) that 'today, Portugal is the most explosively unstable country – the nation nearest to a classic pre-revolutionary situation – in the imperialist world' (Blackburn 1974, 6). He concluded this article with the argument that 'the ambition of constructing a stable bourgeois democracy … [in Portugal is a] phantasy' (Blackburn 1974, 45). This forecast was based on his reading of the economic, social and international context of Portuguese politics. However, if bourgeois democracy was ruled out for the immediate future this did not mean that socialism was a certainty. On the contrary, the fate of Chile might await the masses if the revolutionary left did not learn from history. Luckily, he argued, the left was learning from its previous mistakes, as the Trotskyist grouping LCI had 'vigorously taken up the importance of elections to the Constituent Assembly, and the need for democratization based on proletarian class struggle'. Therefore, Blackburn, in an argument that drew inspiration from Trotsky's analysis of the struggle against fascism in Germany, aimed to generalise this lesson so as to immunise the left against the type of ultra-leftist sloganising that ignored the real importance of bourgeois democratic goals when fighting for socialism (Blackburn 1974, 41-42).

The generally optimistic register of *NLR* was confirmed in issue 91 in May 1975 when the journal welcomed the victory of the Vietnamese over American imperialism in Indochina. With reference to the West the editorial argued that whereas Tet had 'helped detonate the May events in France. The immediate reverberations of the liberation of Indo-China cannot yet be seen, but they will already be silently be making history' (*NLR* 91 1975, 4). The implication was that it was reasonable to be optimistic for the future of socialism. This optimism was repeated in the next issue in which Anderson introduced an interview with Arthur Scargill with the claim that 'the epic struggles against the Conservative Government revealed a class combativity and confidence which ... constitute a formidable obstacle to the Labour Government's attempt to succeed where Heath failed' (*NLR* 92 1975, 1). A few months later Anderson claimed that it was 'only the German Bundesrepublik [that stood] as a bastion of reaction' in a Europe in crisis (*NLR* 96 1976, 1).

However, even before these lines were published – Spring 1976 – the tide appears to have begun to turn against the international left. In particular on 25 November 1975 the left wing of the military was disarmed in Portugal, an action that disorientated the Portuguese revolutionary left which had illusions in the revolutionary potential of the Armed Forces Movement. This action, moreover, set the scene for the creation of a stable bourgeois democracy in Portugal led by Mario Soares (Harman 1988, 308 ff). At a more mundane level, in Britain the Labour government was indeed having more success than its Conservative predecessor in forcing through attacks on the working class (Coates 1980).

Bourgeois democracy thus appeared to have more life in it than Blackburn and Anderson, at least in regard to Portugal, had countenanced. It was from this juncture that an increased sense of political urgency can be detected on the pages of *NLR* in its project of uncovering the basis for the continued resilience of the bourgeois democratic state. Indeed Anderson argued that 'no single phenomenon in the contemporary world has been so central a barrier to socialist revolution, and yet so little engaged or explored in Marxist theory, as the bourgeois-democratic state' (*NLR* 103 1977, 1). *NLR* opened its pages to a new debate on this issue in 1975 when it published an essay by *NLR* committee member Norman Geras; this was quickly followed by substantial interventions by Ernest Mandel, Göran Therborn, Henri Weber, Régis Debray, Adam Przeworski, and Anderson himself.

Therborn's essay addressed two paradoxes: how could a minority class, the bourgeoisie, maintain its rule in a democracy, and why had the nineteenth century theorists who had argued that capitalism and democracy were incompatible been proved so wrong? (Therborn 1977a, 3) His answers to these problems included the claim that capitalism, because it is characterised by the separation of economics from politics, includes an inherent tendency towards bourgeois democracy, while bourgeois democracy had been viable because 'of the elasticity and expansive capacity of capitalism' (Therborn 1977a, 28-30 & 35).

In his résumé of the legacy of May 1968 Debray argued that, with a desire for self-modernisation, the French state would have had to invent the May events if they had not spontaneously occurred (Debray 1979, 52). However, this thesis was hard to square with the actual history of the revolt. As Weber argued, Debray ignored the details of the revolt and was thus blind to the 'anti-capitalist potential of the May movement, [and thus] does not perceive its long term subversive effects'. Weber then agreed with Anderson that a model for socialist advance in the West was necessary, but failed to outline it (Weber 1979, 69-70). Similarly, in his essay on Eurocommunism, he was better at knocking down reformist assumptions than he was at developing a positive revolutionary alternative strategy for the West (Weber 1978, 14).

Ernest Mandel, when pressed on the nature of the difference between the Russian state in 1917 and the modern bourgeois state, in an interview with Weber republished in *NLR* 100 in 1976[45], answered that what 'was specifically Russian was not the duration of the revolutionary crisis, nor the soviet form of self organisation of the masses, nor the tactics utilized by the Bolsheviks to win over the majority in the soviets, nor the concrete form of the decomposition of the bourgeois state' (Mandel 1976, 98). All these features, he argued, could be seen to be general phenomena of the twentieth century revolutionary experience of Europe. The specificity of the Bolshevik experience was not the ease with which they were able to seize power, 'but on the contrary the much greater difficulties they faced on the eve and above all on the morrow of the seizure of power – compared with the possibilities in the advanced capitalist countries of today'. Thus, according to Mandel, the peculiarity of the Russian experience 'lay above all in the limited weight of the working class in the total active population' (Mandel 1976, 98). In addition to this objective factor there existed a subjective factor of some importance. Mandel argued that in the West there did exist a tendency for the 'masses to identify their democratic freedoms … with the bourgeois democratic, parliamentary state institutions'. To ensure that workers did not recoil from revolutionary demands that the state be smashed, Mandel suggested that revolutionaries should be vigilant against ultra-left phraseology that might suggest to workers that the success of any revolution would mean the end of their democratic liberties. The Portuguese Revolution, he argued, had been 'blown off course' by the confusions caused by such overly abstract demands (Mandel 1976, 109-110). Thus, while, objectively, the chances of there being a successful revolution were greater in the West than they had been in the East, this potential could only be actualised if the revolutionary party was aware of the importance of the correct political strategy that should be taken. In particular revolutionaries needed to be aware of the importance of democratic demands.

In his contribution to the debate Geras' argued that bourgeois democracy played the role of 'securing and maintaining the consent of the masses to their own exploitation ... It creates the illusion in the masses that they control this democratic state at least as much as anybody else' (Geras 1976, 58). Geras suggested that Trotsky had understood this when he had argued that in 'a developed capitalist society ... the bourgeoisie leans for support primarily upon the working classes, which are held in check by the reformists' (Trotsky quoted in Geras 1976, 59). The mechanisms through which this subordination is organised are 'incomparably more powerful than those available to ... repressive forms of bourgeois rule'. The pillar of their strength is 'a dense and complex structure of institutions and practices ... of elections, legislative, executive and advisory bodies, political parties, pressure groups and trade unions, newspapers and other mass media, etc. – through which the demands of the masses are processed' (Geras 1976, 60). Unfortunately, despite the strength of this argument, Geras failed to analyse the relative weight of each of these institutions in the legitimation process, and thus his strategic insights remain general and abstract.

Anderson's intervention into the debate in his essay *The Antinomies of Antonio Gramsci* was by far the most sophisticated that was published by *NLR* in the 1970s. Unfortunately, despite its undoubted strengths, its abstract character severely limited its potential as a guide to action. Anderson was aware of this problem, and in both the essay on Gramsci and in *Considerations* he stressed the need for concrete historical investigations to deepen his insights (Anderson 1976b, 41 & 1976a, 110). Unfortunately, he never published his own research in this area.

Anderson introduced his analysis of the *Prison Notebooks* with the argument that Gramsci's most famous conceptual contribution to the socialist vocabulary, the concept of hegemony, had been borrowed from socialists in Russia, and had been encountered by Gramsci as a concept used in the Comintern to explain the political dominance of the proletariat in the class alliance against Tsarism (Anderson 1976b, 15 ff). Gramsci developed the concept from this application to account for the political dominance of the bourgeoisie within Western democracies (Anderson 1976b, 20). However, Anderson discovered major problems with Gramsci's formulations regarding the site of hegemony in the West. At different points in the *Prison Notebooks* Gramsci had formulated the relationship between the state and civil society, and thus the site of hegemony, in three distinct and contradictory ways. In one formulation Gramsci suggested that the state in the West was merely an 'outer ditch' behind which an inner fortress of civil society operated as the site of bourgeois hegemony, while elsewhere he maintained that hegemony operated in a 'balanced' relationship within both the state and civil society, and in a third he submerged civil society into the state (Anderson 1976b, 26 & 31 & 33). Anderson argued that all of these formulations were politically problematic.

The first of these formulations could, Anderson argued, lead to the kind of reformist illusion that he himself had held in the 1960s, and had since been the mistake of Eurocommunism. The second formulation obscured the fact that since coercion was the legal monopoly of the capitalist state, it was juridically absent from civil society and therefore there was necessarily an imbalance between the two arenas. Finally, the third formulation carried with it the problems both of ultra-leftism and reformism, for if civil society was equated with the state then no fundamental distinction could be made between any societal institutions (Anderson 1976b, 27 & 32 & 36). While Anderson argued that the first and third formulations implied the most potentially damaging effects on socialist strategic thought, the weakness with the second formulation was more substantial than simply being the effect of conceptual slippage. Anderson argued that no socialist who engaged in the debates of the inter-war years, with the exception of Bordiga, had fully grasped that the problem of the site of hegemony was only one aspect of a broader problem: the states in the East and West were of a qualitatively different character (Anderson 1976b, 52).

Anderson's formulation of the relationship between the state and civil society in the West, while being based on Gramsci's insights, was more precise, as it was based upon the thesis that he had developed in *Lineages*. His fundamental argument was that as coercion was the legal monopoly of the state in the West, and this state remained a bourgeois state, it remained true that the state required smashing in the Leninist sense. However, as the coercive powers of the modern Western states were incomparably more awesome than those of older states, then the Western states would be much more formidable adversaries than was the Russian state in 1917 (Anderson 1976b, 55). This argument suggested that a specifically Western strategic framework for revolutionary advance, which while incorporating insights from Lenin, transcended the local limitations of his thought, should be developed. Unfortunately, Leninism could not be transcended through a mere addition of insights from Gramsci. For while Gramsci's analysis of the *differencia specifica* of the West was a powerful one, it was not fully thought through. In contrast to Gramsci, Anderson argued that bourgeois hegemony operated both through the state and through civil society: 'the state enters twice' (Anderson 1976b, 32). Thus, at two key levels, there existed a qualitative difference between the Eastern and Western states. First, the former were much weaker instruments of class coercion than were the latter; second, modern Western states were, in addition to their coercive function, also extremely efficient sites of the operation of bourgeois hegemony. Indeed, Anderson argued that this site of hegemony was structured at the heart of the Western states. Bourgeois democracy instilled in the masses the belief that they exercised 'an ultimate self determination within the existing social order'; it thus 'deprives the working class of the idea of socialism as a different type of state, and the means of communications and other mechanisms of cultural control thereafter clinch this central ideological effect'. The 'Western parliamentary state ... is itself the hub of the ideological apparatus of capitalism' (Anderson 1976b, 28-30).

Therefore, in addition to Gramsci's geographical delineation between the Eastern and the Western states, Anderson, drawing upon Althusser, suggested that a deeper temporal delineation should be drawn between them. Gramsci had not fully understood that the states in the East and West existed as very different entities in different historical temporalities albeit in the same chronological time (Anderson 1976b, 50). Given that the central pivot of bourgeois hegemony in the West lay in the operation of democracy itself, 'a revolution will only occur in the West when the masses have made the experience of proletarian democracy that is tangibly superior to bourgeois democracy. The sole way for the victory of socialism to be secured in these societies is for it to represent incontestably more, not less, freedom for the vast majority of the population'. However, this would only be possible in a period of 'dual power'. The problem, in the short term, was that 'the working class in ... the West is some distance away from this threshold'. Anderson concluded that in the short term the united front had 'never been historically surpassed' as a tactic which revolutionaries should utilise to win over 'the conviction of workers' to socialism (Anderson 1976b, 78). However, he failed to explain exactly what he meant by the united front other than that it signified the need to undertake 'deep and serious ideological-political work among the masses, untainted by sectarianism, before the seizure of power could be on the agenda'. He did, however, note that Trotsky was its main 'architect' (Anderson 1976b, 60 & 73).

Trotsky, in the essay to which Anderson refers, argued that the united front tactic was to be used by Communist parties where they commanded the loyalty of a substantial minority of the working class, while reformists commanded the loyalty of the majority. In these circumstances, and as clashes between capital and labour arose, 'the working masses sense the need of unity in action, of unity in resisting the onslaught of capitalism or unity in taking the offensive against it' (Trotsky 1972c, 92). Then, it was the duty of communists to seek unity in action with reformist parties over specific demands. This tactic had two goals. First, it was hoped that the united response would cause the defeat of the bourgeoisie over the specific issue. Second, the communists would prove to the mass of reformist workers that militant action was more successful in combating the bourgeoisie, and thus would facilitate the leftward evolution of the mass of the workers. This argument implied that an independent Communist Party already existed and that these 'clashes' could lead to the politicisation of substantial sections of workers: 'The Communist Party must base itself on the overwhelming majority of the working class. So long as it does not hold this majority, the party must fight to win it' (Trotsky 1972c, 91). Anderson undoubtedly agreed with the general sentiments of this approach. However, he did not attempt to build a new Communist Party, nor did he seek to join one of the competing Trotskyist groups already active in Britain.[46] The basis for this position rested, I would suggest, on his understanding of the difference in the nature of Eastern and Western European states, a difference, he would contend, that neither the Communists nor the Trotskyists had fully comprehended.

However, outside an organisation that could test his ideas in practice, and without the historical research necessary to deepen them, Anderson's insights remained formal and abstract, with no real purchase on the actual struggles of the proletariat. Anderson was well aware of this lacuna in his Marxism: 'any real discussion of the problems of the present would involve many questions to which there has been no allusion here. Such central issues as the interrelation of economic and political struggles in the labour movement, the alliances of the working class in largely post-peasant societies, the contemporary nature of the capitalist crises, the possible catalysts and forms of dual power, the development of more advanced institutions of proletarian democracy – wider and freer than any past precedents – are all omitted here' (Anderson 1976b, 76).

Ironically Gramsci had discussed these in depth in his pre-prison writings. Anderson's limitation of his research on Gramsci to the *Prison Notebooks* thereby had the unfortunate consequence of obscuring almost as much as it illuminated in Gramsci's Marxism. Anderson argued that once bourgeois democracy had first deprived 'the working class of the idea of socialism as a different type of state', it was only then that 'the means of communications and other mechanisms of cultural control ... clinch this central ideological effect'. The obvious weakness with this line of thought is that bourgeois democracy appears to exist without any material mediation. Thus, 'the ideology of bourgeois democracy is far more potent than that of any welfare reformism, and forms the permanent syntax of the consensus instilled by the capitalist state' (Anderson 1976b, 29). In coming to this conclusion Anderson ignored Gramsci's detailed analysis of the way in which the system of hegemony was mediated in Western democracies, noting only his analysis of the role of intellectuals (Anderson 1976b, 21).

By contrast, Gramsci, like Trotsky, argued that the trade union bureaucracy, through their negotiating function at the point of production, played a key role in the mediation of bourgeois hegemony in the West. Indeed, the key lesson that Gramsci learnt in his years as a leader of the PCI, about which he was unable to write in prison, was that the bureaucracy of the labour movement was a crucially important source of legitimacy in bourgeois democracies. 'The trade unions, from Gramsci's point of view, increasingly constituted a central element of bourgeois hegemony' (Boggs 1976, 87). Gramsci's own formulation is hardly equivocal. The trade union bureaucracy, he argued, has developed a 'competitive, not communist character' (Gramsci 1977, 99). Moreover, the bureaucrats 'no longer feel the same passions, the same desires, the same hopes as the masses. Between them and the masses an unbridgeable gap has opened up ... These men no longer see the enemy in the bourgeoisie, they see him in the communists' (Gramsci 1978, 17). Finally, the bureaucracy, because it has quarried out an arena of legal operation within bourgeois society constantly polices that legality against spontaneous eruptions of class anger from the masses below them. 'In these conditions, the trade union discipline can be nothing other than a service to capital' (Gramsci 1977, 268).

Gramsci did not, however, simply condemn the trade unions; he had a dialectical understanding of their role. The acquisition of a legal status was a great victory for the proletariat. However, this victory was structured as a compromise with capital. Thus, the bureaucracy was the organisational expression of bourgeois democracy: 'Industrial legality has improved the working class's standard of living but it is no more than a compromise – a compromise which had to be made and must be supported until the balance of forces favours the working class' (Gramsci 1977, 265). The factory councils were, by contrast, 'the negation of industrial legality ... By virtue of its revolutionary spontaneity, the factory council tends to spark off class war at any moment' (Gramsci 1977, 266). Gramsci wrote these lines in the midst of a revolutionary wave that engulfed Italy after the war (Williams 1975). His goal was to win the struggle for hegemony within the masses against the trade union leaders. Kelly argues that Gramsci's formulation of the nature of the dominance of bourgeois ideology in the West was superior to Lenin's, as Gramsci maintained that it was built into the structure of trade unionism. Thus, Gramsci located the material basis for trade union conservatism within the structures of 'the collective bargaining function of the official' (Kelly 1988, 57-8).

Similarly, Trotsky argued that social democracy was the political expression of the labour bureaucracy and aristocracy: 'The labour bureaucracy and the labour aristocracy are the social foundation for opportunism' (Trotsky 1989, 154). Thus reformism was not simply a false ideology, but was rooted in the experience of workers under capitalism, and had a social basis in the trade union bureaucracy. Moreover, it is upon this layer that bourgeois democracy rested. As Trotsky wrote of Europe generally and Britain in particular: 'If there were not a bureaucracy of the trade unions, then the police, the army, the courts, the lords, the monarchy would appear before the proletarian masses as nothing but pitiful and ridiculous playthings. The bureaucracy of the trade unions is the backbone of British imperialism. It is by means of the bureaucracy that the bourgeoisie exists ... Power must be rested from the control of the bourgeoisie and for that its principal agent, the trade union bureaucracy, must be overthrown' (Trotsky 1983, 47). Social democratic parties were the reverse side of the coin of the trade union bureaucracy; the latter fought to defend economic interests of the working class, while the former pressed for reforms in parliament (Trotsky 1972b, 33). Thus, the division between economics and politics under capitalism had a social basis.

So Gramsci and Trotsky developed similar models of the material basis of bourgeois democracy.[47] Moreover, as Anderson noted, Gramsci's political strategy for overcoming the conservatism of this layer, the war of position, is best understood as his application of Trotsky's united front tactic (Anderson 1976b, 58). The united front tactic is designed not simply to win the masses over from false ideas but to win them over from the influence of those who propagate those ideas. Anderson was silent on this practical aspect of Marxism. This lacuna was symptomatic of a deeper weakness with his discussion of the operation of the system of hegemony. Barratt Brown has noted that Anderson's analysis of the structure of the hegemonic order in the West 'appears to miss the crucial subordination of the labour process and the whole gamut of production relations' (Barratt Brown 1978, 141). This silence meant that Anderson nowhere examined the mediation between economics and politics as it operates under capitalism. Consequently, his model of revolution implied that politics and economics only intertwined in periods of revolutionary crises when the state intervened to prop up bourgeois property rights: 'The development of any revolutionary crisis necessarily displaces the dominance within the bourgeois power structure from ideology to violence. Coercion becomes both determinant and dominant in the supreme crisis' (Anderson 1976b, 44). The problem with this argument lies not in what is said but what is unsaid: there was no implication of a route from non-revolutionary to revolutionary periods in Anderson's analysis. His conclusion may have been to apply the united front tactic but he never explains what this actually meant in practice.

SUMMARY

By the late 1960s Anderson had evolved towards revolutionary Marxism. However, he remained unconvinced that traditional Marxist theory included a satisfactory guide to action in the West. He attempted to overcome this problem by analysing the *differentia specifica* of the state in the West. As we have seen, this project was not without its problems. Thus, despite the undoubtedly impressive nature of his history of the rise of feudalism and absolutism, Anderson's proof of the qualitative distinction between the Eastern and Western states was not as convincing as he believed. Whatever the intellectual limitations of this project, Anderson's theory did underpin his embrace of the politics of the united front. In the next few years, he attempted to apply this policy through cooperation with a wide spectrum of opponents of the new arms race. Moreover, he also engaged with the ideas of other socialists with the aim of giving his own strategic ideas a greater depth.

CHAPTER FIVE

A FLAWED SYNTHESIS

The sense of optimism that overdetermined Anderson's political and theoretical project in the early 1970s became more strained as the decade wore on. If this shift was heralded by the containment of the Portuguese Revolution within the confines of bourgeois democracy (Anderson 1992b, xi), it was compounded in the late 1970s when first President Carter turned up the heat in the Cold War, and then Thatcher and Reagan came to power in Britain and the USA. However, despite these developments, there did exist forces which suggested that the general political context was becoming more favourable to the left. Thus in Britain in the early 1980s three processes suggested a basis for socialist optimism: there was a rebirth of a rejuvenated CND; a left-wing reaction within the Labour Party against the legacy of the 1974-79 government; and growth in the strength of Marxist ideas on the intellectual left.

The socio-political context of the late 1970s and early 1980s was therefore a complex one that generated much political heat as various tendencies attempted to come to terms with the new situation. In an internal document, *New Left Review 1975-1980*, written in 1980, Anderson lamented *NLR*'s failure to develop a comparable analysis of the contemporary conjuncture to the 'substantial attempts' made by 'Hall, Jacques, Gamble or Cliff' (*NLR 1975-1980*, 14). These authors represented a spectrum of opinion from the most revisionist to the most classically Marxist interpretations of Thatcherism. Without agreeing with the detail of any of these positions Anderson was impressed by their power and originality. He aimed to follow their lead and to publish in *NLR* an analysis of Thatcherism that could underpin a viable socialist strategic practice. To this end *NLR* published important essays, first by Anthony Barnett, and then by Bob Jessop *et al.* in the early 1980s (Barnett 1982; Jessop *et al* 1988).

Interestingly, the four authors that Anderson cites in the internal document all argued, in different ways, that socialism was on the retreat in Britain. However, they each drew divergent strategic conclusions from their analyses. Hall, Jaques, Gamble and other writers associated with the Communist Party magazine *Marxism Today* argued that the scale of the setback for the left was such that it entailed that realistic socialist politics in Britain be shifted dramatically to the right: old notions of a workers' revolution were to be relegated to the dustbin of history (Blackledge 2002, 213-216). By contrast, Tony Cliff was a leading member of the Socialist Workers' Party, and, while he outlined what he called the 'downturn' in the class struggle, entailing a more defensive tactical orientation for socialists, he insisted that this perspective did not imply a rejection of the goal of the revolutionary socialist transformation of society (Cliff 1979). In 1980, Anderson was drawn towards an even more optimistic interpretation of the contemporary context.

In this sense Anderson followed the general drift of the British left: Cliff's position sat someway between the extreme pessimism of Hall, Hobsbawm and others around *Marxism Today* and the dominant mood on the British left which was one of extreme, and somewhat naïve, optimism. In fact much of the left became preoccupied with a series of internal battles inside the Labour Party, and Tony Benn's challenge for the deputy leadership, at the expense of a realistic analysis of the ideological and political crisis of the left which had opened a space within which Thatcher began to exercise power. At this moment those editors of *NLR* who were members of the Trotskyist International Marxist Group were carried along in the train of this super optimistic[48] mood and joined, or attempted to join, the Labour Party. Anderson held back from this line of action, but his sympathies seemed with the optimists. It was thus from this perspective that he commissioned Jessop *et al.* to write a materialist critique of the interpretation of Thatcherism associated with Hall and *Marxism Today*.

We can get a sense of Anderson's continuing political optimism from the choice of language through which he expressed his understanding of the key contemporary issue facing British socialists. In *New Left Review 1975-1980* he wrote of the need to analyse the 'changing balance of class forces in Britain today'. This phrase was in fact the title of Cliff's essay on the contemporary context, and reflected his methodological stress on analysing the concrete form taken by the ebb and flow of the class struggle at its theoretical, political and economic levels. However, the critique of *Marxism Today's* analysis of Thatcherism eventually published in *NLR* mentioned nothing of the rise and fall of the class struggle, and instead focused upon the changing nature of Britain's regime of accumulation.

Whatever implications we might read from Anderson's borrowing of Cliff's language to describe the key problem facing the left in the 1980s, Jessop *et al.*'s interpretation was very different. Cliff argued that the British labour movement had experienced a threefold crisis of ideas, leadership and organisation in the 1970s which opened the door to Thatcherism (Cliff 1979, 42). He argued that the recommendations of the 1968 Donovan Commission, that stewards should be integrated into the full-time union machine, had not been, as Hall suggested, dropped for more authoritarian approaches to industrial relations, rather it had proved the decisive weapon in the bureaucratisation of sections of the steward movement (Cliff 1979, 27ff). This organisational process served to isolate stewards from their fellow workers and, in the period of the Social Contract, it reinforced their existing social democratic consciousness. This in turn left them ill-equipped to struggle against the Labour government, and indeed many stewards acted as media for the government's message of national unity during the years of the Social Contract, thus helping to defuse sectionalist militancy. This was especially true of those stewards, influenced by the Communist Party, who were recognised nationally as the leadership of the shop stewards' movement (Cliff 1985, 52). For Cliff, the mid to late 1970s was the decisive moment when the burgeoning militancy of the early 1970s, which underpinned a real if limited growth in socialist consciousness within the working class, was broken by the hegemonic Labourist ideology:

'In the years 1968-74 there was an unstable balance between the political generalisation on the employers side – incomes policy and industrial relations legislation – and the industrial militancy on the workers' side. Such a situation cannot last for long. The unstable equilibrium can lead to one of two outcomes: to political generalisations of the industrial militancy, or to decline of sectional militancy. In fact the unstable equilibrium [was] destroyed by the policies [of] Labourism' (Cliff 1985, 48). It was in the context that Thatcher could appear to be so strong; she could win victories over the workers' movement because the social contract of the previous Labour government 'had sapped both shop floor organisation and economistic militancy' (Looker 1985, 245).

In contrast to Cliff's class struggle analysis, Jessop *et al* argued that Thatcher's rise was premised upon the 'demise of the social democratic power bloc' through the crisis of the Keynesian Welfare state (Jessop *et al.* 1988, 178). Social democracy represented a 'one nation expansive form of hegemony', underpinned by a Fordist regime of accumulation. Thatcherism, by contrast, represented the 'two nation polarisation of society' premised upon a limited movement towards a post-Fordist accumulation strategy (Jessop *et al.* 1988, 179 & 129). At the heart of Thatcher's successes was a 'formidable capacity to work with, rather than against, powerful social and economic trends' (Jessop *et al.* 1988, 151). For Jessop *et al.*, while Thatcher's accumulation strategy was obviously bourgeois, it differed from other capitalist accumulation regimes as it served a social base that was made up of both the petty bourgeoisie and 'significant sections of workers' (Jessop *et al.* 1988, 96). Indeed, Thatcher's strength lay in her ability to forge an alliance that was based upon a material stake in popular capitalism, which she offered to workers in core industries. It was this material basis that underpinned the limited working class ideological support for popular capitalism against the welfare state (Jessop *et al.* 1988, 61 & 167).

While Jessop *et al.* developed their analysis of Thatcherism in an attempt to offer a viable alternative to the pessimistic line coming from *Marxism Today*, their own work was incapable of underpinning a realistic, yet ultimately more optimistic, political perspective. So, while Jessop *et al.* were able to expose the weaknesses with *Marxism Today*'s analysis of Thatcherism, their own obituary of the Keynesian Welfare State implied an equally pessimistic perspective. This was less apparent in the earlier essays that make up his book, for these chapters were written before the collapse of municipal socialism and the defeat of the 1984-5 Miners' Strike. However, the defeat of the miners confirmed for many the obsolescence of class politics, and therefore dashed many hopes for socialism. This context appeared to confirm Jessop *et al.*'s argument that Thatcher's electoral triumphs were underpinned by a new accumulation regime that generated a division within the labour force between a core and a periphery of workers. This argument undercut the materialist basis for class politics, and left Jessop and his colleagues incapable of imagining a socialist alternative to Thatcherism. Thus the most radical goal they envisaged was based upon the development of a reformist socialist version of flexible accumulation (Jessop *et al.* 1988, 140). Returning to this issue in the months prior to Thatcher's resignation, Jessop *et al.* denied the possibility of any socialist political consequences rising from the crisis (Jessop *et al.* 1990, 86). In effect, for them, workers had ceased to be Marx's potential agents of change, and had instead become simple victims of capitalism. Thatcherism's weaknesses would not favour the rebirth of a socialist movement, rather they would strengthen the neo-statist radicals, in particular the 'more statist forces within the Conservative Party' (Jessop *et al.* 1990, 102).

Anderson didn't immediately address this issue in the early 1980s. However, as we shall see below, the type of analysis associated with Jessop *et al.*'s account of the demise of Keynesianism reinforced his increasingly pessimistic reading of the prospects for socialism over the coming decade. In the late 1970s, however, this trajectory lay in the future; at this juncture he aimed to strengthen his Marxism through an engagement with the increasingly powerful interpretations of historical materialism then developing within the British academy.

RAPPROCHEMENT WITH THE OLD NEW LEFT

In 1979 the *NLR* editors of the series of interviews with Raymond Williams, *Politics and Letters,* argued that three forces had helped elevate Marxism to a near hegemonic position on Britain's intellectual left. The first was the work of the British Marxist historians, which had come to 'fruition' in the 1970s; second, and co-temporally, Fabianism had become intellectually 'exhausted'; finally, there had been a 'dissemination of international ideas and idioms among a new generation formed during or after the dramatic struggles of the late sixties' (Williams 1979, 7-8). However, this Marxist culture had only momentarily engaged with the work of Britain's foremost non-Marxist socialist: Raymond Williams. As early as 1966 Anderson had argued that 'the most advanced socialist thought in England is Raymond Williams' superbly intricate and persuasive work ... Any English Marxism will have to measure itself against this landmark in our social thought' (Anderson 1966, 32). *NLR* belatedly began this work in 1976. The first engagement took the form of a highly polemical assault on Williams' *oeuvre* penned by Terry Eagleton. Anthony Barnett, defending Williams, then countered Eagleton's assault. Specifically, Barnett suggested that the cultural forms of the struggle for socialism, about which Williams had much to say, were of central importance to the development of a strategy for socialism in the West (Eagleton 1976; Barnett 1976).

Edward Thompson penned a third intervention into the debate. Thompson had not been published in *NLR* since the editorial split in the early 1960s, and the decision to publish his highly polemical comments on Eagleton specifically, and *NLR* more generally, is of intrinsic significance, for it showed a readiness on Anderson's part to move on beyond old quarrels. While Thompson's essay, *Romanticism, Utopianism and Moralism: the Case of William Morris,* was primarily a reappraisal of the significance of Morris's Marxism, it also contained an afternote on Eagleton's critique of Williams. Thompson argued that Eagleton's Althusserianism had led him towards a form of theoretical elitism. By contrast, the fundamental significance of Morris's Marxism was that he, alone of the Romantics, sought to break with elitism and to 'implant, encourage and enlarge new wants in the present, and imbue the socialist movement with an alternative notation of value, before the rupture'. Thompson related this strategy to Williams' thought. He suggested that Williams' socialism should be understood as an attempt to explain the basis for these 'new values' in the experience of the working class itself. Commenting on this issue, he suggested that 'perhaps we should have theorised more of our substantive findings: and perhaps some of us will' (Thompson 1976a, 110-111). And indeed he did. Thompson subsequently produced a two hundred page polemic against Althusserianism: *The Poverty of Theory*. Moreover, this broadside was aimed not simply at the master, but perhaps even more so against his English epigones; amongst whom Thompson counted Anderson and *NLR*.

In *The Poverty of Theory* Thompson argued that Althusser came 'not to offer to modify [Marxism] but to displace it' (Thompson 1978, 4). Althusser's epistemology 'consists of an idealist mode of theoretical construction' that created a 'self-generating conceptual universe which imposes its own ideality upon the phenomena of material and social existence, rather than engaging in a continual dialogue with these' (Thompson 1978, 13). Indeed, Althusser confused 'empirical procedures, empirical controls, with something he calls empiricism' (Thompson 1978, 32). By contrast, historical materialism, Thompson observed, 'differs from other interpretive orderings of historical evidence not (or not necessarily) in any epistemological premises, but in its categories, its characteristic hypotheses and attendant procedures'. Moreover, these categories were necessarily general and elastic (Thompson 1978, 44 & 57).

Thompson argued that Althusserianism was built upon the weakest elements of Marx's thought. In *Capital* Marx deployed historical concepts to explain capitalism, while in the *Grundrisse* his thought remained trapped within the static structure of political economy (Thompson 1978, 61). It was from within this second tradition that Althusser arose: 'Althusser and his colleagues seek to thrust historical materialism back into the prison of the categories of Political Economy' (Thompson 1978, 68). Thompson saw an ancestor of Althusser's structuralism in Stalin's *Marxism and Linguistics*, and Althusserianism was, like Stalin's Marxism a static system which could not begin to understand history as a process: It was 'unhistorical shit' (Thompson 1978, 108). Against this form of structuralism, Thompson argued, 'I feel myself revert to the poetry of voluntarism' (Thompson 1978, 72). In opposition to Althusserianism, Thompson argued, Marxists should move from the scientific and static analysis of capital to the historical analysis of capitalism (Thompson 1978, 154). To make this leap Marxists should analyse the intentions of actors in real historical time, and, as individuals understand their experiences through culture – the middle term between capitalism and the individual – Marxists were asked to prioritise the analysis of this sphere in their theoretical work. In fact, to the rational case for socialism there should be added a moral argument as individuals experienced their culture through both the media of 'ideas' and 'feelings' (Thompson 1978, 171).

What then was the function of Althusserianism on the left? Thompson asked which group had been the target of Althusser's attack, and found that it was the socialist humanists of the generation of 1956: 'We can see the emergence of Althusserianism as a manifestation of a general police action within ideology, as the attempt to reconstruct Stalinism at the level of theory' (Thompson 1978, 131). Moreover, by insisting that *NLR* was as guilty of these crimes as was

Althusser, Thompson once again threw down the gauntlet to Anderson and his collaborators. Anderson's response to this challenge, *Arguments Within English Marxism*, was much less polemical than had been his *Socialism and Pseudo-Empiricism*. Moreover, it was through this medium that he attempted to fill the gaps in his strategic thought that we noted were conspicuous at the end of *The Antinomies of Antonio Gramsci*.

ARGUMENTS WITHIN ENGLISH MARXISM: A THEORY OF HISTORY

Elliott has characterised *Arguments* as the most sustained exposition of Anderson's credo (Elliott 1995,13). It is indeed so, with, however, the caveat that within half a decade or so of its publication Anderson had retreated from many of its explicit political conclusions. Indeed, by 1992 Anderson had come broadly to accept Fukuyama's obituary of socialism. So we might more precisely say that *Arguments* represents the most sustained exposition of Anderson's credo in his revolutionary socialist phase.

Arguments was written as a theoretical and political response to Thompson's critique of Althusserianism. Nevertheless, Anderson wrote it at a moment when his own understanding of Marxism was evolving. As we saw in chapter three, Anderson's Marxism had been strongly influenced by Colletti in the early 1970s. By the late 1970s, however, he came to reject this interpretation of historical materialism for the more orthodox interpretations associated first with Timpanaro and then with GA Cohen. Timpanaro argued that Colletti's thought was typical of anti-Engelsian Marxism, in that it ignored the real conceptual breakthrough inherent in Marx's 1859 preface to *The Contribution to the Critique of Political Economy* (Timpanaro 1975, 78). Anderson expressed his admiration for these remarks in *Considerations* (Anderson 1976a, 91). Moreover, the 'power' of Timpanaro's thought provided him with the general framework from which he wrote *In the Tracks of Historical Materialism* (Anderson 1983, 8 & 82). However, if Timpanaro offered the 1859 preface as the answer to the idealism of Western Marxism, it was Cohen who most forcefully articulated the philosophical case for the centrality of this essay to Marx's mature work. It was thus towards Cohen's account of Marxism that Anderson gravitated in the late 1970s.

Anderson therefore engaged in his role as mediator between Thompson and Althusser from a position greatly influenced by Timpanaro and Cohen. The book begins with the argument that while Thompson was perhaps the greatest historian of his generation, and Althusser's work was scarred by far too little historical insight, surprisingly, Althusser had formulated the problem of the nature of history far more clearly than had Thompson. Thus, while Thompson equated history with the past *per se*, Althusser, more clearly, argued that a historical fact was one that caused change within existing structural relations

(Anderson 1980, 14). It was towards a comprehension of such social change that Anderson then turned.

Anderson developed his account of social change through a critique of Thompson's magnum opus *The Making of the English Working Class*. He criticised the book at three levels. First, it was marred by the idealistic thesis of 'co-determination', by which Thompson argued that the working class 'made itself as much as it was made'; second, Thompson mistakenly had equated class 'in and through' class consciousness; and third, Thompson had implied that the process of working class formation had, essentially, been 'completed by the early 1830s' (Anderson 1980, 31-2).

Anderson's critique of Thompson's theory of codetermination is perhaps the most persuasive of the three points. For despite Thompson's claim that class formation was an equal product of both objective and subjective circumstances, in practice, he left largely unexamined the structural side of the structure/agency couplet and thus proposed a thesis that could not be 'adjudicated' upon given the evidence cited in his book. Anderson noted several contextual elements that Thompson had left largely unexplored, including the impact of the French and American revolutions, the commercial nature of London and the 'spearhead sectors of the industrial revolution'.

Anderson's criticism of Thompson's equation of class with class consciousness, centred upon the claim that Thompson had made abusive generalisation from a peculiar history that could lead to voluntarist and subjectivist deviations from materialism. Against Thompson's model of class, Anderson cited Cohen's 'fundamental work', of 'exemplary clarity and subtlety', which was 'unlikely to need further restatement' (Anderson 1980, 38-40). Third, in contrast to Thompson's implied claim that the making of the English working class had been closed in 1832 Anderson called for the analysis of the remaking of that class (Anderson 1980, 45).[49] The thrust of Anderson's critique of Thompson's theorisation of class was thus against the idealistic and voluntarist drift that he detected in Thompson's work, and towards a restatement of the materialist insights of Marx which, he believed, Althusser had stressed and Cohen had best formulated. Practically this meant that Anderson took issue with Thompson's approach to the problem of intentionality.

Thompson's model of class implied a 'rehearsal' of Sartre's attempt to construct a model of ordered social relations based upon the interaction of a multiplicity of individual intentional praxes. Anderson argued that Sartre, in the *Critique of Dialectical Reason*, had unsuccessfully attempted to theorise society thus, and in presuming such a framework, Thompson was assuming an untenable account of the structure of social order. By contrast, Anderson argued, 'the problem of social order is irresolvable so long as the answer is sought at the level of intention … it is and must be the dominant mode of production that confers a fundamental unity on a social formation' (Anderson 1980, 53-55). At one level this argument would appear to cohere with Anderson's attempt, in *Passages* and *Lineages*, to map the genealogy and structure of European modes of production and social formations. However, whereas his model of social change had been pluralistic in these earlier works, by 1980 he had moved towards an acceptance of G.A. Cohen's monist and functionalist account of historical development. Cohen had produced an interpretation of Marx, 'whose intellectual force supersedes virtually all previous discussion ... a fundamental work' (Anderson 1980, 72 & 40). Indeed, among Cohen's 'compelling' arguments was a critique of Anderson's own model of modes of production in pre-capitalist societies (Anderson 1980, 72).

Cohen argued that the transition from one mode of production to another was always a consequence of the realisation of the structural conflict between forces and relations of production. As the forces of production developed, the relations of production, which had once facilitated their expansion, slowly began to fetter further development. From then onwards people acted rationally to transform the social relations through revolution (Cohen 1978, 157). Anderson agreed that the 'most fundamental of all mechanisms of social change, according to historical materialism, are the systemic contradictions between forces and relations of production, not just social conflicts between classes generated by antagonistic relations of production alone' (Anderson 1980, 55). He claimed that this stress on structure was characteristic of Althusser's, rather than Thompson's, Marxism: 'Althusser's unilateral and remorseless stress on the overpowering weight of structural necessity in history corresponds more faithfully to the central tenets of historical materialism, and to the actual scientific study of the past – but at the price of obscuring the novelty of the modern labour movement and attenuating the vocation of revolutionary socialism. Thompson's passionate sense of the potential of human agency to shape the collective conditions of life, on the other hand, is much closer to the political temper of Marx and Engels themselves in their own time – but tends to be projected backwards as a uniform weft of the past, in defiance of the millennial negations of self determination in the kingdom of necessity' (Anderson 1980, 58). The problem that Marxism thus needed to face, as Anderson saw it, was how to synthesise these two elements, the voluntaristic and the structural, into a viable interpretation of historical materialism.

Anderson attempted a solution to this puzzle through an analysis of the Marxist concept of agency. While Thompson's *oeuvre* centred on the 'key organising theme' of agency, he had, unfortunately, left this concept unelaborated, and, consequently, his model of active agency elided over three distinct connotations, understood in terms of the goals aimed at by active agents. These three types of goals included agents acting to realize private goals, for example marriage, or public goals that did not seek to remodel social relations, for example wars and diplomacy. However, it was with the third type of agency that Anderson was most concerned – the 'collective project' of the 'conscious creating or remodelling of all social structures'. By contrast with Thompson's elision, Anderson argued, the concept of a collective and transformative agency could be retained 'even on rigorously determinist premises' as 'conscious, goal directed activity'. However, this was only possible if the nature of the goals aimed at, and around which 'everything turns', were themselves analysed (Anderson 1980, 19-21). Thus, Anderson sought to elaborate upon the distinct nature of the goal of socialism, so that he could better conceptualise the novelty of socialist agency.

Anderson argued that the new type of agency, inaugurated by the Russian Revolution, had 'premonitions' in the agencies involved in 'political colonisation, religious heterodoxy or literary utopia in earlier centuries'. More specifically, the French and American revolutions were 'the first historical figurations of agency in this, decisive sense'. The specificity of the Bolshevik Revolution lay in the way in which it was led by individuals who believed themselves to be possessed of a scientific understanding of the social world that enabled them to predict the revolution in advance. In contrast, the American and French revolutions began as 'largely spontaneous explosions'. (Anderson 1980, 20) Thus, Lenin and Trotsky could be differentiated from Robespierre and Washington in that, amongst other attributes, the former, by contrast with the latter, were aware, in advance, that they aimed to transform social relations. The specificity of the socialist project could best be understood as the scientifically predicted transformation of social structures. This formulation of the concept of socialist-agency allowed Anderson both to agree formally with Marx that socialism was predicated upon a novel type of agency, and simultaneously redefine this novel model of socialist-agency so that it could encompass both the Eastern European and Chinese experiences. Anderson's mentor, Isaac Deutscher, had explicitly noted that while Marx had insisted that socialism could only be built upon a new form of agency, his equation of socialism with proletarian self-emancipation could not be maintained if it were accepted that the Eastern bloc and China were in some sense socialist: 'The old Bolsheviks ... believed in revolution from below ... The revolution now carried into eastern Europe was primarily a revolution from above' (Deutscher 1968, 539 & 1987, 514, cf Anderson 1976a, 120). Following a similar line of argument, Anderson replaced Marx's claim that socialism could only be the product of self-conscious proletarian agency with the suggestion that it was the consciousness of the goal that was of prime importance to the socialist project, not the proletarian character of the agency itself.

Following Timpanaro, Anderson's alternative to Thompson's 'voluntaristic' model of agency was intended not to collapse into fatalism, but rather to insist that a cognitive element should be added to the aspirational element in Thompson's account: 'the attainment of communism [is] not only a product of will, but equally and indivisibly of knowledge' (Anderson 1980, 24 & cf Timpanaro 1975, 105). The knowledge to which Anderson refers includes both that of the goal of socialism itself, and the parameters within which material conditions – the development of the forces of production – allow agents to realistically actualise their aspirations. We shall discuss the political consequences of this critique of Thompson's position below.

However, whatever the power of this assessment of Thompson's model of agency, Anderson was unable to outline a coherent materialist alternative to it that was both free of fatalism and voluntarism. He introduced his discussion of agency by noting that the concept had 'two opposite connotations. It signifies at once active initiator and passive instrument' (Anderson 1980, 18). His discussion of agency, as we have seen, then followed Thompson in stressing the former of these associations. Unfortunately, where Thompson had elided over the differing goals of human agency, Anderson makes his own elision between two connotations of active agency as, first, goal directed activity, and, second, the concrete embodiment of such activity. While Thompson may have made some confused comments regarding the nature of the goals aimed at by agents, his discussion, and indeed his entire oeuvre, was aimed at uncovering the real processes whereby working people had in faltering, mediated and never complete ways, attempted to 'become' a collective agent of change through historical processes of struggle (Thompson 1980, 8) Whatever the undoubted merits of Anderson's critique of Thompson's voluntarism, he nowhere addresses this the most salient feature of his work. This is the key elision in Anderson's discussion of the concept of agency. For in the 1980s, as we shall see in the next chapter, he essentially accepted an anthropomorphic conceptualisation of class that rendered it unnecessary that he discuss the contested processes through which activists inside the workers movement, operating within circumstances that were more or less conducive to their success, fought with varying degrees of success to make class agencies. His model, as Kaye points out, 'fail[s] to pose the ... issue of class formation' (Kaye 1995, 240). One example of the malign consequences of this interpretation of Marxism can be seen in his discussion of the 'Crisis of Marxism' of the 1970s.

ANTI-ANTI SOVIETISM

As part of the panorama he painted in *In the Tracks of Historical Materialism* Anderson analysed the 'Crisis of Marxism' of the 1970s. He argued that while this crisis was real, it was 'geographically confined to Latin Europe'. In this region, and within the context of a 'recrudescence of violent anti-communism', many erstwhile Marxists had either renounced Marxism completely, or had become increasingly sceptical 'towards the very idea of a revolutionary rupture with capitalism' (Anderson 1983, 28-9). To explain this phenomenon, Anderson attempted to synthesise both an 'intrinsic' history of the theory of historical materialism, and an 'extrinsic' history, within which this theory 'must first of all be situated within the intricate web of national and international class struggle' (Anderson 1983, 14).

His intrinsic history of Latin Marxism can be briefly stated: Althusser's reply to Lévi-Strauss's critique of Sartre's Marxism 'rather than engaging with Lévi-Strauss's attack on history or his interpretation of humanism, endorsed and incorporated them into Marxism' (Anderson 1983, 37); thence Latin Marxism collapsed into the morass of poststructuralist relativism. What then of Anderson's analysis of Latin Marxism's extrinsic history? Despite his stated aim of situating the theoretical history within the context of the national and international class struggles, his extrinsic history is actually another side to the intrinsic history of the theory. Latin European Marxists had broken too decisively with the Soviet heritage: first, they had too easily been caught up within the orbit of Maoist China, where by 'the early seventies, the momentum of an unrestrained anti-Soviet campaign ... led the Chinese state to an ever closer embrace with the United States government, and an ever more accentuated abandonment of support or solidarity for national liberation movements in the Third World' (Anderson 1983, 73); while, second, they came under the influence of Eurocommunism, which itself grew as a 'critique of the legacy of Stalinism'. Thus, both Eurocommunism and Maoism, despite their radically distinct prescriptions, were products of a 'common point of negative reference' to the USSR. It was the failures of these alternative projects that underpinned Latin Europe's 'Crisis of Marxism' in the 1970s:

What detonated it was the sense of double disappointment: first in the Chinese and then in the West European alternatives to the central post-revolutionary experience of the twentieth century so far, that of the USSR itself.... Maoism appeared to debouch into little more than a truculent Oriental Khrushchevism. Eurocommunism lapsed into what looked increasingly like a second-class version of Occidental social democracy. (Anderson 1983, 74-6)

Thus, for Anderson, the extrinsic history of Latin Marxism was reduced to its failure to guard itself theoretically against anti-Communism: its fortunes, therefore, rose and fell with those of the anti-Communist socialisms to which it was attached. Anderson aimed to guard himself against this fate because he believed, with Deutscher, that the Cold War was the 'product of precisely that global class struggle whose understanding gave birth to historical materialism – a conflict founded on the ceaseless determination of major capitalist states to stifle every attempt to build socialism ... The potential outcome of this conflict transcends the opposition between capital and labour: but its actual spring remains tightly coiled within it' (Anderson 1983, 95-6). Unfortunately, this transposition of the extrinsic history of the class struggle from the point of production to the global arena of the Cold War effectively tied his vision of socialism to the fate of the Soviet Union.

So as a guard against a generalisation of the 'Crisis of Marxism' Anderson developed a politics in this period that can best be described as anti-anti-Sovietism (Elliott 1995, 13). This position was not without a rational basis; it was indeed true that many anti-Stalinist socialists had progressively shifted from articulating left-wing critiques of Moscow, towards operating as intellectual apologists for the West during the Cold War. However, Anderson's position was somewhat paradoxical. For the raison d'être of the New Left was precisely that it sought to explode the duality between Washington and Moscow and to create an alternative left politics to both social democracy and Communism in the West. Anderson's perspective in the early 1980s appears to negate this project. Or rather it appears to repeat a general line that could have been taken from Sartre's *The Communists and Peace*. The rationale for the approach taken by Sartre in this book was that the PCF, in a very real sense, constituted the French proletariat and that an oppositional position to it would inevitably lead towards an anti-proletarian and pro-American politics. In Anderson's new version it appeared to be the Soviet Union that represented the international proletariat. This was, in effect, Deutscher's position in the 1950s, and like Deutscher in the 1950s, Anderson in the 1980s appeared to equate the interests of the international proletariat with the well-being of the Soviet Bloc. Indeed, in 1978 he argued that 'it will be vital for the future course of the Western Left that it be able to reject the fashionable equation ... between the USSR and the USA as two superpowers from which a socialist Europe should be equidistant ... [This] radical verbiage [leads] to a rapprochement with the United States' (Anderson 1978, 28).

To sustain this argument Anderson needed to show that the Russian social formation remained, despite its deformations, in some sense a worker' state. Criticising Thompson's critique of Stalinism Anderson argued that the Soviet Union, 'even delivered from bureaucratic misrule, would ... [continue to suffer from] poverty and shortage ... As every serious Marxist study of the fate of the Russian Revolution has shown, it was the cruel inner environment of pervasive scarcity, allied with the external emergency of imperialist military encirclement, that produced the bureaucratisation of party and state in the USSR'. Anderson maintained that Trotsky's analysis of this process was unsurpassed (Anderson 1980, 25).

In his 1983 essay *Trotsky's Interpretation of Stalinism* Anderson developed this idea. Trotsky had insisted that the Soviet Union could best be understood as a 'degenerated workers' state', and Anderson agreed that this amounted to the most sophisticated categorisation of Stalinism in the Soviet Union. However, Anderson argued, Trotsky's powerful analysis of domestic Stalinism was weakened by a one-dimensional account of the role of Stalinism internationally. With regard to the Soviet Union Trotsky had argued that Stalinism had a progressive character *vis-à-vis* the imperialist states and a reactionary character *vis-à-vis* the Russian proletariat. Externally, however, Trotsky had argued that Stalinism was simply a counter-revolutionary force even though, through the communist parties, it had won the support of some of the best working class militants. Anderson maintained that Trotsky's characterisation of the role of international Stalinism was one-sided, as it could not account for the objectively revolutionary role that had been played by Stalinism after the war, since when Stalinist parties in Vietnam, Yugoslavia, Albania and China had led mass revolutionary movements to victory. Moreover, Anderson maintained that 'European fascism was essentially destroyed by the Soviet Union ... [and] capitalism was abolished over one half of the continent', and 'thereafter the permanent threat of the socialist camp acted as a decisive accelerator of bourgeois decolonisation in Africa and Asia' (Anderson 1984, 126). Stalinism, he argued, should be understood as a contradictory phenomenon, incorporating both progressive and reactionary elements in both its domestic and foreign policies. This meant that in addition to his being critical of Trotskyism's strategy for socialism in the West, Anderson was also critical of what he perceived to be its too critical stance towards the Western Communist Parties.[50]

ARGUMENTS WITHIN ENGLISH MARXISM: POLITICS

In *Antinomies* Anderson argued that prior to the smashing of the capitalist state the socialist movement needed to win over 'the conviction of workers' from an allegiance to the dominant ideology (Anderson 1976b, 78). However, he went on to say very little about how, in practice, this was to be done. In 1980 he went some way towards putting meat on these strategic bones and thus towards closing this lacuna in his work. Anderson's new position was developed in *Arguments* and further elucidated in his introduction to a collection of essays on the New Cold War. In *Arguments* he argued that a moral realism must be added to the left's politics to help it break out of its political isolation. However, in line with his comments on agency, he rejected Thompson's abstract moralism, and insisted that a central 'purpose of understanding the past is to provide a causal knowledge of historical processes capable of furnishing the basis for an adequate political practice in the present'. So, in line with his previous critique of Thompson's politics, he criticised exclusively moral discussions of the case for socialism, as they tended to substitute ethics for 'explanatory accounts of history' (Anderson 1980, 85-86). Nevertheless, he went on to argue that, in contrast to abstract moralism, a 'moral consciousness is certainly indispensable to the very idea of socialism'. This argument had two elements: first, he denied that an abstract moral critique of Stalinism could offer a satisfactory basis for understanding it as a historical phenomenon. Second, however, he insisted that any viable socialist politics required a moral imagination, that is a utopian element, which would act as a bridge linking immediate struggles with ultimate socialist goals (Anderson 1980, 205). Anderson thus at once criticised and welcomed Thompson's moral contribution to socialism.

In the 1977 edition of *William Morris*, Thompson argued that, while it was in 1956 that his arguments with 'orthodox Marxism became fully articulate', his politics had since 1955 existed within the 'Morris/Marx argument' (Thompson 1977, 810). The key continuity over that twenty-year period was the equation of Stalinism with orthodox Marxism. Thus even when, in *The Poverty of Theory*, he located two distinct Marxist traditions – one dogmatic, the other open – and rejected Stalinist dogmatism (Thompson 1978, 188 ff), he maintained that Stalinism was a true heir of Marxism, in particular the 'static' and 'scientific' Marxism of Marx's maturity (Thompson 1978, 168 & 141 & 61). So, the idiosyncrasy of Thompson's Marxist denunciation of Stalinism lay in the way in which it involved a rejection of the scientific pretensions of Marxism. Included amongst the consequences of this argument was that his concept of morality became cut adrift from rational investigation: 'one may not assimilate desire into knowledge' (Thompson 1977, 807).

In contrast to scientific socialism, Thompson's socialism stressed the real creativity of actors. Despite the undoubted strengths of his argument, it did include its own weaknesses. In particular, it led him to systematically downplay the crucial role of material constraints in his explanation for the degeneration of the post-revolutionary Soviet state. Thus, in an article first published in 1956, he had argued that Stalinism was a form of 'mechanical idealism': it was 'socialist theory and practice that had lost the ingredient of humanity' (Thompson 1976b, 69). This, as Anderson was aware, was far from adequate as an analysis of the Soviet social formation (Anderson 1980, 25). More generally, Anderson argued that in divorcing morality from rational investigation Thompson was in danger of succumbing to the worst excesses of Parisian irrationalism. By contrast, Anderson maintained that morality should be understood historically (Anderson 1980, 161-162).

The weakness with Thompson's moralism, according to Anderson, was that in failing to understand morality as a product of history his critique of Stalinism tended towards anachronism. By contrast, Anderson argued that desires – and thus utopias and the moral critique that went with them – could be understood rationally; and in this sense he broke the dichotomy between desires and knowledge by agreeing with Marx that knowledge is in fact a 'fundamental and illimitable human desire' (Anderson 1980, 167). Thus, for Anderson, the fundamental strength of Morris's utopia was its realism: *News From Nowhere* was actually based explicitly upon real antagonisms in Morris's England (Anderson 1980, 164 & 178). Moreover, it was a popular piece that appealed to a mass audience and it did so while maintaining an allegiance to a revolutionary model of the transition from capitalism to socialism (Anderson 1980, 173).

Anderson thus welcomed Morris' intervention as an attempt by a socialist, in conditions where the forces of the revolutionary left were meagre, to break out of the ghetto (Anderson 1980, 171). His utopia, while born of political weakness, therefore was an attempt to overcome this problem. Anderson believed that the contemporary forces of the revolutionary left could learn from this example to help them break out of their ghetto. Not that Morris's utopia was beyond criticism: in particular Anderson pointed to the problem of the simplicity of Morris's future – and the corollary of this – his too romantic critique of capitalism (Anderson 1980, 166). Given this weakness, however, on balance Morris should be seen as an important figure, whose influence should be extended.

In terms of Anderson's own politics this meant that onto his strategic belief in the need to smash the capitalist state, there should be added a morally realistic utopia as a means to make Marxism popular (Anderson 1980, 205). Indeed, in stark contrast to the debate of the 1960s, Anderson re-described his political programme as one that was truer to Morris' legacy than was Thompson's. Thus, while Thompson had successfully latched on to the moral aspect of Morris's thought, he had missed the strategic centrality to Morris' work of his discussion of the need for revolution to break free from the old capitalist state (Anderson 1980, 185). Thompson's political perspective was therefore much more reformist than was Morris's. Anderson noted Thompson's discussion of the Black Acts specifically and the law more generally, as examples of this. Thompson had argued that far from being simply a codification of class rule the law was an arena of conflict. The political corollary of this was that Thompson greatly exaggerated the threat implied by the attacks on civil liberties that were codified into law in the 1970s. Anderson did not believe that these changes were irrelevant, just that Thompson was making too much of them. Thompson was though getting a hearing for his views across a much broader spectrum than the audience for the revolutionary left. It was on the basis of this that Anderson argued for a utopia to be added to Marx's political strategy. For if Thompson's moral outcry could make people listen, then it could be used as a mechanism to draw people into the kind of activity that would tend to further radicalise them and thus help the left break out of its ghetto (Anderson 1980, 205).

Anderson concluded *Arguments* with the case for a morally realistic utopia, which could act as a conduit – a 'transitional demand' (Anderson 1980, 205) – through which revolutionary socialist ideas could pass over to the working class; he argued that the concept of democracy could be used in this way. However, he suggested no actual material basis for this utopia; and in particular, he outlined no incipient ultra-democratic tendencies existing within the system that could be unleashed through a socialist revolution. Rather, his concept of democracy seems unhinged from any proletarian practice as such, and thus his strategic suggestions appeared to be solely propagandistic.

So the ultimate irony of his politics in the early 1980s may be that they suffered from exactly the same weakness that Morris' Marxism had in the 1880s. For while *News From Nowhere* was actually written from somewhere, Morris never developed a political strategy that was able to obtain a purchase on working-class politics (Mahamdallie 1996). He was therefore unable to turn nineteenth-century socialism into a mass force, despite a number of major political successes; and while Morris was the first socialist to take up the fight against reformism (Anderson 1980, 176), his utopia was actually a failed attempt to develop a mass following for the young socialist movement. Indeed, while Thompson downplayed Morris' revolutionary political interventions (Anderson 1980, 185), and while he and Anderson agreed about the significance of Morris's ideological insights, neither fully came to grips with the fact that Morris failed to build a mass revolutionary movement in Britain.

Finally, Anderson's strategic proposals were never posed in concrete organisational terms. This point is important because if it is accepted that experience is no guarantor of interpretation then the framework within which experiences are interpreted becomes centrally important. Logically the acceptance of this position should have meant that Anderson moved forward to examine the nature of the mediations that existed between socialists and working-class experience. This would, of course, lead him to the practical problem of building some form of organisation or party, for, as Lukács argued, 'organisation is the form of mediation between theory and practice' (Lukács 1971, 299). However, nowhere in *Arguments* does Anderson address the problem of building a socialist party. In a sense this is incredible given the importance that classical Marxists have attached to this process since Lenin's day. Indeed, divorced from the act of party-building, Anderson's ideas could never rise from the abstract to the concrete, for, as Lukács argued, 'every theoretical tendency or clash of views must immediately develop an organisational arm if it is to rise above the level of pure theory or abstract opinion' (Lukács 1971, 299). We shall see in the final chapter that Anderson's failure to address this issue has weakened his contemporary strategic orientation.

AGAINST POST-STRUCTURALISM

We have already touched upon some of the themes of *In the Tracks of Historical Materialism* in the preceding sections. In particular, we have seen that by 1983 Anderson argued that the trajectory of all anti-Soviet socialists was towards apostasy. This position was, however, only the minor theme of the book. The book's major theme was that Parisian irrationalism was both a reactionary ideology, and one that a confident Marxism need not fear.

Anderson argued that Marxism was unique amongst the social sciences in that it alone offered a criticism of society that was simultaneously a 'self-criticism' (Anderson 1983, 11). He noted that as he had attempted such a self-criticism in *Considerations*, in *Tracks* he set out to reassess his earlier prognosis. He argued that of the four key predictions that he made in that text, three had, broadly, been proved correct. These were that Western Marxism's specific concerns with aesthetics and epistemology would come to an end; that these concerns would be replaced by a turn to the concrete; and that 'any renascence of a more classical cast of Marxist culture would be virtually bound to involve the spread of the latter to the Anglo-American bastions of imperialism' (Anderson 1983, 19). The unfulfilled prediction, however, was the most important. This was his belief that there would be a 'unification of Marxist theory and popular practice in a mass revolutionary movement' (Anderson 1983, 27). In the place of this optimistic scenario Anderson noted that there had, in fact, occurred a 'Crisis of Marxism' in Southern Europe, while in the Anglo-Saxon world the turn to the concrete did not include a turn to the strategic. The task, which he set himself, was to excavate the foundations of this crisis.

Anderson noted a possible cause for the crisis of Marxism in the power of the post-structuralist challenge to it; however, he remained unconvinced by this intellectual upstart. More pernicious, Anderson argued, was the 'extrinsic history' of Latin Marxism. It was here that he located the true cause of the capitulation before post-structuralism. As we noted above, Anderson explained the Crisis of Latin Marxism as the crisis of the false gods of Eurocommunism and Maoism (Anderson 1983, 76). As these political projects failed, so too did the Marxists who had once looked to them as alternatives to capitalism. Why was Anderson so sure of the validity this extrinsic history of the crisis of Marxism and the rise of post-structuralism? Primarily because he saw that where there had existed fewer illusions in either Eurocommunism or Maoism, then national Marxist traditions had proved much more resilient. For instance in Germany, Habermas, while asking many of the same questions as the post-structuralists, refused to follow their retreat from either socialism or the ideals of the Enlightenment (Anderson 1983, 57-67). So where the left had fewer illusions about anti-Soviet models of socialism, it had proved much more resilient than the left in France and Italy.

As we noted above Anderson also outlined an intrinsic history of the crisis of Marxism. This began centrally with the failure of Althusser to mount a successful defence of Marxism against Lévi-Strauss's alternative. Thus, Althusser endorsed Lévi-Strauss's challenge to Sartre's humanism and his historicism, and where Lévi-Strauss had 'cut the Gordian Knot of the relation between structure and subject by suspending the latter from any field of scientific knowledge ... Althusser radicalised it.... But in an objectivist auction of this sort he was bound to be outbid.... Foucault, proclaiming a full-throated rhetoric of the end of man, in turn reduced Marxism itself to an involuntary effect of an out-dated Victorian episteme' (Anderson 1983, 37-38). What then had this intellectual auction produced?

Anderson argued that post-structuralism was characterised by four themes. First there was the 'exorbitation of language'. Where Saussure had stressed that his model was of strictly limited reference to the analysis of language, structuralism had generalised it and argued that it had a universal validity. Second, and as a direct consequence of this, there was an 'attenuation of truth'. Thus, by contrast with Saussure, who had understood language to be constituted through a series of signs which in turn were each made up of a signifier and a signified, post-structuralism 'repressed the referential' element of the sign. Third, this led in turn to the 'randomisation of history'. Once language was understood to be the general paradigm of society then the concept of causation is lost. Finally, there is the 'capsizal of structures' themselves as the linguistic paradigm consists of a series of signifiers, unconnected to the 'real' world, then the real world cannot operate to limit the structure (Anderson 1983, 40-51). The outcome was thus a theory that was crassly subjectivist and voluntarist.

By contrast with these conclusions, Anderson argued that structure and subject were 'interdependent as categories' and structuralism and post-structuralism, in analysing just one of these elements at the expense of the other, were never able to fully comprehend them (Anderson 1983, 54). However, as we have seen, Anderson's account of this interdependence in *Arguments* did not succeed in integrating what he perceived to be Marx's structuralist theory and his voluntarist practice. He repeated this argument in 1983; Classical Marxism had never offered a coherent answer to the problem of the causal nature of social change: thus a dichotomy exists within Marxism between 'economism on one side, voluntarism on the other' (Anderson 1983, 34).

It was, however, precisely within the parameters of this debate that the structuralists and post-structuralists had developed their critiques of Marxism. The dilemma for Anderson in his rejection of their solutions was that he had nothing better to put in their place. As Aronson argued, Anderson's critique was 'too confident'; it failed to properly admit the real weaknesses that Marxist theory should confront (Aronson 1985, 83). Not that Anderson portrayed Marxism as a finished truth – the postscript to his book was a discussion of possible areas for further research. Rather he, too quickly in Terry Eagleton's opinion, rejected any of the possible insights that deconstruction offered a renewed Marxism, and he was 'too uncritical of Saussure' (Eagleton 1986, 94 & 96).[51]

Meanwhile Anderson looked to Habermas's social theory as a counter to the irrationalism of the post-structuralists. Habermas interested Anderson because he accepted many of the premises of the post-structuralists, while maintaining an allegiance to the Enlightenment tradition. However, Habermas' politics were essentially defensive of bourgeois democracy, and as such offered little in the way of a positive strategy for socialist advance (Anderson 1992x, 330 & 1983, 67). A year after the publication of *Tracks* Anderson sought to remedy this lacuna through the medium of an interview with Habermas. Unfortunately, Habermas failed to utilise the space offered to develop a more robust strategic orientation (Habermas 1992, 181).

Somewhat ironically, given his previous dismissal of English-speaking Marxism, Anderson finally sought solace from the crisis of continental Marxism in the 'steadier and more tough-minded historical materialism' of the Anglophone world (Anderson 1983, 77 & 24). However, he noted, even Anglo-Saxon Marxism had failed to develop a viable strategic analysis of the Western capitalist states. This criticism also applied to the Trotskyists, whose 'too close an imaginative adherence to the paradigm of the October Revolution' undermined their appeal. In particular the 'Fourth International lost its way at the crossroad of the Portuguese Revolution' (Anderson 1983, 79-80). Despite this argument, in 1983 Anderson argued that, while the working class in the West was 'in disarray, … it is much less defeated and dispersed than it was during the last great depression' (Anderson 1983, 105). As they stood in 1983 therefore, Anderson's rejections of Eurocommunism, Maoism and Trotskyism as models for socialist advance in the West, had not yet led to immediate political pessimism.

He did, however, once again, suggest areas for future research. These included the woman question, democracy, and the nature of the post-capitalist societies (Anderson 1983, 88). He also noted that the prospects for nuclear war needed to be examined, as did the nature of the environmental crisis (Anderson 1983, 94). More specifically he argued that the possibilities of socialist democracy, economic planning, gender relations and international relations should be analysed (Anderson 1983, 99). Thus the feeling one gets from reading *Tracks* is of a confident Marxism taking on new problems and accounting for old mistakes. However, within a few short years Anderson had moved from revolutionary Marxist politics towards a version of social democracy that he hoped would be enriched by liberalism. Anderson partially explained this trajectory, as we shall see below, through his reception of Michael Mann's *The Sources of Social Power*.

AGAINST THE NEW COLD WAR

The escalation of the Cold War in the late 1970s demanded a swift response from the left. Edward Thompson quickly threw himself into the rejuvenated CND and its campaign against international militarism. Anderson published Thompson's analysis of the New Cold War in *NLR* and supported the relaunched CND. Moreover, the publication of Thompson's call to arms in May 1980 was followed over the next eighteen months by a fraternal debate over Thompson's analysis in the pages of *NLR* (*NLR* ed. 1982, x). In 1982 this debate was collected in a symposium, edited and introduced by Anderson.

In the lead essay Thompson argued that while it may have been of some comfort to socialists 'to see a cause for [the New Cold War] primarily in Western Imperialism and only secondarily in Soviet reaction. This is now beside the point': the states, East and West, were now 'isomorphic', and the system created by this relation could best be described as one of 'Exterminism' (Thompson 1982, 15 & 21& 5). Thus, capitalist imperialism could not be held solely responsible for the New Cold War. In fact, where imperialism had created its own dialectical opposition in the exploited and oppressed of the subjugated nations, exterminism, by contrast, was a 'non-dialectical contradiction': it produced its other in the military opponent but not an antagonist that it exploited (Thompson 1982, 24). So, while class struggle would continue, it could not act as the basis for an anti-war movement. Such a movement would, it was hoped, grow from the humanistic appeal by Thompson and his collaborators to the people of Britain and Europe. This political position had all the hallmarks of the voluntarism for which Anderson had previously criticised Thompson's Marxism; how then did his materialist critique of this model operate in practice?

The rest of the *NLR* book was taken up with detailed criticisms of Thompson's thesis from a series of left activists and intellectuals. In particular, *NLR* editorial committee members Fred Halliday and Mike Davis – in analyses that were described by Anderson as 'fundamental' (Anderson 1983, 96) – sought to emphasise the role of the West in unleashing the new conflict. Davis's argument was fundamentally a rehearsal of Deutscher's analysis of the Cold War as the 'class struggle on a world scale', within which the politics of CND should be closer to those of the USSR than to those of the USA (Davis 1982, 42). Davis maintained that since 1945 the USA had been fighting a losing war against socialism and the New Cold War was a product of this growing crisis

(Davis 1982, 47 & 51). Indeed, there had been a successful socialist revolution on average once every four years since the war; it was this against this background that the USA was reacting (Davis 1982, 47). Davis went on to argue that Thompson's methodology was closer to Weber's than it was to Marx's, as he had divorced militarism from class antagonisms, leading him towards a form of theoretical pluralism (Davis 1982, 37). This was an apt point, however, the *NLR* editorial members faced a similar problem when they attempted to explain the Sino-Soviet split.

This weakness is evident in Fred Halliday's essay. Halliday argued a similar general case to Davis. However, for him a key causal factor in the New Cold War was the anti-Soviet policies of the Chinese which had played a key role in sparking off the new conflict between the East and the West (Halliday 1982, 312). But what was the cause of the Sino-Soviet dispute itself? While Halliday did not give an answer to this problem in this essay, in his book on the subject he maintained that the basis for the split was ideological: the Chinese were aggrieved by Moscow's pro-*détente* policy in the 1950s (Halliday 1986, 160). However, a few years earlier he had argued that 'so deep is the Chinese conflict with the Soviet Union that it is easy to forget how without foundation it is' (Halliday 1976, 185). Similarly, Anderson suggested that while Chinese anti-Sovietism was 'initially intelligible enough', it became 'increasingly unbalanced and hysterical' (Anderson 1983, 73).

These arguments obviously opened the door to theoretical pluralism, and they did so just as Michael Mann developed a social theory of tremendous power in precisely that area where Anderson's own Marxism was weakest: the relationship between the state and capital. In his book, *The Sources of Social Power*, Mann argued that there were four sources of social power, each irreducible to the others: the political, military, ideological and economic (Mann 1986, 2). Mann was a member of CND and as such sought, like Anderson, to explain the New Cold War in order to combat it. Unlike the Marxists, however, Mann had no ulterior motive for insisting on a monist account of historical development. In particular, he argued that 'capitalism and militarism are both core features of our society but they are only contingently linked' (Mann 1984, 28). This position was the logical extension of the *NLR* analysis of the Sino-Soviet split: for if militarism can exist without capitalism then it certainly cannot be reduced to it. In 1982 this was only the implied position of *NLR* and Anderson; what changed to make it more explicit?

Anderson was aware of a core element of what was to become Mann's 1986 book as early as 1980 (Anderson 1980, 92). This fact thus casts a shadow of doubt over his own comments on his move away from revolutionary Marxism in the mid 1980s. This shift in his perspective, he claimed, was in part a consequence of the reverberations in academia on the publication of Mann's book;

for its publication now meant that it was 'immediately clear' that there 'existed a developed analytical theory of the pattern of human development, exceeding in explanatory ambition and empirical detail any Marxist account' (Anderson 1992b, xii). He explained his own evolution away from revolutionary socialism as in part a consequence of this discovery. However, Anderson did not move away from revolutionary socialism until the mid-1980s. In addition, he also produced a powerful critique of Mann's book when it was first published in 1986. In this review he argued that, despite its many strengths, *The Sources of Social Power* lacked a comparative element, and consequentially Mann both underplayed moments in the history of civilisation that seemed to contradict his own thesis; and, where he did devote space to detailed discussions of particular institutions, the lack of a comparison with other similar institutions weakened his case. Thus, Mann had produced an idealistic and implausible analysis of the role of Christianity in fostering the development of capitalism, in part because he had not compared it with other religions that also encompassed multi-state systems (Anderson 1992n, 84). Furthermore, Anderson argued that the theoretical infrastructure of Mann's thesis was questionable. Mann's concept of political power did not 'possess the same categorical autonomy as the others', it always rested upon either military or ideological power (Anderson 1992n, 77). A complete materialist critique would thus have to unite the ideological, military and economic aspects of power.

This was not the last word to be said on the subject. Anderson argued that Chris Wickham had penned the most powerful and sustained critique of Mann's thesis (Anderson 1992h, 217). Wickham argued that 'Mann's position only appeared to be non-materialist because the state has not yet been theorised sufficiently as an economic form' (Wickham 1988, 67). Moreover, Mann and other 'post-Weberians' were taking the lead in analysing the development of the modern world precisely because Marxists had allowed them to do so. Thus, Wickham suggested, Marxists should rise to the challenge posed by historical sociology. In particular, he argued that Anderson's sequels to *Passages* and *Lineages*, which might fill this gap, were 'fourteen years overdue' (Wickham 1988, 78).

Ironically, however, as we saw in the last chapter, Anderson's history floundered precisely over the issue of the state as an economic form. As we have seen, Anderson juxtaposed, in *Lineages*, a pacific capitalist mode of production to its antipode militarist mercantilism. It is evident that Anderson did not consider capitalism as it had actually evolved as a pacific system, just its generic form. This is very similar to Mann's solution to the problem of the relationship between economic and political power: 'militarism derives from geopolitical aspects of our social structure which are far older than capitalism' (Mann 1984, 28). This did not mean that capital and state could be separated in reality, in fact the 'link between capitalism and the state was growing closer' (Mann 1986, 454). Thus Mann concluded the first volume of *The Sources of Social Power* in words that could have been written by Anderson: 'The capitalist mode of production ... is a purely economic abstraction. Real life capitalism ... actually presupposed, and embedded within itself, other forms of power, especially military and political power' (Mann 1986, 495).

Given this understanding of the relative permanence of military competition, Mann was able to outline a more realistic analysis of the militarism of post-capitalist societies. He argued that while there may exist many good reasons for combating capitalism, its supposed innate militarism was not one of them. Rather, 'politically speaking neither the capitalism of the West, nor the state socialism of the Soviet Union, are the key enemies of those who desire peace and survival today. The enemies are rather the common geopolitical pretensions of the superpowers' (Mann 1984, 45). Mann's analysis of the autonomy of military power was the element of his book that most impressed Anderson, to such an extent that, in addition to his increasing political isolation as the 1980s progressed, he was also experiencing a theoretical pull away from Marxism (Anderson 1992n, 83).

This theoretical pull from Marxism was coupled with Anderson's increasing isolation from Britain's political left. This development at first appears somewhat counter-intuitive given the orthodoxy of Anderson's critique of Thompson's thesis. However, Anderson was at least as critical of the organised Marxist left as he was of Thompson. As we have seen, Thompson argued that what was at stake in the New Cold War was 'the extermination of our civilisation'. Moreover, this was 'not a class issue' and 'certain kinds of revolutionary posturing and rhetoric, which inflame exterminist ideology ... are luxuries we can do without' (Thompson 1982, 28). By contrast, Anderson argued, while 'a shared interest in human survival now unites exploiters and exploited, ... class struggle has not been suspended or even reduced by the thermonuclear age – it has only been deformed and displaced' (*NLR* ed. 1982, viii). Thus, socialism was an ever more necessary objective of the struggle against militarism, but one that was more difficult to achieve. His hope was to solve this conundrum through the unification of the two elements of socialism: the utopian and the rational; 'the notions of peace and revolution' must be united through this merging.

Thus, Anderson began with Thompson but moved on to argue for a socialist perspective for CND and European Nuclear Disarmament (END). The basis for this argument was logical: 'War', he argued, 'is a determinate activity... peace is not. It is the sheer absence of war, and as such intrinsically negative ... peace must acquire a tangible social shape capable of inspiring the positive dreams and loyalties of millions ... what could that shape be if not socialist?'

(*NLR* ed. 1982, xii) So while Anderson agreed with Thompson's perspective for building CND and END in as wide a constituency as possible, he wanted to go further than this, to argue positively for socialism within these organisations.

But what would be the medium for this message? Halliday argued that socialists should support Tony Benn's challenge for the leadership of the Labour Party (Halliday 1982, 324). By contrast the *NLR* interviewers, including Anderson, of Tony Benn in 1982 rejected the argument that socialists should join the Labour Party. They argued that the Labour Party 'remains very much a corporatist, union based party' that had in fact 'never been socialist'. Moreover, they suggested that socialists might build independent organisations of their own: 'is there not something to be said for the course taken in other European countries, where groups of socialists have broken with the inherited structures of the labour movement to form new left parties' (Benn 1982, 117 & 123). Additionally the *NLR* interviewers argued both that significant numbers of socialists existed outside the Labour Party – 'the Communist Party and the Socialist Workers Party being the most prominent' – and that these organisations had experienced significant successes, 'in the Anti-Nazi League, for instance' (Benn 1982, 121-122). The implication was that Anderson would have preferred to work outside the Labour Party.[52] This sense is reinforced by Anderson's positive introduction to David Coates' critique of the strategy of working within the Labour Party (*NLR* 129 1981, 1). However, while the Communist Party may have supported Anderson's anti-anti-Soviet position, the Socialist Workers Party would certainly have not.[53] Moreover, the Communist Party certainly did not share his belief in the need for violent revolution; and while the Socialist Workers Party did, its Trotskyism meant that Anderson would dismiss its model of revolution as bearing a too close relationship to the Russian experience. Thus, in the early 1980s Anderson found himself isolated from the Labour, Communist and Socialist Workers' parties in Britain; while simultaneously feeling the pull of Mann's theoretical alternative to historical materialism.

CHAPTER SIX

THE RETREAT FROM REVOLUTION

Thus far we have documented Anderson's theoretical and political evolution towards a self-confident Marxism from the 1960s to the 1980s. In this chapter I outline the process through which his understanding of Marxism, in the wake of a period of defeats for the left, led him from the mid 1980s to reject the possibility of a socialist transformation of society. This did not lead him to extol a totally pessimistic political perspective; rather he attempted from then onwards to outline a realistic reformist political programme.

We noted in the last chapter that Anderson's work of the early 1980s, while written in the context of major setbacks for the international left, was overdetermined by a sense of confidence emanating from the growth of the Labour left, the expansion of CND, and the growing hegemony of Marxist ideas on the intellectual left. However, these forces all proved transitory. Thus the CND demonstration of October 1983, while massive, proved to be the highpoint of the movement, rather than a precursor of greater things to come. Moreover, the scale of Labour's defeat in the 1983 general election convinced many activists of the need to moderate the Party's message. With hindsight it seems that the highpoint for the Labour Left's campaign was Tony Benn's unsuccessful attempt on the Party's deputy leadership in 1981. Finally, despite Anderson's critique of post-structuralism, postmodernist rhetoric appeared to sweep everything before it as the 1980s wore on. So all of the three areas from which Anderson had taken inspiration in the early 1980s had, by the end of the decade, disappeared.

The retreat of the Labour left, the decline of CND, and the ascendancy of post-Marxist ideas on the academic left all occurred within the context of the general downturn in workers struggles from the mid 1970s, as we noted in the last chapter. The retreat of the workers' movement against first Labour's Social Contract and then the Thatcher government's Ridley Plan[54] culminated in 1985 with the defeat of the Miners' Strike. For the next few years the eddy currents that had previously mediated against the successes of neo-liberalism were reduced to a low background noise.

Unfortunately, this crisis for the left was not a narrowly British concern. Across the West in the mid 1970s there occurred a 'stabilisation of bourgeois rule', through the medium of revitalised reformist institutions and organisations, followed, in the 1980s, by a move to the right led by Thatcher and Reagan (Harman 1988, 339 ff). In step with this process many Western leftist intellectuals produced a series of theoretical justifications for their own flight to the right. In Britain this tendency was epitomised by the journal *Marxism Today*, but nevertheless found echoes far beyond its readership. Christened by Ralph Miliband the 'new revisionism', this political and theoretical movement offered less a viable 'way out of the crisis' than 'another manifestation of that crisis' (Miliband 1985, 6).

However, Thatcherism proved to be less stable than the pessimistic analysis associated with the new revisionist current assumed. Within a year of the Tory chants of 'ten more years', to celebrate Thatcher's 'first decade' in Downing Street, the Poll Tax rebellion acted as a catalyst which saw them abandon her ignominiously to the political wilderness. John Major, her replacement, managed to hold on to power in the 1992 general election by combining a retreat over the Poll Tax with an ideological shift in Tory Party rhetoric from Thatcher's open class warfare to the more centrist discourse of a 'classless society'. However, on Black Wednesday September 1992, within six months of winning the election, Major lost what was for the Tories their major electoral asset: their perceived credibility as guardians of the economy. Moreover, a month later the government's decision to impose a massive pit closure programme across the country resulted in two huge demonstrations of the British working class within a week, and polls that declared more than 90 per cent of the country supported the miners. From that moment onwards the defeat of Major at the next general election seemed to be just a matter of time. These two events threw into doubt the pessimistic dismissal of a working-class socialist challenge to capitalism associated with the journal *Marxism Today*. However, where once Anderson would have welcomed such a development, in the early 1990s these events seemed hardly to register with him. By contrast, the collapse of the Soviet Union and her East European allies compounded his feeling of pessimism that had originated with the crisis of Western Keynesianism. In this context the ups and downs of the class struggle seemed but small fry on Anderson's Olympian radar.

MARXISM AND HISTORY

In the last chapter I outlined Anderson's understanding of classical Marxism as expressed in *Arguments*. In this chapter I explore his application of that model, and show how he was able to draw reformist political conclusions from it. Anderson first applied his model of Marxism in two essays that expressed the breadth of his learning: *Geoffrey de Ste. Croix and the Ancient Greek World* and *Marshall Berman: Modernity and Revolution*.

In the first of these Anderson posed three minor 'queries' that 'do not touch on the central theoretical statement of' Ste. Croix's 'great work' (Anderson 1992j, 12 & 1) In his book, *The Class Struggle in the Ancient Greek World*, Ste Croix applied, utilising the most modern research, classical Marxism to the problem of the nature and dynamic of antiquity. He suggested that antiquity's long-run evolution could only be understood as a consequence of the changing nature of the extraction of surplus-labour from slaves (Anderson 1992j, 10). While Anderson heartily accepted this thesis, he noted that there were problems with Ste. Croix's discussion of women in classical antiquity, with his discussion of the role of class struggle itself in shaping history, and with his discussion of the dynamics of the slave mode of production (Anderson 1992j, 12).

With regard to women, Anderson challenged Ste. Croix's suggestion that they constituted a separate class in classical antiquity. Anderson persuasively argued that women, who themselves owned slaves, and women, who were themselves slaves, could on no account be considered to be part of the same class, irrespective of the levels of oppression experienced by the former (Anderson 1992j, 13).[55] As to the class struggle, while Anderson welcomed Ste. Croix's critique of subjective models of class, he suggested that in his history Ste. Croix had perhaps gone too far in the opposite direction: indeed, Ste. Croix ironically said very little about actual class struggles in antiquity, despite the title of his book. This, Anderson posited, was because he had actually noticed that 'the real mechanism' that accounted for the rise and fall of antiquity was not class struggle *per se* but the developing contradiction between 'forces and relations of production'. However, in stressing these blind forces Ste. Croix had underplayed the conscious element of agency that existed even in antiquity. Anderson agreed with Ste. Croix that slavery was slowly undermined as the geographical limitations of the Roman Empire were reached and the source of slaves, as the spoils of war, dried up. However, he suggested that Ste. Croix had ignored the gradual weakening of the ideological hold of Rome over slaves, as previously heterogeneous groups of slaves were brought together and thereafter were able to develop a common culture of resistance to the Empire (Anderson 1992j, 17-18).

This review was first published in 1983 and is further evidence of the power of the interpretation of historical materialism outlined in *Arguments*. Centrally this involved an allegiance to the Marxist case that the dynamics of any mode of production are rooted, not simply in class struggle, but in the conflict between forces and relations of production. But how did Anderson understand this conflict to operate under conditions of advanced capitalism? A clue to this is given in his essay *Modernity and Revolution* within which he took issue with Marshall Berman's account of modernity and modernism as presented in his book *All that is Solid Melts into Air*. Anderson argued that Berman's vision of modernity, as an epoch of remorseless change and development, while admittedly 'powerful', was one-sided. The key to Anderson's charge lay in his claim that Berman had chosen as characteristic modernist writers, writers who actually 'preceded modernism proper' (Anderson 1992k, 32). Thus, Berman had analysed a series of nineteenth century writers – Goethe, Baudelaire, Pushkin, Dostoevsky – whilst high modernism was an early twentieth century phenomenon. This elision in Berman's account was a corollary of his utilisation of the Hegelian, rather than the Marxist, conceptualisation of historical time. Consequently, he flattened out history and politics in his survey, as he both failed to analyse the sharp political and aesthetic rifts that were characteristic of modernism, while, simultaneously, failing to distinguish modernism adequately from capitalism (Anderson 1992k, 33).

Anderson argued that modernism could best be understood as a response to a particular 'cultural field of force triangulated by three principal coordinates'. The first of these was the 'academicism' of art that was characteristic of European culture in the epoch when – up until between 1914 and 1945 – the *ancien regime* still ruled. The second was the 'still incipient, hence essentially novel, emergence within these societies of the key technologies or inventions of the second industrial revolution'. Finally, there existed the 'imaginative proximity of social revolution' (Anderson 1992k, 34). Thus modernism was an artistic movement whose conjuncture existed from around the end of the nineteenth century to around 1914 at its height, and for another thirty years or so in a less pure form. Anderson defended this periodisation of capitalism through reference to Marx claim that 'bourgeois society would experience an ascent, a stabilisation and a descent' (Anderson 1992k, 31). Capitalism would thus appear to be more complex than modernization theory would suggest. Specifically, Anderson rebuked Berman for abstracting society out of his account of modernism.

However, criticisms have been made of Anderson's own account of historical conjunctures. First, and specifically in relation to modernity, Callinicos has argued that one element of Anderson's conjunctural explanation is particularly weak. This is his utilisation of Arno Mayer's characterisation of the pre-war

European state system as 'pre-eminently pre-industrial and pre-bourgeois' (Mayer 1981, 17). Callinicos, basing his arguments on those of Hobsbawm and Stone, argues that the European state system at the turn of the century was in fact modern and bourgeois (Callinicos 1989, 43). The salience of this argument is of fundamental importance to Anderson's political evolution in the 1980s. For, as we shall see below, if his argument as to the archaic nature of the pre-war European state system is wrong, then the direction of his political evolution over the last decade is thrown into question.

More generally, Osborne has argued that a fundamental contradiction exists between Anderson's formulations of the structure of a mode of production as articulated in *Arguments* and in *Modernity and Revolution* respectively. As we saw in the last chapter, Anderson had argued in *Arguments* that it was the 'mode of production that confers a fundamental unity on a social formation' (Anderson 1980, 55). Osborne points out that in 1980 Anderson had criticised Althusser's attempt to unify 'different sectoral times' through his concept of a 'ruptural unity'. However, by 1983 Anderson's concept of conjuncture closely resembled Althusser's ruptural unity (Osborne 1995, 26 & Anderson 1980, 76). Osborne argues that Althusser's concept, by its very nature, 'rules out the development of the whole as a whole' and therefore makes impossible the 'thinking of the transition from one mode of production to another'. Thus, as different levels develop along different temporalities, breaks can only be understood to exist together as conjunctures: no fundamental unity can be ascribed to the system. Conversely, Marx insisted, 'modes of production must themselves be combined into an ongoing total history' (Osborne 1995, 25-26). Anderson, in *Arguments*, attempted to do just this: 'the relevant time in which all regional histories should be convened is not an empty grid of dates, but the full movement of the social formation as a whole' (Anderson 1980, 75). Osborne argues that Anderson failed to carry through this prescription when he wrote *Modernity and Revolution*, and therefore failed to explain 'modernity as a historical category' (Osborne 1995, 26). Thus, Anderson, in *Modernity and Revolution*, like Althusser, defined events only relationally. This, in turn, related to his application of Saussure, in whose system, as we have noted above, even the concept of diachrony 'does not refer to a temporal mode of existence, but to the mere succession of semiological systems one upon another' (Fabian quoted in Osborne 1995, 27).

This appears to be how Anderson understood modernity. For where Berman saw only continuity, Anderson saw only change. The pivot of this change was the stabilisation of bourgeois democracy in the mid twentieth century. 'It was the Second World War ... which destroyed all three of the historical coordinates under discussion, and therewith cut off the vitality of modernism. After 1945, the old semi-aristocratic or agrarian order and its appurtenances were finished, in every country. Bourgeois democracy was finally universalised'. 'At the same time Fordism arrived in force. Mass production and consumption transformed the West European economies along North American lines. There could be no longer be the smallest doubt as to what kind of society this technology would consolidate: an oppressively stable, monolithically industrial, capitalist civilisation was now in place' (Anderson 1992k, 37).

Anderson argued that 'Modernism was the product of a historically unstable form of society and an undecided epoch, in which drastically variable futures were lived as immediately possible – among them ... socialist revolution ... Since the Second World War, the West has passed into an opposite constellation ... capitalism has anchored itself in the structures ... of liberal democracy and consumer prosperity to become a self reproducing order' (Anderson 1992k, 53-4). These final lines formed part of the postscript to the original essay, published in 1985. In 1983 Anderson argued the weaker case that the potential for revolution was only a 'seeming' rather than a definite absence (Anderson 1992k, 44). Not that this fact was to be celebrated, far from it: while 'postmodernism makes a spurious virtue out of that necessity', the crippling nature of the bourgeois order 'is another reason for remaining true to the hope of a passage beyond this world order' (Anderson 1992k, 54-5). However, as the 1980s wore on he became increasingly convinced that an alternative to capitalism was ever more remote. One exception to this rule lay in the Third World where 'a kind of shadow configuration of what once prevailed in the First World does exist today' (Anderson 1992k, 40).

If Osborne is correct, then Anderson's application of a conjunctural analysis of modernity presupposed an insurmountable gap between past and present historical moments: implying that the politics of these past conjunctures need not have any relevance to modern politics. This general position underpinned Anderson's more substantive case that the bourgeois-democratic state was a phenomenon of which Marxists, operating prior to 1945, had no experience, implying in turn a distancing of his thought from those classical Marxists who had developed their ideas prior to 1945. These two assumptions thus helped ease Anderson on a trajectory that took him away from revolutionary politics. This political evolution was reinforced by a third element of his Marxism: his understanding of the concrete nature of the contradiction between forces and relations of production as it expressed itself under capitalism.

We noted in chapter three Anderson's dissatisfaction with the labour theory of value. Moreover, we saw in chapter five how Anderson had argued that Cohen's reconceptualisation of the Marxist concept of the mode of production had an 'intellectual force [that] supersedes virtually all previous discussion' (Anderson 1980, 72). Cohen had in fact developed a reconceptualisation of Marxism that was not built upon the labour theory of value. Now in

Arguments Anderson does not outline the nature of the conflict between forces and relations of production under advanced capitalism, while, in *Karl Marx's Theory of History*, Cohen does. He argues that the conflict expresses itself as a disproportionality crisis. That is, a crisis whereby the anarchic structure of capitalist production produces both under and over-employment in various sectors of the economy (Cohen 1978, 306 ff). Marx, by contrast, had argued that capitalist crises generally occur as a consequence of the falling rate of profit, which is itself a product of the accumulation process (Rosdolsky 1977, 376-82). These two models lead to very different political conclusions. The former implies that some form of state planning could solve the crisis-prone nature of capitalism, while the latter explicitly denies that capitalist crises can be reformed away. As we shall see below, Anderson's application of orthodox Marxism to the problem of the crisis of British capitalism in the 1980s led directly to reformist political conclusions. These conclusions imply that his understanding of the nature of the conflict between forces and relations of production under capitalism was closer to Cohen's than it was to Marx's.

THE POSSIBILITY OF REFORMISM

In the late 1980s Anderson returned to the themes of *Origins* and *Components*. In two essays, *The Figures of Descent* (1987) and *A Culture in Contraflow* (1990), he updated, utilising his new more materialist interpretation of Marxism, these earlier theses. As we noted in chapter two, Gregory Elliott has suggested that Anderson's republication of these four essays, alongside *The Notion of Bourgeois Revolution* and *The Light of Europe* in *English Questions* in 1992, obscured a break in his thought (Elliott 1998, 31). Elliott makes the valid point that whereas directly strategic counterparts, *Problems of Socialist Strategy* and *A Critique of Wilsonism*, had accompanied the essays from the 1960s, the later essays had no such stable-mates. Elliott argues that Anderson's decision to leave the earlier strategic interventions to the gnawing criticism of the mice, rather than to see them republished, distorted the impression given of his *oeuvre*. A consequence of this elision over the political orientation of the former essays gave the impression in *English Questions* of academic continuity, rather than of a break between the radical critique of the early years from the outsider with the developed thoughts of an academic insider in the 1980s. The general thrust of Elliott's point is undoubtedly correct. However, as Elliott admits, *The Light of Europe* did contain some strategic recommendations, and Anderson did publish a much more directly political essay in the 1980s. While this essay, *Social Democracy Today*, was not as substantial a political intervention as were the essays from the 1960s, we can still learn from it about both Anderson's political evolution and his continued desire to develop a realistic socialist political perspective.

Figures opens with a brief introduction to the debates between *NLR* and Thompson and Poulantzas from the 1960s. This résumé is followed by a lucid outline of Marx's and Engels' evolving evaluations of the nature of the British state in the nineteenth century. Anderson then moved on to reaffirm his previous argument that an early entrepreneurial ideology had been subverted in Britain at the hands of an aristocratic culture in the nineteenth century. *Origins*, he argued, conflated this fact with the opinion that this marked a '*differentia specifica* of England among major capitalist societies'. This second element to his original argument was 'wrong'. He based this new conclusion on a reading of Arno Mayer's *The Persistence of the Old Regime*, in which Mayer, generalising from Anderson's earlier thesis, had argued that aristocratic hegemony to be the norm rather than the exception across nineteenth-century Europe (Anderson 1992g, 128-9; Mayer 1981).

Given that a continuing aristocratic hegemony was the lynchpin of the thesis of *Origins*, the prospects for the original thesis seemed to be somewhat circumscribed assuming the truth of this new evidence. Indeed Anderson remarked that 'the problem of the historical source of the British crisis in the mid twentieth century remains intact'. (Anderson 1992g, 129). The rest of the essay was then an attempt to locate the specificity of the British state, which, he suggested, underpinned its national 'malady' (Anderson 1992g, 121).

The English aristocracy could be differentiated from its European cousins, Anderson argued, in two important respects: first, it had the 'longest consecutive history as a capitalist stratum proper'; while, second, 'the Hanoverian and Victorian landowning class ... was the wealthiest in Europe' (Anderson 1992g, 130-132). These two facts combined to form the basis for Britain's specificity. Wealth gave the aristocracy leisure, which in turn opened the door to its involvement in politics. Thus, the aristocrats were able to run the state, and as they were a capitalist stratum they ran it, after 1688, in a capitalist manner, assuring that no fundamental antagonism existed between themselves and the industrial capitalists. Thereafter, with just a minor fine-tuning, the state was able to incorporate the industrial capitalists into the elite after 1832 (Anderson 1992g, 141). The sting in the tail took the form of the aristocracy's relationship to merchant capital and thus the conditions upon which the industrialists were incorporated into the elite.

Anderson argued that whereas agrarian capital was the first incarnation of capitalism in England, merchant capital was its second. Indeed, he suggested that the merchant capitalists were the key element that tilted the balance towards the parliamentary landowners during the civil war, ensuring their victory over the old order. Anderson argued that alongside the establishment of parliamentary sovereignty, the Glorious Revolution of 1688 'laid the modern foundations of the City'. This in turn underpinned England's uniqueness: 'The

Hanoverian epoch saw an increasingly intimate connexion between the dominant landed and moneyed interests, even if this never extended to social fusion'. These two super-rich fractions of capital ruled together throughout the nineteenth-century while industrialists were always 'typically much smaller figures' (Anderson 1992g, 136 & 139). So, even after 1832, industry was the relatively poor cousin that remained marginal to the running of the state. Anderson compared this situation with those in the USA and Germany, where industry was always incomparably wealthier than agriculture and thus had a much more central role in the running of the state.

The first element of Anderson's explanation of Britain's crisis in *Figures* is in essence then very simple: Britain never developed the kind of modern state necessary to maintain its early industrial might. As in the 1960s Anderson justified this position historically with a fairly straightforward genealogy. In the context that I have outlined above, Britain industrialised. Industrialising first, she had an open field and duly dominated the world economy in the mid nineteenth century. However, precisely because of this early, easy lead, the British state was never forced to intervene within the economy in the way that its competitors did, to pull the economy up by its bootstraps so that it could compete with earlier industrialisers. Industry did not feel it necessary to struggle against the dominant elite in the British state to transform the operation of the state. Moreover, because the 'decentralised gentry' had prevented the development of an absolutist state in the seventeenth century a strong state was never on hand to offer its services in the context of the new challenges of the nineteenth century: the 'stabilised Victorian state was exceptional in the austerity of its means and the simplicity of its functions'. The British state thus 'exonerated from economic, military and cultural tasks ... devoted itself to the most limited range of traditional duties ... The key functions of the state ... were largely imperial'. Finally, the Treasury dominated the British state, which in turn was subordinate to the needs of the City (Anderson 1992g, 142-144). However, the City's main arenas of activity were pre-industrial: the 'trafficking of Government securities' and the 'discounting and insurance of foreign trade'. The City, moreover, developed autonomously from manufacture: 'two economic sectors thus grew up side by side under the Pax Britannica without intrinsic structural connection other than a common imperial framework' (Anderson 1992g, 138).

This structure of state inaction had as its logical conclusion the Thatcher government's programme of deregulations in the 1980s; which 'could only mean more deindustrialisation'. By contrast, Britain's competitors had developed regulative structures that had facilitated their more rational economic strategies. Britain needed to follow their lead because 'the rectification of disadvantage requires ... a centralising force capable of regulating and counteracting the spontaneous molecular movements of the market'. Anderson noted that four distinct structures of regulation[56] had been instituted in advanced capitalist countries since the war. The first, in France, consisted of a 'highly trained and cohesive technocracy' which directed economic advance; second, in Germany, it was the banking system that 'performed comparable functions'; in Japan a third structure combined elements of both the French and the German models; finally, in Austria and Sweden, organised labour played the directive role. In Britain, unfortunately, labour was 'corporate', and the international orientation of finance capital precluded it from playing a similar role to its German counterpart; and while a capable administrative class evolved to police both imperial and domestic social conflicts, it developed no head for economic planning (Anderson 1992g, 187-90).

One factor that helped explain the lack of an instinct for planning in the British establishment also explained the subordination of the Treasury to the City. The British elite had been educated in the Arnoldian public school system, whose values were 'markedly anti-industrial from the outset' (Anderson 1992g, 147). Given that these schools were the institutions that gelled together the nation's elite, their anti-industrial bias was of profound consequence, affecting a malign influence throughout the ideology of the British ruling class. Thus, the Arnoldian public schools were, first, anti-industrial in outlook and, second, pivotal in manufacturing the culture of Britain's rulers in the nineteenth century. Moreover, these schools were able to act as a medium for an anti-entrepreneurial ideology because of the prior existence of an elite aristocratic culture in Britain. Anderson's argument was therefore an attempt to provide a materialist grounding for the cultural analyses of England's decline. How persuasive is this argument?

Anderson's view that the English aristocracy had been a capitalist stratum long before 1640 is based upon the work of Robert Brenner, and suffers from similar weaknesses to this model (Anderson 1992g, 130; Blackledge 2003). Brenner has argued that capitalism developed in England on the basis of the transformation of class relations in the countryside: English capitalism's first manifestation was as agrarian capitalism (Brenner 1985). A weakness with Brenner's otherwise very powerful account of the nature of transition from feudalism to capitalism is that, in emphasising the *longue durée* at the expense of the political moment in the transition, he has tended systematically to downplay the importance of the English Revolution itself in the transition, and he has on occasion almost written it out of the transition altogether (Brenner 1989). However, despite some formulations of his position that can be read to this effect, in 1993 he published a 700-page monograph on the revolution itself: *Merchants and Revolution*. In this book Brenner argues that the traditional social interpretation of the transition was untenable: 'by the era of the Civil

War, it is very difficult to specify anything amounting to a class distinction of any sort within the category of large holders of land, since most were of the same class' (Brenner 1993, 641). Thus, the available evidence could not sustain the idea of a rising bourgeoisie confronting a feudal aristocracy. However, he was convinced that the revisionist challenge to the old social interpretation was even less compelling. The revisionists had reduced the Civil War to a conflict over particular individual and group interests within a general ideological consensus. Against this position Brenner pointed out that 'analogous political conflicts over essentially similar constitutional and religious issues broke out on a whole series of occasions in the pre-Civil War period' (Brenner 1993, 648). Thus, Brenner maintains that a social account of the Civil War is indispensable, while insisting that the traditional Marxist account of the revolution is indefensible. In his alternate social interpretation of the Civil War Brenner suggests that, while the landowners as a whole had been transformed into a capitalist class in the previous centuries, the monarchy maintained its position at the head of the state via a medieval legacy. Monarchs, he argued, 'were no mere executives, but were great patrimonial lords' (Brenner 1993, 653). Moreover, 'the king was largely politically isolated from the landed class as a whole until the autumn of 1641' (Brenner 1993, 643). The fundamental conflict at the heart of the English Revolution was thus between this 'patrimonial group', who derived their wealth from politically constituted property rights, and the rest of the landowning class.

However, as Anderson has noted, even these formulations have shied away from providing Brenner's analysis of the Revolution with a firm materialist foundation. Anderson criticises Brenner's utilisation of Weber's concept of 'patrimonial' to describe the Stuart monarchy as a 'self contained household' against which the revolution was fought. Such a concept is necessary to Brenner's schema because he rejects the view that the monarchy, because it rested upon feudal forms of exploitation, fettered the expansion of capitalist relations of production. Brenner discards the traditional characterisation of the Stuart monarchy as feudal because he understands feudal property relations to be 'politically constituted', while the Stuarts rested upon economically constituted, that is capitalist, property relations. Consequentially, Brenner does not explain the revolution as a conflict between feudal and capitalist forces. However, while Anderson agrees with Brenner's general characterisation of the dominant relations of production in early seventeenth century England, he suggests that feudal property relations could be constituted 'ideologically', in addition to being constituted politically. Thus, he argues, citing the authority of Brian Manning, that the monarchy could be understood as feudal given the 'ideological role' that it played up to the revolution (Anderson 1993c, 16-17). So Anderson, while agreeing with Brenner's fundamental argument that the aristocracy was a capitalist class, sought to strengthen Brenner's general case by attaching onto it the added complexity that the monarchy could be understood through the ideologically feudal role that it played.

However, Anderson's citation of Brian Manning as authority for this argument is somewhat disingenuous. Manning did indeed argue that when Charles fled to York in 1642, 'the monarchy was reduced to its bare essence – the sentiment of loyalty to the person of the king'. Unfortunately for Anderson and Brenner, Manning goes on to argue that 'the monarchy was seen to rest, not upon the love of the people, but upon the interests of a class. For positive assistance the king had to turn to the nobility and greater gentry' (Manning 1991, 319-20). Moreover, Manning points out that 'as the war went on parliamentarians increasingly came to see the conflict, not so much as a struggle against the king, as a struggle against the aristocracy' (Manning 1991, 326). Developing this argument in a later study Manning has suggested that while the 'wealth of the peers and gentry rested on the ownership of land', there was 'an important distinction in the type of income: in the upper levels the main part of income came from the rents of tenants, but for many in the lower levels it came from the sale of agricultural produce' (Manning 1992, 51). Indeed Manning has specifically criticised Brenner's account for ignoring the growth of industry up to 1640. Interestingly, Manning does write that Brenner's empirical findings, relating to the role of merchants within the revolution, cohere with his own much more classical thesis that it was the 'middling-sort' who were the driving force behind the revolution (Manning 1994, 85). However, he suggests that the growing importance of this group needs to be related to the development of industry, a development stressed by Dobb and ignored by Brenner. In ignoring these developments Brenner, according to Manning, fails to explain why 'industrial districts – not all of them – provided a main base for the parliamentarian and revolutionary parties' (Manning 1994, 86). This materialist explanation of the conflict between feudal and capitalist elements in the revolution can be deepened utilising insights articulated by Christopher Hill.

Hill has argued that the monarchy, the biggest landowner in the pre-revolutionary era, derived much of its wealth in a feudal manner through feudal tenures, and that it is only if we understand the political importance of this fact that we can develop a materialist understanding of the revolution itself. Thus Hill suggests that the abolition of feudal tenures during the English Revolution underpinned the agricultural revolution of the next century. The abolition of feudal tenures occurred after the first civil war in 1646, was confirmed in 1656, and its acceptance was, according to Hill, 'one of the unspoken conditions of the Restoration' (Hill 1997, 321). So, while it is true that the capitalist nature of much of English agriculture in many respects pre-dated the revolution, it is also true that the capitalist elements within English society had to win a revolution in order to fully realise the potential of the new system which they had nurtured. Moreover, this revolution had to be won against a feudal state that was more than ideologically constituted.

Anderson's underestimation of the nature of the material break in the nature of the English state after the revolution is evident in his claim that 'the victory of decentralised gentry rule, through a landowner parliament and unpaid justices of the peace, blocked this path towards a modern state in England' (Anderson 1992g, 142) This compares with Hill's claim that the English Revolution was a world historic turning-point after which 'state power was ruthlessly used to foster economic growth' (Hill 1990, 20). Hill's position seems the more realistic account of the state that was to become the world's dominant imperialist power in the nineteenth century.

In addition, Anderson's argument that the City operated under a pre-industrial prerogative can only be maintained on the implausible assumption that the City's international orientation was anti-industrial and that industry did not support this orientation. Anderson attempted to justify these claims through a discussion of the debate over tariff reform at the turn of the twentieth century. He noted that industrial capital was divided over this issue, and that the empire exacerbated these divisions. On the one hand, certain elements of industry, which were cushioned from the full force of international competition by their utilisation of the protected markets of the empire, tended to support Free Trade; while on the other, the pro-tariff party had its appeal undermined by the specific nature of any proposed reforms; the English debate over tariff reform differed from those in Germany and America because urbanisation had progressed much further in England, such that the number of winners from the increased cost of food from domestic suppliers in the wake of the imposition of tariffs would be far outweighed by the number of urban losers from the consequenses of this policy. This, Anderson argued, was tariff reform's 'Achilles heel': 'Chamberlain's scheme had appeal only for high-cost colonial farmers. There was no rural electorate at home that could compensate for the urban unpopularity of increased food prices. The cause of industry was thus compromised by the connexions of empire in a way that occurred nowhere else' (Anderson 1992g, 150-151).

Critics of Anderson have challenged the argument that the interests of the City and of industry were opposed. Callinicos has pointed out that 'British industrial capital is not coextensive with manufacturing industry in Britain', since much of it is international in orientation. The international orientation of the City is thus not foreign to industry. Moreover, with respect to the 1980s speculative boom, Anderson 'ignores the involvement of British industrial companies in the surge of financial speculation'. In addition, the disengagement of the financial markets 'from the circuits of productive capital' that Anderson maintains is a peculiarly British phenomenon is, according to Callinicos, 'a general phenomenon' rooted in the 'global crisis of capitalism'. Thus, Britain's malaise was just an 'extreme case' of the general response to the common predicament of the industrial economies in the 1980s (Callinicos 1988, 104-105).

Additionally, Barratt Brown has argued that, while it was the City that eventually broke Chamberlain's attempted tariff reform strategy, the division over tariff reforms was not a division between a parasitic City and productive industry. The division was one between the City that was integrated with some fractions of industry, and wanted to invest internationally and did not want to be fenced in by empire, and other sections of industry that needed protection from foreign trade (Barratt Brown 1988, 31). Thus, the delayed introduction of tariff reform in Britain can best be understood if the British economy is not understood primarily as a distinct national capitalist unit, with the international economy outside it, but rather as a constituent part of the international economy: for, as Hobsbawm argues, 'vast sections of the British economy which depended on international trade had nothing to gain by protection' (Hobsbawm 1969, 243). To denounce the British elite as anti-manufacturing because it did not introduce tariff reform earlier is thus anachronistic; for implementing earlier tariff reforms would have hurt as much industry as it aided. The split within the ruling class was thus not between industry and City but within industry itself: 'the main division was between those industrialists apart from the shipbuilders, who used iron and steel and were happy to obtain cheaper and better quality steel from Germany, or in the USA, and those in the heavy industries whose products were being challenged in this way' (Barrett Brown 1988, 33). The City's international orientation, which swung the day against Chamberlain's reform strategy, thus cohered with some sections of industry while conflicting with others. Barrett Brown argues that because Anderson misunderstood this process it led him to misdiagnose contemporary trends in international capitalism.

However, while Anderson argued that Britain's missing corporate strategy accounted for its economic decline, he could not locate any viable mechanism through which a similar strategy could be developed in Britain in the late 1980s. So, while reformism was possible in theory, in practice it was untenable. 'The radical internationalisation of the forces of production ... that defines the spearhead forms of capital in the final year of the twentieth century promises to render all national corrections ... increasingly tenuous in the future. The British crisis has no solution in sight; and perhaps the time in which one was possible ... has passed'. Furthermore, 'no bourgeois society ... will be immune from the unpredictable tides and tempests of an uneven development whose elements are acquiring a well nigh meteorological velocity around the world across all frontiers' (Anderson 1992g, 192). This was Trotsky's position from the beginning of the century. Anderson's dilemma was that while he accepted Trotsky's pessimistic perspectives for the prospects of reformism, he increasingly could not share his optimistic alternative of world proletarian revolution. This pessimistic diagnosis of the Trotskyist strategy for the West was reinforced in Anderson's analysis of bourgeois democracy.

In *Origins*, and *Modernity and Revolution* Anderson argued that fully formed bourgeois democracies were post-1945 phenomena. He deepened his articulation of this argument in *Figures*. Developing an idea first suggested in *Origins* and developed in *The Notion of a Bourgeois Revolution* he argued that 'between the initial bourgeois revolution that breached the old order and the final completion of bourgeois democracy as the contemporary form of the capitalist state, there typically lay violent intervening convulsions that extended the work of the original upheaval and transformed the political framework of the nation' (Anderson 1992g, 155). These new convulsions, which modernised the western European states, were primarily brought about by the events of the Second World War, before which these states were essentially archaic pre-capitalist structures (Anderson 1992f, 156 & 129). Britain's specificity lay, at least in part, in her victory in the Second World War: she 'alone had now never experienced a modern second revolution', and thus had never developed a modern system of democracy, nor did she develop a modern state: the work of 1640 and 1832 still required completion (Anderson 1992f, 155 & 1992c, 17 & 1992f, 156).

In Europe, by contrast, second revolutions had occurred between 1939-45. The implication was thus that the regimes that had experienced revolutionary outbursts after the First World War were in fact *'ancien regimes'* (Anderson 1992k, 35). A corollary of this argument is that not only could the Russian Revolution not act as a legitimate model for socialist strategy in the modern West, but also the events in Germany of 1918-33 held at best only limited lessons for socialists, as this state was not a modern bourgeois democracy. This pessimistic diagnosis of the possibility of repeating he triumphs of Lenin and Trotsky was reinforced by Anderson's analysis of the modern working class.

Anderson's re-engagement in 1987 with the problem of the nature of the English working class was the area of the most marked continuity with the analysis associated with *Origins*. There is, however, an important difference: while in 1964 hope took the form of Wilson, in 1987 there seemed to be no hope at all. The heart of Anderson's analysis of the British working class remained the 'deep caesura', noted in *Origins*, between Chartism and the rest of British labour history (Anderson 1992d, 23 & 1980, 47). However, while in *Origins* the basis for this break remained ideological, in *Figures* it is given a more materialist slant. The radicalism of Chartism was explained by the structure of the English working class at the time, and its subsequent moderation by its modern structure.[57] Artisans and hand workers dominated an economy up to 1848, where 'the machine driven factory was the most advanced rather than the most typical unit'. It was only in the second half of the nineteenth century that there emerged the modern labour movement forged in factory production (Anderson 1992g, 157). This new movement was characterised by a profound schizophrenia, which had not affected its predecessor: politics and economics were tightly separated.

The specificity of the new English working class thus lay in the contrast between its high degree of 'industrial organisation' compared with its exceptionally weak 'political project'. Politically, 'British labour as an organised force was a captive client of the Liberal party down to the end of the century after which the Labour Party grew as part of the liberal revival' (Anderson 1992g, 157-60). Subsequently, Labour's path to power was no road of its own making. The First World War destroyed the Liberal Party, while the Second World War created the conditions for massive state intervention. Indeed the smooth transfer of power to the Conservatives in 1951 showed just how little the Labour Party had affected the 'structures of Britain's imperial economy' (Anderson 1992g, 164).

As Looker argues, 'read as an account of the Labour Party there is little new or original here – Miliband's *Parliamentary Socialism* mapped this terrain decades ago'. However, Anderson went beyond Miliband, in assuming that Labourism set the 'structural limits to working-class consciousness and activity' (Looker 1988, 17). Thus, whereas previous Marxist analyses of the English working class had shown the impossibility of the Labour Party seriously challenging the status quo, Anderson deepens this thesis, to dismiss the potential of English working-class anti-capitalism. This dismissal is premised upon the claim that 'the English 1848 closed a history' (Anderson 1992g, 157). By this he meant to suggest that the political and organisational legacy of Chartism was almost nil: the new factory proletariat had no use for the old ideology. What, is striking, therefore, about Anderson's analysis of Labourism is the way that it is first, founded upon a mechanical model of the relationship of consciousness to industrial structure, while second, it is equated, anthropomorphically, with the politics of the working class itself. The two are, of course, intimately related; for if Labourism is the natural politics of a certain industrial structure, then to describe the history of the Labour Party is to describe the history of the working class.

This conceptualisation of the nature of the English working class as an essentially passive reflection of England's social structures is built upon his reading of Cohen. In the second of his general criticisms of *The Making of the English*

Working Class Anderson, as we noted in the previous chapter, rejected what he perceived to be Thompson's conflation of the concepts of class and class consciousness, and supported this argument with the claim that Cohen's 'concept of class as an objective relation to the means of production, independent of will or attitude, is unlikely to need further reinstatement' (Anderson 1980, 40). Anderson's argument in *Figures* appears to be that his outline of the objective coordinates of England's social structure is sufficient to explain the nature of the consciousness of England's proletariat:

> The British Labour movement never exhibited one unchanging essence; but nor did it display indefinite variation. Through every transformation and vicissitude, its history developed within a set of structural limits that placed strict bounds on its identity. The modern form of that binding has been Labourism. (Anderson 1992g, 168)

Interestingly, this mechanical reading of the relationship between social structure, class and class consciousness goes beyond even Cohen's, for whom the phrase 'Making of the English Working Class' was acceptable, despite his criticisms of Thompson, so long as it was meant to connote the process whereby the English working class moved from being a class in itself to acting as a class for itself; rather than connoting the process whereby the class itself was made (Cohen 1978, 77). Anderson, in as far as he neither traced the processes of the ebb and flow of socialist class consciousness within the English proletariat, nor discussed the possibility of such a development, appears to have moved beyond even the objectivism of Cohen to accept a crudely mechanical explanation of the relationship of social structure to political consciousness: in effect, inverting Thompson's voluntarism rather than correcting it. As Bob Looker argues, 'Anderson ... has failed to grasp what Thompson's analysis of the English working class clearly demonstrated; the issue isn't a matter of conceptual distinctions but of real movements rising through class practice' (Looker 1988, 27). Whatever the sources of Anderson's position, his fatalistic understanding of Marxism implied that revolutionary politics could never be on the agenda in Britain. This pessimism combined with his understanding of crisis theory to suggest that not only was reformism the only potential strategy for the left, but also that in certain circumstances it could be a viable strategy for the left. In 1987 Anderson could not see any structures that could make reformism viable, and so his political pessimism ran deep. This pessimism possibly explains the political conclusions of *A Culture in Contraflow*.

If, in *Figures*, Anderson had returned to the debate occasioned by the publication of *Origins*, the publication of *A Culture in Contraflow* marked his reassessment of Britain's academic culture two decades after the publication of *Components*. Moreover, as in *Components*, *Culture* was aimed as a riposte to the dominant ideology. However, whereas in the 1960s Anderson had argued that this ideology had found its natural spokesmen in those who held the hegemonic university chairs, in the late 1980s he argued that there had been a sharp reversal in fortune within the academy, so that the left now held sway in the universities. These radicals then found themselves under attack from an increasingly dogmatic Conservative government. So, whereas in 1968 Anderson had assaulted British academic traditions, two decades later his reassessment of this culture was much more generous.

Anderson argued that while academia had been attacked from the left in the 1960s, it was now being assailed from the right. He set himself the task of explaining this paradox. His answer was that the radicalised graduates of the 1960s and 1970s had reached the necessary 'numerical mass' to furnish the basis for a militant academic culture in the 1980s. This in turn explained the antagonism that came from the Conservative government. These radicalised students had further been the beneficiaries of a lively radical culture that had existed as a minority culture since the war and had been represented chronologically from earlier days through the graduates of the Communist Party Historians' Group, through the New Leftists, to the critical journals of the late 1960s and early 1970s and onto the feminists (Anderson 1992g, 195-6).

These two elements combined to furnish academia with a broad left milieu of considerable talent. Anderson argued that this broad milieu did not collapse under the impact of Thatcherism, but 'resisted and grew' (Anderson 1992h, 196). Thus Anderson congratulated the left (himself) for the intellectual development of this current from the 1960s. 'A period which began with Althusser and Gramsci, Adorno or Lacan pioneered by journals like *NLR*, ended with Habermas and Bourdieu starring in a chastened *TLS*, and Derrida or Foucault admired by an *LRB*[58] recanting its suspicion of deconstruction' (Anderson 1992h, 202). The attacks from the right were therefore to be explained as a consequence of the victory of the left within academia. Not that there were no right-wing academics; rather, 'the new right had always been relatively weak in the academy, and lacked the cadres to impose its vision at large' (Anderson 1992h, 198). Moreover, the decline of Conservative support amongst lecturing staff (down to 20 per cent in 1987), was interpreted by Anderson as an heartening sign, even though many of these had moved not to the Labour Party but to the Liberal and Social Democratic Alliance – then to be split equally between the two parties once Labour had 'moved towards normalcy again'. Interestingly, it was the shift towards support for the Alliance that most impressed Anderson, for this involved a 'weakening of automatic allegiance to constitutional tradition'. So while 'authoritarian populism was redrawing the electoral contours of the country to the advantage of capital, in this domain the hegemonic legacy weakened'. This radicalisation was reinforced by the 'growth of the transatlantic presence' whose result was that 'Englishry in its worst, caricatural form declined' (Anderson 1992h, 198-204).

Anderson then moved to paint, on broad canvas, the main themes of this radical culture, before concluding his essay with the argument that while in the 1960s a timeless ego had filled the vacuum created by the lack of a major sociology, in the 1980s sociology 'became overarching' and 'historical time re-entered reflection; material life took on a new referential weight; sexual difference won lodgement'. However, whereas this culture existed on high, below this layer there did not exist 'any significant political movement as a pole of attraction for intellectual opposition'. The vehicle that had been chosen by the reformers to break the political logjam of Thatcherism – Charter 88 – was both too radical to be taken up by the Labour leadership and too moderate to begin to put right the consequences of a decade of Tory rule. Thus, the vacuum created at the radical end of politics by the 'long crisis of Labourism, the short life of the Alliance [and] the retirement of Communism', had not been filled (Anderson 1992h, 299-301).

Ironically this pessimistic conclusion was published, in two parts in 1990, between the Poll Tax riot and Thatcher's removal from Downing Street. The Poll Tax saw Thatcher hoisted by her own petard. She introduced this piece of crude class legislation, whereby all progressive elements to local taxation were abolished, in a fit of overconfidence in the wake of the defeat of the Miners' Strike of 1984-5. Unfortunately for Thatcher the Poll Tax precipitated a huge campaign of non-payment and civil disobedience, culminating in a great demonstration of 250000 and riot in March 1990. This movement was a first sign of the re-emergence of class politics after the defeats of the 1970s and 1980s, against which the Tories responded by ignominiously discarding Thatcher as Party leader, and giving their policies a much more egalitarian spin. Interestingly, Anderson neither registered the part played by the Poll Tax riot in Thatcher's downfall, nor did he address his essay to those that had rioted (Anderson 1992i, 302-3).[59] This dismissal of a real workers' movement reflects Anderson's static model of working-class consciousness.

Whatever the coherence of Anderson's implicit dismissal of the anti-Poll Tax movement, a more immediate paradox springs to mind. While in 1983 Anderson had launched an attack on post-structuralism, in 1990 this target did not warrant a critical mention in his analysis of Britain's academic culture. Why not? The obvious answer would be that its growing hegemony would undermine Anderson's thesis of the radicalism of academia, given his previous assessment of post-structuralism's malign influence. However, Anderson was not simply silent over the issue; rather he, as we have seen, welcomed the reception of Derrida and Foucault onto the pages of the *London Review of Books*.

So there exists a lacuna at the heart of *Culture* around the issue of post-structuralism and its intellectual stable-mate postmodernism. The weakness with Anderson's argument is evident, at least in part, in his own text. He showed how, in the history departments, the revisionist critics of Marxism were becoming increasingly dominant (Anderson 1992h, 293). Moreover, one of the most important leftist intellectuals in the field of sociology, Anthony Giddens, based his theory of action partially on insights from Derrida and thus produced a theory that 'was to understate considerably the typical pressures of social determination' (Anderson 1992h, 209). Similarly, Anderson noted the idealist bent in the aesthetics of Raymond Williams, but did no more than note Terry Eagleton's qualified warm reception of post-structuralism as a 'relay to feminist concerns' (1992a, 239 & 241).

Despite the very real attacks aimed at the academic left from the establishment in the 1980s, against which Anderson was undoubtedly right to protest, the left was by no means as hegemonic as his argument suggested. Moreover, the weaknesses of the left's own formulations disabled it from successfully responding to the backlash. A more rounded Marxist response would have begun, as Anderson had done, by initially and unconditionally defending the left against the right. However, it would then need to perform a radical criticism of the idealism and other weaknesses of the academic left. For it was in these areas that the left had shown itself open to attack from the right in the first place. In this sense something more akin to *Arguments* was needed. For it was around the dichotomy of subject and structure that the left's theoretical reply to post-structuralism was weakest. However, while we have seen in the last chapter that Anderson had attempted to produce a solution to this problem, he had ultimately failed to forge a path out of the structure/subject dichotomy. Moreover, his own structuralism not only disallowed him from solving this problem but also weakened his critique of the idealism of the post-structuralists. So while Anderson could offer solidarity to a beleaguered left within the academy, he could not offer it the tools with which it might have begun to repulse the ideological as well as political offensive.

The lack of a polemical edge in his account of academic radicalism is evident in his more general overview of the left under Thatcher. Anderson argued that the 'liveliest vehicle of response to the new order became the reconverted *Marxism Today*'. Moreover, while he noted that there had been controversies amongst socialists, he maintained that despite these, a 'basic solidarity on the left was rarely breached' (Anderson 1992h, 197). Unfortunately, this formulation obscures the very real passion that was inspired by left-wing debates in the 1980s. To be against Thatcher was the only commonality; on strategic and tactical questions much blood was spilt (Blackledge 2002). This was especially true after the defeat of the Miners' Strike, when *Marxism Today* in particular played the intellectual role of challenging the hard left's opposition to Kinnock's project of modernising the Labour Party (cf Callinicos 1985, Carlin & Birchall 1983, Saville 1990, Miliband 1985). Indeed *NLR* had published Miliband's powerful polemical critique of this phenomenon (Miliband 1985). Anderson's implicit dismissal of these disputes is indicative of his inability to get a purchase on just how far many of these left academics had moved to the right under Thatcher.[60]

The corollary of Anderson's refusal to address the problem of postmodernism in his essay was therefore his positive appraisal of the politics of academia. However, if he had been true to the thesis of *Tracks* he would have been forced to take on a much more polemical stance to academic left politics. This would have been especially true of his relationship to the journal *Marxism Today*, which more than any other left journal had helped proselytise for the postmodernist discourse. To say that this was a fruitful venture flew in the face of his own negative appraisal of post-structuralism as outlined in *Tracks*: four years earlier his tone had been much more strident.

SOCIAL DEMOCRACY AND COMMUNISM IN THE 1980s AND 1990s

As we have noted, there was something of a paradox in Anderson's relation to reformism in the mid-1980s. For he at once accepted the abstract possibility of a reformist solution to capitalist crises, while remaining pessimistic as to the possibility of a concrete solution to these crises in a new global order. In 1986 he returned to the problem of social democracy, nominally the historical agency of reform. In *Social Democracy Today* he outlined the trajectory of European social democracy, which he divided into Northern (UK, Germany, Scandinavia, Austria, Belgium and Holland) and Southern (Greece, Spain, Portugal, Italy and France) zones.

In the former, social democrats first entered government to act as 'shock absorbers' against the social crisis after the First World War. Once in government 'its inter war record was a barren one' as it implemented economic policies of impeccable neo-classical orthodoxy. However, in the wake of the Second World War, the changed international circumstances – specifically, the installation of 'Keynesian economic management at the heart of capitalism ... [and] a powerful wave of popular radicalisation', underpinned by the 'generalisation of Fordism', combined to allow social democracy to both 'ameliorate and strengthen' the Western capitalist states. In particular, the creation of welfare states represented a 'genuine social gain for labour'. Unfortunately, as the Keynesian consensus collapsed in the 1970s, social democracy proved itself incapable of offering a distinctive solution to the alternative proposed by the neo-liberals. Social democratic governments thus implemented orthodox neo-classical economic policies. As a consequence of this, in both Britain and

Germany, social democratic parties were ejected from office 'as large numbers of their working-class supporters went over to local conservative parties', which in turn established popular right-wing regimes (Anderson 1986, 22-23).

Southern social democracy, by contrast, entered office just as their Northern cousins lost it. This reflected the growing maturity of the Southern economies. These now could no longer be ruled by force alone; compromise with the increasingly politically important proletariat was essential. However, the new social democratic regimes did not repeat the welfare reforms of their Northern predecessors; rather, at best, under Mitterrand, early reform programmes were discarded under the impact of global economic crisis, resulting in a 'fiasco'. They did, though, promise one progressive legacy: 'democratization'. For in these countries the 'incompletion of bourgeois democratic tasks' opened up an objective space for reforms. Unfortunately, Southern social democracy's record was 'very modest' in this regard, the insistent pattern being 'one of political greed and lack of principle' (Anderson 1986, 25-28).

Anderson then prophesied that these parties – both Northern and Southern – would evolve in the direction of a convergence with the American Democratic Party. This perspective filled him with dread, as the 'final corruption and disappearance of the heritage of the Second International ... would compound an historic regression' that had begun with the collapse of the tradition of the Third International. Anderson believed that there would be 'no shortage of bellwether intellectuals to theorize this sort of shift'. However, these would be challenged: 'in the rank and file of both communist movements of the South and the social democratic movements of the North of Europe forces of ferment and resistance exist'. This, he argued, was an apposite arena for 'revolutionary socialist' political intervention (Anderson 1986, 28).

Thus, Anderson outlined, by contrast with the thesis developed a year later in *Figures*, a conflict between social democratic parties and their traditional voters. However, this position should not be taken to imply that he believed, even in his revolutionary period, that socialist revolutionaries would automatically gain from this situation. In the essay *Communist Party History*, presented as a conference paper in 1979 and subsequently published in 1981, Anderson argued that there had only been two instances in European history when masses of workers had switched allegiance from social democracy to revolutionary socialism: between 1919 and 1923, and from 1942 to 1945. On both of these occasions two forces had interacted to produce a favourable situation for revolutionaries: first, the existing order was delegitimised, while second, an alternative to the status quo was given a practical focus. Thus, in the first period, the First World War had demonstrated the barbarity of Western civilisation, while the Russian Revolution had offered an alternative to it. In the second period, Nazi occupation forced many across Europe into conflict with their authorities while the victories of the Red Army after Stalingrad offered hope for a better future (Anderson 1981, 152-5). This analysis implied that only when there occurred a combination of a colossal crisis and an external source of hope could proletarian disillusionment with social democracy lead to gains for revolutionary socialism.

This relatively pessimistic perspective seemed to be confirmed by Anderson's understanding of changing voting patterns in the 1980s. He argued that, in Britain and Germany at least, working-class voters had shifted towards voting for the dominant bourgeois party during this decade. Thus, in the context of economic crisis, but without the existence of an external political alternative to capitalism, proletarian disillusionment with social democracy had not led to gains for revolutionary socialism but on the contrary to a strengthening of conservatism. In 1994 he was to repeat this argument, citing the findings of psephologist Ivor Crewe to substantiate his point (Anderson 1994d, 10). This position dovetailed with Anderson's broad acceptance of the authoritarian populist position that had been developed by the milieu around *Marxism Today* in the late 1970s and 1980s (Anderson 1992h, 200).[61]

This pessimistic political perspective was given added weight in his introduction to *Mapping the West European Left*, published in 1994. This essay covered much of the same ground as *Social Democracy Today*, albeit in a less strident tone. However, whereas the former essay had ended with Anderson positing a conflict between the rank and file and the leadership of the labour movements in the West which would open the door to revolutionary politics, in the latter he suggested a much more pessimistic scenario. In particular, he argued that two material developments had undercut the socialist project in the West: first, as he had previously argued in *Figures*, 'the internationalisation of capital flows ... has made it increasingly difficult to' plan any national economy; second, the traditional constituency of the socialist tradition – the white, male, manual working class – has been fragmented along lines of race, occupation, age, gender and skills. Thus, the socialist project had been undermined both 'objectively and subjectively' (Anderson 1994d, 11-14).

Moreover, if globalisation and class fragmentation had helped to undermine the socialist project, then events in the Soviet Union and Eastern Europe appeared to finally undermine the revolutionary socialist tradition: while 'the collapse of Communism far from strengthening ... [social democracy] has for the moment further weakened it. For all mutual disclaimers the two were joined as heirs of nineteenth century socialism. The victory of capitalism over the revolutionary attempt to replace it was never likely to leave untouched the reformist endeavour, also compromised by the idea of some social transformation' (Anderson 1992i, 324).

Anderson had first expressed his dismay at the collapse of Communism in the concluding sentences of *Culture*: 'the year 1989 closed an epoch. Since then, the collapse of the Communist order in Eastern Europe and the approach of federation in Western Europe has struck away mental fixtures of left and right' (Anderson 1992h, 301). This train of thought was developed in his 1992 response to Fukuyama's seminal essay, *The End of History*. Anderson's reply, entitled *The Ends of History*[62] at first appeared to be much more open-ended than Fukuyama's celebration of liberal capitalism. Thus, socialism, understood as an alternative to capitalism, might end in 'oblivion, transvaluation, mutation or redemption' (Anderson 1992x, 375). However, while he hoped for redemption the thrust of his essay suggested that oblivion was his own expected outcome.

Surveying the remains of the socialist project Anderson argued that it had been built upon four pillars: first, the 'historical projection' of the increasing socialisation of the forces of production; second, the 'collective labourer' as agent of change; third, the political objective of 'the deliberate planning of the social product by its citizens, as freely associated producers sharing their basic means of livelihood in common'; finally, socialism's central ethical value was the ideal of equality. Commenting on the validity of these claims in the 1990s Anderson argued that in all of the four areas socialist assumptions had been found wanting. However, all was not lost, for while the physical concentration of the forces of production might be declining the 'technical interconnexion ... has enormously increased'. Thus, the objective basis for socialism remained. Moreover, the abject failure of capitalism to deal with either the growing environmental crisis or growing social polarisation provided the basis for an ethical indictment of capitalism as a system. Additionally, despite the proven inefficiencies of centralised command planning, socialists had risen to the challenge of theorising the democratisation and socialisation of the market (Anderson 1992x, 358-362).

However, Anderson argued that Marx's predictions regarding socialist-agency were much more questionable: the industrial proletariat had 'declined in absolute numbers in the advanced economies, and in relative size as a proportion of the world's population, while, at the same time, the number of all those who depend on wages for their livelihood has vastly increased'. Furthermore, with the entry of women into the paid labour force, 'the human potential of opposition to the dictates of capital has become more truly universal'. Unfortunately, the globalisation of capitalism had not drawn the resistances together, but scattered and outflanked them: 'the case against capitalism is strongest on the very plane where the reach of socialism is weakest – at the level of the world system as a whole' (Anderson 1992x, 366). Where did this leave Fukuyama's thesis?

In *The Ends of History* Anderson rejected what he considered to be crude replies to Fukuyama. Fukuyama's own thesis was relatively straightforward: Hegel was substantially correct; Western bourgeois society did mark the end of history. Hegel's mistake was to telescope this process; his analysis was two centuries premature. Fukuyama's argument was based upon his analysis of the collapse of the alternatives to liberal capitalism. Thus, he argued, but for the details, fascism had been ousted as a serious challenge at the heart of the world system in 1945; second, Communism had followed a similar path in the late 1980s, while aristocratic rule had ended in 1918. Fukuyama did not argue that non-liberal states would never emerge in the future. Rather, he suggested that at the system's core such an outcome would be impossible. Wars would continue for the foreseeable future, as would systemic conflicts between liberal capitalism and decaying communist, fascist and fundamentalist states. However, history, quite literally, was on the side of liberal democracy.

Anderson dismissed simplistic arguments that juxtaposed Fukuyama's thesis to, for instance, the contemporary events in the Gulf or Bosnia; maintaining that 'an effective critique [of Fukuyama] must be able to show that there are powerful systemic alternatives he has discounted' (Anderson 1992x, 336). With the collapse of Communism, and welfare reformism undermined by globalisation, such an alternative did not exist. 'The central political fact today is that there are no programmes claiming to overcome capitalism left ... history does appear to have come to its term' (Anderson 1992x, 343). Anderson, however, quickly turned from this paraphrase of Fukuyama to the problems of the latter's model. These problems did not lie in an unseen alternative to capitalism, but rather in the limits of liberal capitalism itself. Just because one or two Newly Industrialising Countries had broken into the international premier league it by no means followed that others could follow suit. In this sense Fukuyama had committed the 'fallacy of composition'. Moreover, there existed real environmental limits to the growth of consumption in the rest of the world to Western levels: 'If all the peoples of the Earth possessed the same number of refrigerators and automobiles as those in North America and Western Europe, the planet would become uninhabitable' (Anderson 1992x, 352-353).

These were problems with Fukuyama's utopia, not alternatives to it. As to the socialist alternative, Anderson argued, as we have seen, that four options were possible: first, like the seventeenth-century Jesuits in Paraguay, oblivion could be its final resting place; second, like the Levellers, a transvaluation of the heritage could occur; third, like the Jacobins, the heritage could be mutated; finally, like liberalism, it could be redeemed after its nadir. This last alternative seemed, on one level, the least likely to Anderson. Thus, he argued that while liberalism had proved itself capable of rising from the ashes through its ability to incorporate elements of a foreign doctrine – social democracy, Communism had 'tried to modernise itself in a similar fashion, by introducing elements of the rule of law and of competitive markets but the result was a complete failure' (Anderson 1992x, 375). As to the other alternatives, Anderson concluded that 'no one can say' which would be in the end fulfilled (Anderson 1992x, 372). However, simply because Communism's attempt to redeem itself through the incorporation of liberal practices had failed, this did not prove that such a failure would necessarily be the fate of social democracy if it were to choose a similar course of action.

Thus, Anderson had, by the early 1990s, developed a coherent, yet highly pessimistic, evaluation of contemporary international politics. It was to his great credit that, in these circumstances, he sought, once again, to develop a realistic and viable politics for the left. This new politics was premised upon an element of his earlier revolutionary thought. Anderson's analysis of various types of capitalism in *Figures* implied his general agreement with the disproportionality theory of crisis that was held by Cohen and Aglietta. Given such a theory of crisis, then a regulative structure could conceivably underpin the creation of a full employment, welfare state regimes. So Anderson's rejection of Marx's theory of crisis opened the door to his acceptance of the potential viability of a reformist political strategy. What he needed was an agency that could implement this strategy.

THE NEW POLITICS: CITIZENSHIP IN A NEW EUROPE

According to Elliott, Anderson's political perspective in the 1990s can be best characterised by its realism. Confronted by a new world, he refused to retreat into dogma but rather has attempted to develop a viable progressive politics for the new era (Elliott 1998, 243). This argument contains much that is valid. Indeed, Anderson's entire career can be read as a series of attempts to develop a viable socialist politics in various circumstances. However, his political reorientation in the 1990s was premised upon certain contestable assumptions and led to some highly unrealistic conclusions. Incontestable, however, was the fact that by the end of the 1980s both social democracy and Stalinism were in deep crisis. For more than a decade social democratic parties across Europe had proved themselves incapable of solving the crisis of capitalism; while, more dramatically, Communism in Eastern Europe had, between 1989 and 1991, collapsed. Anderson's response to these two failures was the basis for his new politics.

Ironically this realistic political reorientation began with a positive, if critical, assessment of the utopia of Roberto Unger. For Unger the collapse of Communism and the failure of social democracy need not imply the demise of any conceivable alternatives to the status quo (Anderson 1992q, 132). He then set himself the goal of formulating the basis for a more radical alternative. Anderson disagreed with much of the detail of Unger's proposals, but could only welcome the general direction of his work; and while its lack of a model of agency gave it a 'dream like quality', Anderson concluded that the dream 'is a salutary and emboldening one' (Anderson 1992q, 148). The direction of Unger's utopia set the parameters for Anderson's political evolution in the 1990s. So while he critically accepted Fukuyama's obituary of socialism, this did not, in the first instance, lead him to a political paralysis caused by despair. Rather, he attempted to formulate a perspective through which socialists could best reorient themselves in this new world. Communism may have been dead, but social democracy remained alive, if in ill health. Anderson thus aimed at a realistic reformulation of the reformist project. In essence, he argued, social democracy could be reinvigorated through its incorporation of the best elements of liberalism and then given a new lease of life in a regulated Europe.

A possible arena for convergence with liberalism had been implied at the heart of Anderson's thought from the early 1960s. Thus his argument in *Origins* that 'the unfinished work of 1640 and 1832' must be completed; or, as he rephrased the same essential argument in the 1980s, that a second bourgeois revolution was necessary to 'modernise the state ... [and thus] reinvigorate the economy' (Anderson 1992d, 47 & 1992g, 156). In both cases Anderson's thesis implied that liberalism had much to offer the British left. Despite this, his evolution from the 1960s was towards revolutionary socialism, if it did not include an ultimate embrace of orthodox Trotskyism. However, Anderson's distance from Trotskyism did not simply relate to Trotsky's perceived overestimation of the universal significance of the Bolshevik revolution. As important was his belief that none of Trotsky's attempts at analysing Western social formations had been as successful as his analysis of 'atypical' Germany. In particular he reproached Trotsky for underestimating the 'traditional organization of the petty-bourgeoisie' in his writings on France and for incorrectly characterising the Second World War as simply an inter-imperialist conflict (Anderson 1976, 119 & 1980, 154). These criticisms implied that the petite bourgeoisie could act as a progressive social force domestically, and that even Anglo-American capital had acted as a progressive force in the war against fascist Germany. Thus, Anderson's criticisms of Trotsky's critique of the French Popular Front implied that a common front could be forged between liberals and socialists against political reaction.

Anderson made this position explicit in his 1988 review of Noberto Bobbio's work: 'the synthesis of liberalism and socialism has so far failed to take. That is not to argue that it must ... it is too soon to say' (Anderson 1992p, 129). Indeed, far from being two mutually exclusive traditions, socialism and liberalism contained many points of intersection. Such key figures in the liberal tradition as Mill, Russell, Hobson and Dewey had all in their own ways been close to one form or other of socialism (Anderson 1992p, 87-9). This potential convergence between Anderson's socialism and the liberal tradition came to fruition in 1991 after the collapse of Communism. Anderson argued both for a new model of citizenship and for constitutional reform.

To turn around the British economy's cycle of decline Anderson looked to proposals made by the proponents of the idea of social citizenship. 'Norms of social responsibility' should be fostered within firms, while employers should be given greater 'representation in private enterprise'; second, there should be a commitment to full employment; next 'a basic monetary income' should be guaranteed; fourth, the resources committed to public education should be expanded to match those in the private sector; fifth, sexual oppression should be tackled through universal access to maternity entitlements. These seemingly disparate reforms would be united under the ideology of 'social citizenship': a term taken by Anderson from Marshall, as developed by Mann (Anderson 1992i, 352).

Mann argued that an ideology of citizenship need not fall into the trap of contrasting conservative dynamism with socialist fairness, but would rather show that equity would give a fillip to economic dynamism. 'Labour is not for caring rather than wealth. In fact democratic socialism has a superior theory of how wealth is created in modern society: through a fair society based on the cooperation of free citizens. Social citizenship is not a charitable urge – it is the way towards a more productive, more generally creative society' (Mann 1985, 19). Similarly, in 1949 Marshall had argued that social citizenship would foster increased dynamism as it would facilitate the creation of the optimum conditions within which one could 'put one's heart into one's job and work hard' (Marshall 1996, 46). This ideology, Anderson argued, 'now holds out the best promise of practical advances in the equity and emancipation in Western Europe at large' (Anderson 1992i, 353). However, the ideology did not float freely but was predicated by Mann upon the transformation in mid-century British capitalism through Keynesian macro-economic management. 'In macro-economics social citizenship involves a commitment to Keynesian principles' (Mann 1985, 20). As we have seen, Anderson has consistently argued that Britain lacked a regulative regime capable of underpinning such a political superstructure. Moreover, he had come to believe that the globalisation of economic activity undermined any hope of remedying this situation. How then could social citizenship be underpinned? Anderson opened his answer with the claim that Britain had never developed the necessary stepping-stone to the creation of social citizenship: political citizenship (Anderson 1992i, 353). Moreover, given that national Keynesian strategies were moribund, social citizenship must be underpinned by a European regulative regime.

Figures concluded on the pessimistic note that globalisation had smashed the opportunities to reinvigorate the British economy. Four years later, Anderson articulated a solution to this problem. Britain lacked a modern state comparable to the French, German, Swedish and Austrian models. It was still 'archaic', and this archaism was most evident in Britain's lack of a written constitution' (Anderson 1992i, 338). However, as a response to the 'authoritarian' nature of the Thatcher regime a constitutional opposition had developed in Charter 88. This was founded in 1988 on the back of 'the impotence and division of the opposition to the Thatcher regime in the 1980s' (Anderson 1992i, 347). The strength of Charter 88 lay in the way that it set itself the task of overthrowing the aristocratic elements of the British constitution and thus of creating the kind of modern bourgeois democracy capable of organising the *dirigiste* regime necessary to turn around Britain's cycle of decline. The problem for Britain was that this had happened across the rest of Western Europe in 1945 – before globalisation. How then could the regime succeed in a qualitatively different world? Anderson's hope was that the two birds of political and social citizenship could be killed with the one stone of European integration. However, his hope that the move towards a more unified Europe would underpin the evolution of political citizenship appears to be much more realistic than his hope that this process could also lead to the development of social citizenship. Regarding political citizenship, he argued, 'sooner or later the Westminster system will in any case be undone by federation in Europe which no major British party yet accepts and none will be able to resist' (Anderson 1992i, 351). This process would overcome Charter 88's problem of agency. To succeed, Charter 88 obviously needed the political support of one of the main parties. The Tories could be expected to oppose its demands while Liberal support was largely irrelevant as they were politically marginalized by the institutions that they aimed to change: this left the Labour Party. Unfortunately, while individuals within the party supported the Charter, the party as a whole, in 1992, did not.

Anderson suggested a number of reasons for Labour's refusal support electoral reform. First, the first-past-the-post system offers the Labour Party the ultimate prize of majority government without an, 'extremely unlikely', majority national vote; second, 'what ultimately makes it difficult for Labour to conceive or advocate any democratisation of the state … is that it is itself, brazenly and obdurately, far less democratic even than the unreformed *ancien regime* at Westminster … the block vote was always the working-class version of the rotten boroughs' (Anderson 1992i, 349). Other (better) social democrats on the continent had won proportional representation after 1945; in Britain alone Labour failed ever to raise the demand (Anderson 1992i, 343). So, where European social democracy had helped create modern states that were able to develop *dirigiste* strategies that underpinned a social-democratic consensus, Britain was barred from creating a social citizenship by the lack of political citizenship.

Lord Rees Mogg wrote of Charter 88; 'royalists can sleep easily in their beds because the temper of the debate was too reasoned for there to be a threat' (quoted in Barnett 1994, 51). Anderson, however, had an answer to this dilemma. In 1990 he had recognised that Charter 88 was unable to solve the problem that it had set itself, for it was both too radical for Labour to take up and too moderate to take on radical Conservatism (Anderson 1992h, 300). In 1991 he saw a potential solution to this problem in the process of European integration (Anderson 1992i, 351).

I have already shown that as early as 1961 Anderson had supported European integration as the lesser evil compared to British isolationism. Similarly in the early 1970s *NLR* distinguished itself on the hard left by its firm pro-European stance (Nairn 1972). In the 1990s Anderson returned to this issue. Interestingly, in the interim much of the British left had shifted from an anti to a pro-European position. This itself was a response to a general feeling of despair within the labour movement, especially after the defeat of the Miners' Strike, when the general consensus appeared to be that not only had militancy failed, but also that national constitutional measures were largely impotent in the face of Conservative dominance. Progressive European legislation, it was hoped, would force on the Tories from without, what the Labour Movement was incapable of forcing from within: reform. This political shift paralleled that towards constitutional reform, for many on the left argued that the political hegemony of the Conservative Party could be prevented by, amongst other structures, a system of proportional representation, which would undermine any future tyranny of the minority. Anderson helped articulate both of these perspectives.

Anderson's general perspective towards the question of European integration was based upon two premises. First, globalisation had led to 'the attenuation of democratic forms in the major capitalist societies'. In these conditions 'the construction of effective supranational sovereignties is the obvious remedy to the loss by national states of much of their substance and authority'. The EU, he maintained, was significant in that it marked the first steps in this process, and as such 'it is clear that a major task of the Left will be to press towards the completion of a genuine federal state in the community with a sovereign authority over its constituent parts' (Anderson 1992x, 364-5). Second, and against his left-wing critics,[63] he argued that the *sui generis* character of Britain's crisis needed an explanation that they were unable to offer. His explanation was that Britain had an archaic state structure, and that European integration was the only viable medium through which that state could be politically modernised (Anderson 1992i, 329-337).

In 1996 Anderson returned to the debate on Europe. In two essays he provided an overview of the history of European integration and a résumé of potential prospects for its future. The first essay was written as a critical commentary on Alan Milward's account of European integration. Milward had argued that the process of European integration had been set in train by democratic pressures from below that existed across Europe after the war, and whose goal was the 'rescue of the nation state' through the pooling of certain elements of sovereignty. Anderson argued that this account of the process of integration was untenable because the domestic policy goals, upon which Milward premised his account, could have been realised through much more moderate means than the level of integration that had already been achieved in Europe (Anderson 1997a, 58). Moreover, there was no democratic involvement by any of the European electorates before the British referendum in 1975 (Anderson 1997a, 62)

Other forces were necessary to explain the process of integration. Anderson argued that four elements combined initially to push forward the process of integration. The first was the role of the USA in promoting a strong unified Europe as a bulwark against the Soviet threat. Second, the French sought to rein in Germany before it was able to play a fully independent role in Europe again. Third, the Germans wished to return to the rank of a great power and saw that cooperation with the French could be a suitable medium for this. Finally, and tying together these first three themes, was the 'federalist vision of a supranational Europe developed by, above all, Monnet' (Anderson 1997a, 66 & 59).

Monnet was able to realise his vision because of the influence of these three factors. However, his vision could not be reduced to these other elements (Anderson 1997a, 60). According to Anderson, Monnet's 'genius' was to initiate a system with an incremental 'inertia' of its own (Anderson 1997a, 68). Once created the Common Market developed towards its self-transformation into the EU (Anderson 1997a, 69). Thus Monnet had combined the 'ambitions of Napoleon [with the] methods of Taaffe' (Anderson 1997a, 69). Underlying this process of integration in the early years was also a shared belief in Keynesian economic management. A slightly different pattern emerged after 1985 when both the Single European Act was signed and Jacques Delors became president of the Commission. The act was predicated upon the return to neo-classical economic policies, while Delors insisted upon pushing through its logic by using the full powers invested in him by the act (Anderson 1997a, 66 & Urwin 1995, 238). The reactionary nature of these policies was all too apparent to Anderson, and yet he supported further integration. Why?

Milward argued that the progressive aspects of the EU were a product of the involvement of the masses in the decision-making process: the EU was progressive because it was democratic. Anderson, by contrast, pointed out that the process of European integration had been negotiated by elites, with next to no popular participation (Anderson 1997a, 62). However if this were true, then where did any possible future progressive elements of the EU originate? Anderson's answer was that it was in the social-democratic strategy of Delors that hope for progressive reform was to be located (Anderson 1997b, 131).

However, the Single European Act was predicated upon the return to neo-classical economic policies, and the Maastricht Treaty of 1991 was a compromise between German and French capitalists over price stability, whose logic was the erosion of the European welfare states. Where were Delors' ideals here? Anderson initially seemed to suggest that Maastricht offered nothing but attacks on the conditions of the mass of Europeans. It implied the 'revolutionary prospect' of the end of the last vestiges of the Keynesian limitations on the free market that had protected workers for half a century; Europe would mean less, not more, state. However, so revolutionary were these consequences that they posed 'the question of whether in practice it might not unleash the contrary logic ... Would there not soon be overwhelming pressure to reinstitute them at supranational level, to avoid an otherwise seemingly inevitable polarization of regions and classes within the Union?'(Anderson 1997b, 130-131)

Anderson conjectured that this indeed might have been Delors' 'gamble' at Maastricht (Anderson 1997b, 131). This somewhat naïve confidence in Delors' motives was matched by an equally naïve belief in the continued functionalist inertia towards European integration. He argued that while the widening of the Union may appear to lead inextricably towards institutional gridlock, this would create the 'functional necessity [of] a much more centralized supranational authority than exists today' (Anderson 1997b, 143). Therefore, while social-democratic values were implied by their absence in the Maastricht Treaty, Britain – the greatest champion of the widening of the Union in the hope that this process would undermine the tendencies towards the deepening of its structures – would be hoist with its own petard, as widening functionally led to deepening.

On what was this optimism based? In part at least Anderson saw hope where Hayek feared to tread. Thus, in his 1992 essay *High Jinks at the Plaza*, he argued that Hayek's pro-European position of 1939 – based on his view that a distant European state would be less open to democratic pressure to buck the market than the existent states – was 'less a logical deduction than an empirical wager' (Anderson 1992c, 19). In 1996 Anderson developed this argument by suggesting that Hayek had retreated from his earlier position by the mid-1970s, for fear that the opposite scenario might work itself out (Anderson 1997b, 131). But this would only happen if the French allowed themselves to pay the massive costs implied by the Maastricht convergence criteria. Contemporary events in France implied that this was far from a certain prospect. Anderson suggested that the wave of strikes in France, caused by the Chirac government's welfare cuts as it attempted to reach the Maastricht convergence criteria, could be the basis for the collapse of the agreement (Anderson 1997b, 136). Anderson thus concluded that a 'radical indeterminacy' existed in the three main areas of Europe's future – Maastricht, German dominance through the application of the convergence criteria, and the widening of the Union (Anderson 1997b, 144). In each case conclusions either conducive to business or ordinary Europeans lay in embryonic form within the existing structure. The implication was that the role of the left was to intervene in this contested arena to best help fulfil Delors' hidden agenda.

Anderson returned to this issue in 1999 when he located Lafontaine as a possible medium of a regulative regime in Europe (Anderson 1999a, 16). Indeed, he suggested that with the victory of the SPD in the German general election, the Left would control Britain, Germany, France and Italy. 'Let us hope', he argued, 'that the European Left as a whole proves capable of acting as the party of movement rather than the party of order once again' (Anderson 1998f, 93). This desperate plea was dashed later that year when Lafontaine resigned after much criticism from within business circles.[64] This occurred shortly after the publication of Anderson's essay *The German Question*, and while certainly confirming his argument that 'Germany will not be a dull place', it appeared to fundamentally undermine his hopes that social democracy might play a progressive role in Europe.

However, even assuming Anderson's reading of Delors' strategy, there are deeper structural problems with his whole analysis. As we have seen, he has based most of his economic comments since the early 1980s on the regulation school's approach to understanding the post war economy.[65] Like Cohen, the regulation theorists Aglietta and Lipietz held to a disproportionality theory of crisis. Moreover, both agreed that capitalism could overcome its crisis-prone tendencies by instituting some form of social-democratic class compromise at the national level (Brenner and Glick 1991, 116 & Cohen 1978, 316).[66] However, there were problems with the regulation approach. Most importantly it was weakest when it came to relating the national and international aspects of the economic crisis. As Brenner and Glick argued, the regulation model is unable to explain the 'simultaneous and general character of the crisis on an international scale' (Brenner and Glick 1991,102).

Brenner's own answer to the question posed by the general crisis of the world economy from the 1970s was published as a special issue of *NLR* in 1998. In this essay he argues that the specificity of capitalism lies in the way that it systematically encourages the growth of the forces of production. However, 'given capitalism's unplanned, competitive nature, realization problems cannot be assumed away'. Brenner argues that if capitalists had a perfect knowledge of their competitors' actions, and could adjust to the developing situation, then 'cost cutting technical change poses no problem'. Unfortunately, in the real world of capitalism, 'individual capitalist producers can neither control nor predict the market for their goods'. Capitalism is thus characterised not by planning, but by risk taking and a process of what Schumpeter called 'creative destruction'. Unfortunately, Brenner suggests, 'Schumpeter may ... have underestimated the potentially destructive side of creative destruction' (Brenner 1998, 24-26). In the *Themes* to that issue of *NLR* Anderson argued that Marx had found a worthy successor in Brenner, whose thesis had finally unveiled the mystery of the world economic crisis. Anderson thus appeared to have moved from a loose allegiance to Aglietta's analysis of the post-war economy to cite Brenner as his economic authority. Overviewing Brenner's thesis Anderson wrote: 'it was when German and Japanese products started to penetrate the American market on a major scale, with a massive growth in international trade during the 1960s, that the conditions for the downturn were prepared'. This occurred because 'successful competition in manufacturing typically requires the sinking of large amounts of investment into complexes of fixed capital. These, however, will tend to become outdated ... The competitive pressure of the latter arrivals then inevitably depresses the rate of return on the older enterprises ... The result is a pattern of overcompetition forcing down the rate of profit throughout the branch concerned ... Once such competition becomes generalised ... downturn becomes inevitable' (*NLR* 229 1998, iv-v).

This framework allows Brenner both to begin his analysis from the standpoint of relatively distinct national blocs of capital and yet explain the synchronous shift of the world economy into crisis after 1973. However, it contradicts Anderson's earlier analysis of the globalisation of the world economy, for, unlike Brenner, Anderson's earlier comments on the process of globalisation included the argument that this process had much deeper roots than simply the increase in world trade. Indeed, in *Figures*, Anderson had argued that globalisation had included the 'internationalisation of the forces of production' (Anderson 1992g, 192). Similarly in *The Light of Europe* he noted 'the internationalisation of capital flows', and argued: 'the national spaces presupposed by Keynesian demand management has been steadily reduced' (Anderson 1992i, 312 & 319). Brenner's model of a world of interacting, yet essentially distinct, national blocs of capital, sits uneasily with this analysis. However, Brenner's model of crises of overcompetition does imply that crises can be suppressed, if competition is suppressed, and thus does provide a basis for Anderson's hopes for a regulated Europe. Indeed, Brenner's vague conclusions as to the prospects for global capitalism offers a potential vision of a crisis free

Europe.[67] However, if Anderson's own thoughts on globalisation are even partially correct, then the hope that one section of the world economy can isolate itself from the rest and enshrine a progressive regime seems very unrealistic. Moreover, Brenner has recently cast doubts on the possibilities of a continued expansion of the US economy, suggesting that the USA today finds itself in an ominous situation, similar to that of Japan ten years ago just before its bubble burst, and from which a serious risk of a descent into recession is likely, a move that will, in all likelihood, set off an international recession (Brenner 2002, 276 & 278). This pessimistic diagnosis of world economic prospects would appear to undermine Anderson's hope for a Europe-wide statist reform strategy, and indeed he has recently argued that 'the Union is not a state, and the prospects of anything like one emerging are dwindling' (Anderson 2002e, 26). Somewhat counterintuitively, Anderson, as we shall see in the next chapter, appears to have responded to this, his increasingly desperate reading of the parameters of contemporary politics, with a move towards a more resolutely oppositional political stand.

CHAPTER SEVEN

POSTMODERN RENEWALS

In the mid-1980s Anderson exchanged the editors chair at *NLR* for a professorial chair in history at UCLA. This move came in the wake of the general downturn in the class struggle across the West that we noted in chapters five and six. In America this downturn took a peculiar form: while across Europe ex-revolutionaries were to be found rushing to join the social democratic parties, the American left found itself pulled into the orbit of the Democratic Party. As Mike Davis argues, the 'decline of the social movements of the 1960s', combined with an 'organic crisis of the trade-union and community-service bureaucracies', fostered a shift by the new left into the Democratic Party: the graveyard of radical American politics (Davis 1986, 297). However, the pull of the Democratic Party – a thoroughly bourgeois party, quite distinct from European social democracy – was felt less by American academic Marxists than was the comparative attraction of the European social democratic parties on their European counterparts; and when this difference was combined with the relative weakness of the American revolutionary left, 'US scholars' found themselves 'under even greater pressure than their European counterparts to become purely academic socialists' (Callinicos 1984, 124).

In 1987 Russell Jacoby famously bemoaned this 'academisation' of the American left; a process which, he argued, had helped put an end to the American 'public intellectual' (Jacoby 1987, 4). Academisation, Jacoby argued, had a double effect on the American left: first, it fostered a theoretical style that was impenetrable beyond specialist academic audiences; second, most of the theory thus produced had little relationship to 'critical political and social events' (Jacoby 1987, 158). While there is undoubted power to Jacoby's analysis of the death of the public intellectual in general, and Marxist public intellectuals more specifically, his argument is of limited analytical appeal. Callinicos argues that Jacoby's structural explanation for the demise of public intellectuals in the US overlooks the crucial role played by tradition in explaining the divergent trajectories of the post-1930s and post-1960s American lefts: 'The major political experience shared by many New York Intellectuals was their involvement in the Trotskyist movement, which sought systematically to relate rigorous theoretical enquiry to practical involvement in the public world. Habits acquired in this context stayed with the New York Intellectuals even after they had moved on to very different political commitments. By contrast, the generation of 1960s left intellectuals tended to encounter versions of Marxism – Western Marxism or often highly Stalinist variants of Maoism – which made it much more difficult to combine critical theory and political practice' (Callinicos 1990, 4). Thus, according to Callinicos, the tradition from which the American left of the 1980s had evolved helped foster its relative divorce from political practice. It might be assumed, according to this model, that Anderson's heterodox-Trotskyism would have immunised him from a similar fate. Indeed, as we shall see, Anderson returned to a more overtly political presence in the late 1990s and early twenty-first century. However, Anderson's Trotskyism had been of an Olympian variety from the first, owing as much to the Western Marxist tradition as it did to the organiser of the October Revolution. Indeed, the academic character of Anderson's thought helps account for what Elliott calls his 'bizarre bibliocentrism' in judging the work of his North American peers as 'a steadier and more tough minded historical materialism' than that affected by the Latin European 'crisis of Marxism' (Elliott 1998, 177; Anderson 1983, 77).

In fact, as numerous authors have argued, the work produced by the North American Marxist left cannot adequately be understood outside of the context of its own peculiar crisis of Marxism; as 1960s radicalism died away in the 1970s. Many would agree with Wohlforth that in the 1970s and 1980s 'the American left became an increasingly isolated and aging group of radicals recruited during the 1960s' (Wohlforth 1994, 223). However, while in this period much of the left 'vanished or was left to atrophy, other parts ... persisted and even gained strength over time' (Boggs 1995, 202). Unfortunately, as the mass labour militancy, predicted by some in the 1960s for the 1970s, failed to materialise, the trajectory taken by the bulk of the North American left was away from Marxism and towards 'life-style and identity politics' (Eagleton 2000, 126; Aronowitz 1996, 94).

This general trajectory was not, however, a simple product of the left's pragmatic reaction to events of the 1970s, but rather reflected the theoretical tradition from which the American new left had emerged. Thus, Ahmad points out that American Marxist theory of the 1970s and 1980s was barely influenced by the materialist tradition associated with writers around the journal *Monthly Review*, but was indelibly marked by the culturalist tradition of Western Marxism, a heritage which reinforced the attraction of identity politics for the American left (Ahmad 1992, 4-5). John Bellamy Foster has argued that in taking this trajectory 'many US radicals [were] doubtless simply trying to be practical and realistic'. However, the political perspectives of these radicals moved from Marxism towards something similar to the politics that C. Wright Mills had once characterised as 'liberal practicality' (Bellamy Foster 1990, 266). In fact, Sharon Smith argues, the political separatism entailed by identity politics came almost naturally to the American New Left in the wake of the retreat of 1960s radicalism. She argues that as the bulk of the American new left had broadly accepted the Frankfurt School argument that the working class had been 'bought off' by consumer capitalism, they consequentially looked elsewhere than to the class struggle of workers for the locus of social change. In particular Maoist and Third Worldist notions of the struggles of oppressed nations translated easily into support for the language of the autonomous struggles of oppressed groups within the USA: 'Separatism was on the cards logically, for the New Left was focused on the needs of all oppressed groups to organise themselves' (Evans quoted in Smith 1994, 7). Smith argues that 'beneath the bold veneer' of many of the programmatic statements of the separatist movements, was often to be found 'standard liberalism' (Smith 1994, 5).

Parallel pressures affected even those who maintained a commitment to an explicitly Marxist framework. Thus Fredric Jameson combined a sophisticated Hegelian Marxist theory with, argues Eagleton, much weaker political judgements. Eagleton explains this paradox through the combination of the pressures felt by Jameson of the relative quiescence of organised American labour in the decades after 1968, and the tradition from which his Marxism had evolved – Lukács as interpreted through an Adornian lens (Eagleton 1986, 63 & 76; Jameson 1981, 297). In fact, once we recognise the importance of this tradition to Jameson's stance within the academy we can begin to comprehend weaknesses with Jacoby's critique of academic Marxism. For Jacoby, Jameson is the most significant exemplar of the academisation of the American left: Jameson's 'world is that of the university: its jargon, its problems, its crises ... his writings are designed for seminars' (Jacoby 1987, 167). However, other academic Marxists have produced much more explicitly political work. In this sense a comparison of Jameson with his English counterpart, Terry Eagleton, is suggestive. From a similar position within the academy Eagleton has criticised Jameson's *oeuvre* for its lack of a polemical edge: 'he is in no sense a polemical or satirical writer – essential modes, to my mind, for a political revolutionary'

(Eagleton 1986, 71). This criticism does not merely concern an issue of style. Eagleton argues that Jameson's Hegelianism leads to a tendency in his work for him to 'subordinate political conflict to theoretical *Aufhebung*' (Eagleton 1986, 76). Thus, the Western Marxist tradition, out of which Jameson emerged helped push his thought towards an accommodating relationship to the academy: indeed, in downplaying the sense in which Marxism seeks to 'grasp history as structured material struggle' Jameson's Marxism tends towards the 'merest academicism' (Eagleton 1986, 73-4). Analogous criticisms of Jameson's Hegelianism have been made, as we shall see below, by Callinicos and Norris.

Interestingly, both Eagleton and Callinicos share with Anderson a similar heritage from within the heterodox Trotskyist tradition. However, while this heritage informed both Callinicos's and Eagleton's polemical relationship to both postmodernism generally and Jameson's interpretation of the postmodern world more specifically, Anderson was to warmly recommend Jameson's general account of the contemporary epoch. How can we begin to explain the divergence between these two broad approaches to Jameson's *oeuvre*? One answer to this might be that Anderson's idiosyncratic reception of Jameson can be understood, at least partially, as a corollary of the way in which he assimilated Trotskyism through a lens built from components supplied by Deutscher and Western Marxism. This lens, as we have seen, informed both his hugely pessimistic reading of the collapse of Stalinism, and his pessimistic judgment on the potential for the growth of a socialist consciousness within the Western proletariat. These factors, as we shall see, are of importance to his analysis of the rupture between the modern and postmodern worlds. In contrast to Jameson and Anderson, Callinicos and Eagleton developed two much more political analyses of the rise of postmodernism. They essentially explained the reception of postmodernist discourse in the 1980s as a consequence of the toll taken by the defeat of the radicalism of the late 1960s and early 1970s on a layer of leftists who, in the 1980s, benefited from the rise of the 'new middle class' under Reagan and Thatcher. This social layer had become disillusioned with the left, but could never, unembarrassingly, embrace the traditions of the right: irony thus became its dominant trope, and postmodernist rejections of grand narratives its theoretical self-justification (Callinicos 1989; Eagleton 1996).

JAMESON AND POSTMODERNITY

In 1998 Anderson returned to the themes of modernism and postmodernism, previously analysed in his critique of Marshall Berman. In *The Origins of Postmodernity* he sought to assess Frederic Jameson's *oeuvre*. *Postmodernity* begins with an overview of the development of the concept of postmodernism. As with the concept of modernism, that of postmodernism originated in the 'distant periphery' of the world system. Both came from Hispanic America;

the first in the 1890s; the second in the 1930s. From its inception by Federco de Onis as an aesthetic concept describing 'a conservative reflux within modernism itself', the term mutated over the next two decades until Arnold Toynbee deployed it as an 'epochal rather than an aesthetic category'. Writing in 1954 Toynbee described the period from around 1870 as the 'postmodern age' (Anderson 1998a, 3-5). This usage was echoed by the radical American poet Charles Olson who, in the aftermath of the Chinese Revolution, spoke of a dawning postmodern age, whose future could be seen via the 'light ... in the East' (Anderson 1998a, 10). By the late 1950s the category of postmodern was, by contrast, being deployed by C. Wright Mills and Irving Howe in a pejorative sense as compared to the period of modernism. While a few years later Leslie Fielder and Amatai Etzioni inverted this appreciation to describe the post-1945 period as a postmodern age, characterised by the advent of true democracy (Anderson 1998a, 12-14).

All these applications of the category of postmodernism were, Anderson informs us, improvisations; the concept truly came of age in the late 1970s. This point of maturation began with the publication of the journal *boundary 2* in the autumn of 1972. Subtitled a *Journal of Postmodern Literature and Culture* this journal took its themes from Olson. However, whereas Olson's characterisation of the new age was coloured by his communist sympathies, the new journal allowed these radical political considerations to pass out of sight, such that *boundary 2* failed to unite any form of political stance with its cultural theory and became 'essentially a literary journal' (Anderson 1998a, 16). This lacuna in postmodernist thought was filled at the end of the decade from two widely diverse political perspectives: in 1979 Lyotard published *The Postmodern Condition* in Paris, while a year later Habermas outlined his alternative vision of the contemporary world in his lecture *Modernity – an Incomplete Project.*

Both of these writers came from within dissident factions of the Marxist tradition. However, Anderson notes that neither brought very much of this intellectual heritage to their analyses. In particular neither attempted a 'real historical interpretation of the postmodern'. Thus Lyotard built his critique of all grand narratives upon a reading of developments in the natural sciences (Anderson 1998a, 45 & 26). Interestingly, Anderson notes that the version of Marxism held previously by Lyotard was marked by a 'vehement anti-Communism', and suggested that this fact accounted in part for his apostasy (Anderson 1998a, 29). However, this line of argument, reminiscent as it is of that outlined in *Tracks*, was not redeployed by Anderson to account for Lyotard's shift from Marxism to postmodernism.

By contrast with Lyotard, Habermas had attempted to defend the Enlightenment tradition. He believed that modernism's ultimate weakness lay 'not so much [in its] lack of vigilance towards the market, as [in] too much trust in the plan'. Unfortunately, the corollary of this position was that while Habermas in his later works 'reaffirmed the ideals of the Enlightenment [he] denied them any chance of realisation' (Anderson 1998a, 43-44). This position approximates to Anderson's politics in the mid-1980s, when, as we have seen, he had unsuccessfully looked to Habermas to furnish the left with a political alternative to postmodernism.

At this point Anderson introduces the thought of Fredric Jameson. Unlike Habermas, Jameson offers the beginnings of a radical politics for the postmodern age. According to Anderson, Jameson's *oeuvre* marked the culmination of the Western Marxist tradition, but also 'enormously magnified' the traditional object of enquiry of that tradition and thus 'exceeded' it (Anderson 1998a, 71 & 73-4). Jameson achieved a total explanation of the contemporary world, explaining postmodernism as a culmination of five processes: first, the capitalist economy had been transformed from around the 1960s into 'multi-national capitalism'; second, in his analysis of the fragmentation of the subject, Jameson claimed that postmodern man had lost any active sense of history; third, he expanded the postmodern 'across virtually the whole spectrum of the arts'; fourth, he argued that while class was still a central category in the postmodern world its referent had changed dramatically from the modern period: crucially, the experience of class had been fragmented across regional, gender and racial lines. Finally, Jameson refused to condemn, moralistically, the postmodern age but instead sought to develop a 'totalising comprehension' of it (Anderson 1998a, 54-66).

This appreciation of Jameson, as the culmination of Western Marxism, contradicted somewhat Anderson's earlier obituary of that tradition. Interestingly, Anderson noted that while he had previously understood the militancy of the late 1960s and early 1970s as the herald of the rebirth of the revolutionary Marxist tradition, he had now come to accept that the defeat of this movement had opened the door to a new flowering of Western Marxism; a tradition which grew in close contact with new, non-Marxist, modes of thought (Anderson 1998a, 71). Anderson did continue to believe that the late 1960s marked a real historical watershed, which he characterised by the transition of the economic itself as 'life itself becomes so pervaded by the symbolic systems of information and persuasion that the notion of an independent sphere of more or less a-cultural production increasingly lost meaning. Henceforward, any major theory of culture was bound to encompass more of the civilization of capital than ever before. The traditional object of Western Marxism was enormously magnified' (Anderson 1998a, 73). Thus, the scene was set for Jameson's expansion of the field of enquiry of Western Marxism.

The element of Jameson's thesis to which Anderson was most attracted was his predication of the category of postmodernism upon a qualitative transformation in the nature of the world economy. Jameson had argued that it could not be stressed too much that postmodernism was a period whose existence depended upon 'some radical break or coupure, generally traced back to the end of the 1950s or the early 1960s' (Jameson 1991, 1).[68] Developing Jameson's insights, Anderson argued that a radical break in the nature of the system could be located, but that the transition was a long time coming. In particular he updated his model of modernism as outlined in his essay *Modernity and Revolution*. Accepting arguments made by Peter Wollen, Anderson argued that his own previous analysis of the demise of the modernist epoch had been too 'abrupt' (Anderson 1998a, 83 & Wollen 1993). Whereas he had previously held that the end of the Second World War had marked the closure of the modernist epoch, he now became convinced that 'the quarter century after the end of hostilities ... seems in retrospect an interregnum, in which modernist energies were not subject to sudden cancellation, but still glowed intermittently here and there, where conditions allowed in an inhospitable environment. It was not until the turn of the seventies that the ground for an altogether new configuration was prepared' (Anderson 1998a, 84).

Wollen had based his periodisation of the twentieth century political economy on the writings of the French regulation school (Wollen 1993, 36 & 68). However, Anderson made no explicit link between his periodisation of the contemporary world and that of the regulation theorists, despite his previous positive appraisal of their work. Rather, he developed a new conjunctural analysis of the postmodern world to supplement his conjunctural analysis of modernism. As with his account of modernism, Anderson argued that postmodernism could be understood as an epoch whose coordinates were triangulated by three processes. Recapitulating his account of the moment of modernism, Anderson wrote that he had argued that it was best understood as a field of force triangulated by, 'an economy and society still only semi-industrial, in which the ruling order remained to a significant extent agrarian or aristocratic; a technology of dramatic inventions, whose impact was still fresh or incipient; and an open political horizon, in which revolutionary upheavals of one kind or another against the prevailing order were widely expected or feared' (Anderson 1998a, 81).

Postmodernism, by contrast, was triangulated by a 'the constellation of a *déclassé* ruling order, a mediatized technology and a monochrome politics' (Anderson 1998a, 92). By this he meant that, while modernism 'virtually defined itself as 'anti-bourgeois', postmodernism is what occurs when, without any victory, that adversary is gone'. Anderson did not mean by this that he accepted John Major's claim to have created a classless society. Rather, he insisted that while gross inequalities and inter-generational immobility remained, the bourgeoisie, as understood by Weber as a group defined by common values and norms, had vanished; Bill Gates had taken the place of Flaubert's bourgeoisie (Anderson 1998a, 84-6). Second, he suggested that where once new technology was exciting it was now commonplace. In particular the invention and mass use of the television had changed everything and saturated the world with an imagery that constituted a 'Niagara of visual gabble' (Anderson 1998a, 89). Not that Anderson believed that these images were meaningless: television stations transmit 'discourses that are wall to wall ideology, in the strong sense of the term. The intellectual atmosphere of postmodernism as doxa rather than art, draws many of its impulses from the pressure of this sphere' (Anderson 1998a, 89). Finally, he suggests that while it was true that the political left had been defeated in the 1970s, Callinicos and Eagleton had underestimated just how decisive this defeat had been. In particular he stressed the significance of the collapse of Communism and the abandonment of the reformist impulse by the Western social democratic parties. Together, Anderson concluded, these changes suggested that 'capitalism as a whole [had] entered a new historical phase' (Anderson 1998a, 91-92).

So while modernism was a world of 'sharp demarcations', postmodernism was characterised by the fact that 'what moves is only the market' (Anderson 1998a, 93 & 114). Not that Anderson believed that the postmodern world was without conflict. Rather, 'new poles of oppositional identification have emerged in the postmodern period: gender, race, ecology, sexual orientation, regional or continental diversity'. However, these 'have today constituted a weaker set of antagonisms' than that offered by Marx's proletariat to the traditional bourgeoisie (Anderson 1998a, 104). The problem was thus posed of how to confront this new 'common nonsense of the age' (Anderson 1998a, 115). Anderson maintains that both Eagleton and Callinicos had misjudged their opponent in their polemical zeal to oust it: 'Postmodernism is the cultural logic of a capitalism not embattled, but complacent beyond precedent. Resistance can only start by staring down this order as it is' (Anderson 1998a, 118).

Similarly, Anderson rejected the alternative politics offered by postcolonial theory. Indeed, in rejecting the claims of postcolonial theory to have located an alternative to the metropolitan postmodern world in the ex-colonies, Anderson retuned his own picture of the contemporary world. Whereas, in his essay *Modernity and Revolution*, he had argued that the uneven development of international capitalism meant that in some areas, where full capitalist modernization had yet to take hold, elements of the modernist conjuncture remained to this day, in *Postmodernity* he argued that, given the contemporary 'incomparably greater degree of cultural penetration of the former Second and Third Worlds by the First ... the influence of postmodern forms becomes inescapable' (Anderson 1998a, 121).

Given the omnipresence of postmodernism, it appears that the mistake of both Eagleton and Callinicos has been to attack it from without. Jameson, by contrast, not only accepted that postmodernism is the dominant form of the day but also that it could be periodised. Thus, Anderson notes that Jameson celebrated the early 'creative release' of postmodernist thought in the 1970s and yet bemoaned postmodernism's 'regression' thereafter. So his most recent essays have been political interventions within postmodern culture that have engaged with this regression from the left in the hope that the trajectory of postmodernism could be changed. Anderson concluded: 'Jameson's voice has been without equal in the clarity and eloquence of its resistance to the direction of the time', and that the only viable modern left politics could develop from within postmodernism itself (Anderson 1998a, 135-136).

To make sense of this latter claim Anderson differentiated between what he termed the 'citra' and the 'ultra' forms of postmodernism. The first 'can be taken as all those tendencies which, breaking with high modernism, have tended to reinstate the ornamental and more readily available; while the ultra can be read as all those which have gone beyond modernism in radicalising its negations of immediate intelligibility or sensuous gratification' (Anderson 1998a, 102). Postmodernism is therefore, like modernism, 'a field of tensions' and the arena of culture is a 'battlefield' (Anderson 1998a, 135 & 134). Correct politics should thus start from within the cultural field rather than, as with Callinicos and Eagleton, from outside the ballpark. So Anderson remained true to his long-term commitment to radical politics – the left he insisted must 'fight for a real alternative' to the right (Anderson 1998e, 81) – but insisted that the parameters within which such politics might operate were much more narrowly defined than either Callinicos or Eagleton imagined.

RENEWALS

Anderson has developed this argument in his recent manifesto for the re-launched *NLR*. At the heart of this programme is the claim that the principal characteristic of the past decade is 'the virtually uncontested consolidation, and universal diffusion, of neo-liberalism' (Anderson 2000, 10). Anderson is aware that the neo-liberal agenda has not gone unchallenged, and briefly notes, among other counter currents, the labour upsurge in France in 1995. However, he dismisses the significance of these events with the claim that 'capital has comprehensively beaten back all threats to its rule' (Anderson 2000, 16). Comparing the context of the launch of the first *NLR* with that of the present day, Anderson writes that then a third of the planet had broken with capitalism, the discrediting of Stalinism in 1956 had unleashed a vital process of the rediscovery of authentic Marxism, while, culturally, there had been a qualitative break with the conformism of the 1950s (Anderson 2000, 7).[69] Today, by contrast, American capitalism has reasserted its international primacy; European social democratic governments are implementing policies designed to follow the American model; the Japanese economy is experiencing a slump; the Russian catastrophe has produced no popular backlash; and the Western Powers have asserted themselves successfully in the Balkans (Anderson 2000, 11-12). He concludes *Renewals* with the claim that despite upsurges against neo-liberalism in the 1990s 'no collective agency able to match the power of capital is yet on the horizon' (Anderson 2000, 17).

The ideological form taken by the new neo-liberal consensus is that of 'the 'Third Way' of the Clinton-Blair regimes' (Anderson 2000, 12). This new 'organic formula' of neo-liberalism differs from the 1980s Thatcher/Reagan version in that it makes 'gestures of social conciliation' (Anderson 2001a, 6). Commenting on the prospects for this ideology in the wake of the 2000 US Presidential elections, Anderson initially argued that George W. Bush's victory probably would not herald a return to 1980s style conservatism: Third Way neo-liberalism 'is under little threat' (Anderson 2001a, 21). However, eighteen months later he was less confident that the Third Way had survived either Bush's election or the governmental changes in Europe: 'there is no longer an 'organic formula' of internal neo-liberal hegemony across the whole advanced-capitalist world' (Anderson 2002e, 27). Unfortunately, while the ideological garb worn by the various neo-liberal regimes might vary, neo-liberalism itself was safe from the threat of the anti-capitalists of Seattle and elsewhere. Where does this leave *NLR*? Anderson suggests three possible positions that socialists could take in such an unpromising conjuncture: accommodation, consolation or resignation (Anderson 2000, 13). Commenting on each he writes that while 'clamorous renegacy is quite rare ... the depth of actual accommodation can be seen from episodes like the Balkan War, where the role of NATO was simply taken for granted ... by a wide band of opinion that would not have dreamt of doing so ten or twenty years back'. Consolation, on the other hand, could be explained as an understandable, if misguided, 'propensity to over-estimate the significance of contrary processes ... to nourish illusions in imaginary forces'. The third alternative, resignation, is, he argues, rarely articulated, but involves a 'lucid recognition of the nature and triumph of the system ... without any belief in the chance of an alternative to it' (Anderson 2000, 13-4). In contrast to these positions, Anderson argues that *NLR* should combine 'uncompromising realism' with a refusal to accommodate 'to the ruling system'. Thus, the journal should 'support any local movements or limited reforms, without pretending that they alter the nature of the system'. Indeed, it should 'bend the stick' resolutely against any accommodation to the market (Anderson 2000, 14 & 21).[70]

How has Anderson expressed this perspective in the re-launched *NLR*? A full answer to this question cannot be settled after only a couple of years. However, on the evidence available to us we can say that Anderson has succeeded in consistently acting as a critic of 'the system' without repeating the mistakes he made in the 1960s of naïvely impressing earth shattering socialist potentialities upon each new movement. Unfortunately, his aim of immunising *NLR* against consolationary rhetoric, with a dose of 'uncompromising realism' has, it seems, sometimes led him towards a timid embrace of other, at least equally naïve and unrealistic political perspectives.

Anderson signalled the stance of the soon to be re-launched *NLR* in 1999 when, through the medium of a review of the work of Timothy Garton Ash, he engaged in the debate over the war in the Balkans. He concluded the essay, *A Ripple of the Polonaise*, with a scathing, realist, interpretation of the imperialist calculations underpinning the general Eurasian policy of the US, including the linked efforts to expand NATO eastwards and to bomb Serbia, that should be read by all those whose naivety led them to accept the official humanitarian interpretation of these processes (Anderson 1999b, 10). This analysis was followed in 2001 with an interpretation of the US presidential elections, within which Anderson refused to be pulled by the liberal stream towards a critical support for Gore against Bush. While accepting that the Democrats and the Republicans were 'not interchangeable', he insisted that the 'lesser evil' argument, articulated by many on the left to garner support for Gore, acted to invoke an 'inoperative' evil to mask an 'operative' alternative (Anderson 2001a, 16 & 18). Specifically, as most American presidents had pursued similar domestic policies since the Second World War – the result of institutional gridlock, then Bush's reactionary domestic policy would be largely inoperative. By contrast Gore was a keen reactionary in the international arena, while, before the Afghan war at least, the worst that could have been said about Bush in this field was that he was ignorant of it.[71] Generalising his critique of the lesser evil argument to Britain, Anderson refused to be swayed by the inoperative threat of William Hague's Tories into supporting the operative evil of Blair's Third Way in the 2001 General Election (Anderson 2001a, 20 & 22).

If, in both *A Ripple of the Polonaise* and *Testing Formula Two*, the strengths of Anderson's perspective were expressed, then his overview of the Palestinian conflict, *Scurrying Towards Bethlehem*, illustrate how his powerful analytical skills could be distorted as he sought to square a 'realistic' diagnosis of the conflict with a non-resignatory politics. In this essay Anderson provides a historical account of the context of the contemporary conflict in Palestine. On the back of a bravura portrait of the history of European Jewry, anti-Semitism and Zionism, up to the 'massive operation of ethnic cleansing' that gave birth to the state of Israel, Anderson locates the roots of the present conflict between

Zionists and Palestinians within a broader history of imperialism (Anderson 2001b, 12). He goes on to shows how the first Intifada, beginning in 1987, originated as a Palestinian reaction to the oppression that they experienced at the hands of the American backed Zionist state, and that the Oslo 'peace process', which grew as a reaction to the Intifada, was a sham: 'after eight years, the IDF remains in complete control of 60 per cent of the West Bank, and 'joint' control of another 27 per cent; a network of new Israeli-only roads built on confiscated land divides and encircles the residential enclaves under Palestinian authority; the number of Jewish settlers, who monopolise 80 per cent of all water in the occupied territories, has virtually doubled; the per capita income of the Palestinian population fell by one quarter in the first five years after the Accords, and has since collapsed further'. As Anderson observes, 'in these conditions, nothing was more certain than continuing acts of popular rebellion': and thus the second Intifada began in September 2000 (Anderson 2001b, 18-19). Unfortunately, 'no matter how brave their resistance to the IDF, the Palestinians are too weak to have much hope of obtaining justice themselves' (Anderson 2001b, 28). What then can be anticipated for the future of Israel and the Palestinians?

Traditionally, many Marxists had agreed that the Palestinians alone could not liberate themselves: only a socialist revolution in the Middle East, led by the Arab working class, could realise their liberation, and maintain democratic rights for Jews (Marshall 1989, 207-8). Anderson no longer believes in the viability of the socialist alternative to capitalism, and consequentially, in the Palestinian context, this means that he accepts that Jewish and Palestinian nationalisms are both essentially fixed. He thus proposes that two more or less equal states be created, one Palestinian the other Israeli, along lines suggested by Mandron (Anderson 2001b, 25 & Mandron 2001). Unfortunately, as he himself acknowledges, this suggestion does not appear to be even 'remotely practical politics' (Anderson 2001b, 26). Despite this caveat, his hope is that Arab leaders will turn away from their own, and Arafat's, traditional response to conflict in Palestine: of running, pathetically, to the White House. Anderson's belief in a radical alternative to this reaction involves hope for the development of 'genuinely independent regimes on the Nile or in Mecca', whose reality 'would put the existence of the Zionist connexion into perspective'. 'The day the Arab world stop scurrying to Washington – should that ever come – Israel will be forced to disgorge its incommensurate gains. Short of that, Zionism is not likely to be moved' (Anderson 2001b, 30).

Unfortunately, despite the grandeur of Anderson's historical overview of the problem, there is an overwhelming sense that he is grasping at straws in his conclusion. Chomsky, in a formidable work on the subject, stresses Israel's geopolitical role as Washington's 'strategic asset' in the Middle East;

and argues that the 'unique' relationship between the USA and the Zionist state rests upon Israel's proven ability to back American interests with force whenever the oil producing states began to challenge US hegemony in the area. If Chomsky is right then it would seem that any movement towards genuine independence in the Arab world would be met, not by a weakening of the ties between America and Israel, but by their strengthening. Anderson's faint hope for Palestine therefore appears somewhat misplaced. More so because the agents of reform that are implied by his analysis – the Arab and Israeli elites, are precisely those that have presided over the continuing subjugation of the Palestinians. Anderson locates no basis for a change in their interest at this level. Indeed, even assuming that a more reasonable division of Palestine be achieved, it is not apparent how this could be distinguished from what Chomsky calls 'the Labour/Likud program of establishing a Bantustan-style settlement' (Chomsky 1999, 563).

However, Anderson's discussion of the condition of Israel does point beyond his own perspectives, to an outlook that is much closer to that held by traditional Marxists. He notes that Israel, in following American neo-liberal policies, has become 'one of the two most unequal societies in the world' (Anderson 2001b, 22). Unfortunately, the deeply racist structure of Israeli society has mediated the consequences of this social polarisation, such that two right-wing forces compete for control of the Zionist state – a rich liberal capitalist faction and a poorer religious fundamentalist section (Anderson 2001b, 23). This condition seems to act as a specific confirmation of Anderson's generally pessimistic diagnosis of postmodern culture. However, it is precisely the peculiarities of the Zionist state that mark its politics as anomalous on an international scale; elsewhere social polarisation does seem to be fanning the flames of revolt. Indeed, Israeli neo-liberalism is just one aspect of a market revolution that has swept the Middle East for two decades or more. In the vanguard of this movement is Egypt where, as Alexander argues, 'the cumulative effect of years of free market reforms has eaten away at support for the regime'. Elsewhere the neo-liberal project is less advanced: in 'Lebanon, Iran and Syria, the effects of economic liberalism have so far been contradictory. In all these countries a section of the ruling class has been able to link the idea of free market reform with the hope of political liberation'. Alexander suggests that this ideological masking of the real consequences of neo-liberalism will become increasingly strained if and when the world economy enters into recession, and the price of oil falls. Indeed, even in Saudi Arabia over recent years, Saudi citizens – as opposed to foreign workers – have seen their relationship to 'their' state placed under stress (Alexander 2001, 65-6). Alexander concludes that this situation has led to the development of what she calls 'the objective conditions for a large-scale revolutionary crisis ... in a number of Middle Eastern countries'. Unfortunately, the leadership of the Arab masses has not, subjectively, matched these objective conditions. At this level the failed traditions of nationalism and Islamicism compete for hegemony over the Arab workers and peasants (Alexander 2001, 69-75). Need this situation go on indefinitely? Anderson himself argues that 'no stasis is permanent' (Anderson 2001b, 29). However, while he looks for an agency from above to break this particular deadlock, it seems at least as likely that American imperial oppression of the area, when combined with the growing economic misery produced by the liberalisation of the Middle Eastern economies, will create the conditions for the potential growth of a politicised working-class militancy that could upset the regional status quo. In fact, just as Alexander's hopes for the growth of a socialist movement in the Middle East is premised upon a new recession, Anderson suggests, more generally, that Third Way neo-liberalism 'is likely to dominate the scene' only 'so long as the global economy holds up' (Anderson 2001a, 22).[72] The implication of his analysis, however, is that if the world economy goes into crisis the choice opened up for humanity lies simply between variations of the neo-liberal paradigm.

Fortunately, Anderson's assertion that 'what moves is only the market' can be contested at a number of levels (Anderson 1998a, 114). First, if Osborne's and Callinicos's critiques, noted in chapter six, of his periodisation of capitalism are correct, then both his general model of historical conjuncture, and his specific characterisation of the *differencia specifica* of the modernist conjuncture, are untenable. He has failed adequately to show that we live in a qualitatively different epoch from those who made the European revolutions of the twentieth century.[73] Of course the key continuity between the present day and the epoch of high modernism is the fact that the demands of capital accumulation lie necessarily in contradiction to the interests of the exploited wage labourers, upon whom that process rests. This process, as Anderson showed in *Arguments*, creates an objective unity to the interests of workers. Unfortunately, he seems to ignore this, his previous analysis of the salience of class, in his more recent writings on the experience of class fragmentation, along lines of gender, race, skill, age and occupation, under postmodernity (Anderson 1994d, 11-2). While the experience of such fragmentation is undoubtedly real, it fails to address the issue of how, through struggle, workers can challenge this fragmentation and begin to develop a consciousness of themselves as a class.[74] As we saw in chapter five, even at his most orthodox Marxist, Anderson held to a mechanical and static model of the relationship that existed between class consciousness and class structure, which necessarily lent itself to political impressionism. So, ironically, from a structuralist model of class, Anderson, has moved to outline what is in effect a model of class consciousness that merely describes the fragmented market location of workers.

In fact, through this description Anderson is partially engaging with the ideological experience of workers' in struggle; unfortunately, it is the experience of defeat which he reflects, and beyond which, moreover, he appears incapable of conceiving an alternative. Thus, as the general pattern of the class struggle in the West in the 1980s and 1990s has been on the downturn, so Anderson increasingly stressed the fragmentary nature of class. Indeed, his model, like Weber's, appears incapable of conceptualising the possibility of historical change,[75] such that his contemporary discussion of class fragmentation is overly objective and static, and appears blind to processes that are acting to draw together the proletariat into a collective agency of change.[76]

By contrast, Kim Moody has deployed a more dynamic model of class formation in his analysis of contemporary political and economic trends. In his work on the rebirth of working-class struggles against capitalism from the mid-1990s he has suggested that 'if any picture of the globalisation process necessarily involves some overwhelming 'gloom and doom' analysis, it is the return of class confrontation in recent years that offers the hope' (Moody 1997, 4). Moody argues that in a whole series of countries from the first to the third world 'it was the working class itself, led or at least accompanied by its unions, that was taking on the right-wing/neoliberal (conservative) agenda that had come to dominate the politics of most nations' (Moody 1997, 10). Moreover, against the argument of those that say that the working class is increasingly fragmented and thus politically marginalized, Moody argues that 'what these theories overlook is what is most basic about capitalist society: the capital-labor relationship, the 'social relations of production'' (Moody 1997, 150). Indeed, this relationship ensures that the 'fight option' has been taken by increasing numbers of workers internationally in the last few years (Moody 1997, 193). Furthermore, 'as the twenty-first century approached a rebellion against capitalist globalisation, its structures, and its effects had begun ... At the centre of the rebellion were the working class and its most basic organization, the trade union' (Moody 1997, 269). Interestingly, given Anderson's tendency to read the opinions of the working class from those of its leaders, Moody notes that 'the rebellion seemed unlikely because so many of its official leaders were reluctant warriors' (Moody 1997, 270). In contrast to the conservatism of this layer, the influx of new groups of workers into the labour process carries with it more positive than negative consequences. 'In the heat of mass action international differences, ethnic and gender diversity, and old sectoral divisions ... appeared as strengths among both the strikers and the working-class public that expressed almost universal support for these movements' (Moody 1997, 272). Indeed, James Petras has argued that these 'large scale social mobilisations explicitly rejecting part or all of the neoliberal agenda call into question the assumption of 'consolidation'. They open the perspective of the decay of neoliberalism and construction of a political alternative based on a different socio-economic model' (Petras quoted in Moody 1997, 7).

More recently, both Pierre Bourdieu and Noam Chomsky have argued that the global anti-capitalist movement that has emerged from the end of 1999 marks a potential turning point in the fortune of radical politics (Chomsky 2000 & Bourdieu 2000). How does this movement relate to the workers' movement? Moody begins a sober discussion of this issue by differentiating the process of globalisation into four phases: first, capitalism's inherently expansionary drive to accumulate; second, the political process of negotiated trade and investment agreements; third, the ratification of these agreements; fourth, the implementation of these agreements (Moody 2001, 297-8). Moody argues that the anti-capitalist movement has been most interested in the second of these phases, the labour bureaucracy with the third, and striking workers with the fourth (Moody 2001, 298). Without mythologizing what occurred with the 'Teamster and Turtles' alliance at Seattle and similar developments at Quebec, Nice and elsewhere, Moody's aim is to build upon these movements to win over the rank and file of the workers to anti-capitalism. He argues that for the anti-capitalists to achieve this goal they must systematically address all four of the phases of globalisation (Moody 2001, 293 & 299). Thus, without loosing sense of the difficulties involved for socialists, and the limitations of what has been achieved, Moody's analysis has the strength of at least recognising the possibilities opened up by the present conjuncture.

Moody's account of the strengths and weaknesses of contemporary international labour politics is built upon an analysis of a previous twenty-year history of proletarian retreat in the face of neo-liberalism, and coheres generally with the reading of the present conjuncture offered by Callinicos and Eagleton. Moreover, Moody's thesis appears to combine the kind of objectivist account of class that Anderson maintained was essential in *Arguments*, without loosing sight of the ebb and flow of the process of developing class consciousness to which Thompson was so acutely aware.[77]

Moody's arguments suggest, contra Anderson, that it is possible for ordinary working people to see through the 'Niagara of gabble', to the underlying class relations. In fact Anderson's suggestion to the contrary rests upon one of the weaker elements of Jameson's thought. Jameson's defence of the proposition that the economic and the cultural cannot be separated in late capitalism shows him at his most Hegelian. Callinicos has argued that while Jameson has attempted to unite Althusserian and Lukácsian concepts of the totality, this has been particularly unsuccessful in his account of postmodernism. Thus, rather than developing a complex model of the totality, Jameson has instead produced a 'homology' within which a supposed break in capitalism simply gives rise to a depthless postmodern age (Callinicos 1989, 128-32).[78] Jameson himself looks to Adorno as a guide to political issues in the postmodern world: 'Adorno was a doubtful ally when there were still powerful and oppositional political currents from which his temperamental and cantankerous quietism could distract the uncommitted reader. Now that for the moment those currents are themselves quiescent, his bile is a joyous counter-poison and a corrosive solvent to apply to the surface of 'what is"' (Jameson 1990, 249). Unfortunately, while, as we have noted above, the downturn in the class struggle from the mid-1970s could help explain the re-emergence of Adornian Marxism, even in periods of relative political quiescence there do exist counter-currents that can act to maintain more activist interpretations of Marxism. Indeed, Mike Davis has criticised the exiled Frankfurt School in Los Angeles for

> 'exhibiting no apparent interest in the wartime turmoil in the local aircraft plants nor [were they] inclined to appreciate the vigorous nightlife of Los Angeles's Central Avenue ghetto, Horkheimer and Adorno focused instead on the little single family boxes that seemed to absorb the world-historic mission of the proletariat into family-centred consumerism under the direction of radio jingles and Life magazine ads' (Davis 1990, 48).

In fact, while most commentators would agree that television was important to the process of the diffusion of the dominant ideology, this insight needs to be combined with awareness that television is not omnipotent; its reception is mediated by the experiences of its audience. Ironically, if Jameson's ideological totality is too Hegelian, because it is too homogeneous, its articulation in consciousness is too Althusserian, because, like Althusser, he tends to dissolve experience into ideology (Palmer 1990, 44-5).

There does exist, however, a large literature on the topic of the reception of televised ideology that is critical of the overly pessimistic reading of the power of television. Thus, during the British strike wave of 1978-9, Stuart Hood argued that large sections of the strikers actively deconstructed the reactionary television messages that were aimed at them. They 'rejected the preferred reading of the events they saw pictured on their screens and judged both the events and the television representation of them in the light of their own experiences as workers and trade unionists – in the light of their class consciousness' (Hood 1980, 22). Similarly, David Morley analysed the viewers of the *Nationwide* programme along class lines. He concluded that different groups – shop stewards, trade union officials, apprentices, students and managers – read the programme in distinct ways. In particular, shop stewards developed the most 'oppositional' reading of the programme; they 'rejected' attempts by television journalists to interpret their grievances, and then reinterpreted the 'implicit theory of the origins of wealth', espoused on *Nationwide*, and 'explicitly moved on to substitute for it a version of the labour theory of value'

(Morley 1986, 117). Philo and Miller argue that such divergent readings of media messages derive from the contestation between groups that are based upon the 'material fact of conflicting power and interest'. Divergent interpretations of the ideological messages encoded through television were not, they insist, simply based on the plurality of opinions held by viewers. Rather, the plurality of opinions was itself based upon the life experiences of people. Thus, the dominant ideology, as mediated through television, was more likely to be accepted for issues about which viewers had little or no experience, and less likely to be accepted in areas were they themselves had a first hand knowledge. This would still suggest that the limitations of individual experiences would imply only at best a fragmentary break with the dominant ideology. However, Philo and Miller insist that viewers are able to generalise from misinterpretations and lies told of their experiences on television to open the possibility of breaking with the dominant ideology. Thus, through a combination of their experience and their logic, individuals could potentially develop a scientific understanding of their own material position within society, and thus of their real interests (Philo & Miller 2001, 52ff). Anderson nowhere asks the kind of questions that might make this type of oppositional reading of televised ideology become apparent, and in this sense he seems to confirm Marshall Berman's argument that he had lost 'touch with the stuff and flow of everyday life' (Berman 1984, 123)

In contrast to Philo and Miller's nuanced analysis of the contested reception of ideology through the mass media, Anderson claims that the ideology propagated by television is so strong that it constitutes a doxa. This term, associated with the work of Pierre Bourdieu, was developed to underpin an extremely pessimistic diagnosis of the acceptance, by the oppressed, of their awful conditions of life. Marxism, Bourdieu once said, had grossly 'overestimated the capacity for resistance'. This was in part because the Marxist concept of ideology was not firm enough to account for this acquiescence by workers in the status quo (Eagleton and Bourdieu 1994, 268). In contrast to the concept ideology, Bourdieu used the idea of doxa to express the way that power is naturalised 'so that no social arrangement different from the present could even be imagined' (Eagleton 1991, 157).[79] Anderson's broad acceptance of this argument informs his analysis of Jameson's political project. Commenting on Jameson's 'by-passing' of Gramsci in his 'resumption of Western Marxism', Anderson wrote, 'who can say that his intuition was wrong? The grandeur of the Sardinian is stranded today, amid the impasse of the intellectual tradition he represented, plain for all to see. The current of history has passed elsewhere. If the legacies of Frankfurt or Paris or Budapest remain more available, it is also because they were less political' (Anderson 1998a, 131). This interpretation of the contemporary conjuncture seems to be confirmed by the defeat of the striking shop stewards noted above, despite their oppositional readings of the media. However, Anderson's pessimism follows from this, and other similar, defeats only if we ignore the concrete form of organisation through which the shop stewards interpreted the televised ideology. Conversely, it was surely Gramsci's key political argument in the early 1920s that shop steward organisation was not a sufficient base from which to challenge capitalism. His championing of Leninism from this point on shows the importance he placed on the concrete organisational forms through which experiences were to be mediated.

While Anderson wrote his 'farewell' to Gramsci before the rise of the anti-capitalist movement, his position doesn't seem to have softened in the post-Seattle period. Thus, where Anderson had previously suggested that radical politics requires a utopian core, he now argues that 'three decades of nearly unbroken political defeats for every force that once fought against the established order', has robbed humanity of such a vision, and has instead bequeathed a postmodern doxa of dystopian despair which will not be challenged until radicals 'regain the social ground, of institutions and ideologies, systems and states' (Anderson 2004, 71 & 76). However, despite this claim, the struggle from below goes on, and with it, as Gramsci wrote, the 'struggle of political 'hegemonies' of opposing directions' continues. In his attempt to comprehend this struggle, Gramsci argued that actors have 'contradictory consciousnesses' that incorporate elements from both their practical activity, and from the historically received dominant ideology. The socialist critique of the received dominant ideas is therefore to be built upon the actual practical activity of working-class actors; and the socialist goal of unifying theory and practice is thus best understood to be 'part of the historical process, whose elementary and primitive phase is to be found in the sense of being 'different' and 'apart', in an instructive feeling of independence, and which progresses to the level of real possession of a single and coherent conception of the world' (Gramsci 1971, 333). Now, while this feeling of 'difference' is structured into capitalist relations of production, it only manifests itself in consciousness through class struggle; and can only move to victory, according to Gramsci, through a Leninist revolutionary party (Gramsci 1971, 334).

Unfortunately, after early schematic attempts to address the problem of political organisation in the 1960s, Anderson has never re-engaged with this issue. This should not be very surprising to students of his work, as his mechanical conceptualisation of the relationship of class structure to class consciousness implies the irrelevance of such an organisation. Moreover, his Deutscherism has had the effect of forcing an elision in his conceptualisation of socialism from Marx's 'the real movement that abolishes the present state of things' (Marx & Engels 1970, 56-7), to the goal of a statised economy. Assuming this elision, it was only natural that the collapse of the Soviet Union led him to become increasingly pessimistic about prospects for socialism. This pessimism has been reinforced as globalisation undermined *dirigiste* accumulation regimes in the West. So, while he might sympathise with the contemporary anti-capitalist movement, he cannot conceive of its victory.[80]

CONCLUSION

In 1956 the combined political reverberations of the Anglo-French invasion of Egypt, the Russian invasion of Hungary, and Khrushchev's secret speech included, in Britain, the formation of a self-styled New Left. This New Left was composed of an impressive amalgam of dissident elements from both the Labour and Communist parties, alongside unaligned individuals and members of the Marxist groups. Originally this milieu seemed full of promise; however, within six years of its emergence the New Left collapsed, and its leading members were largely dispersed. Perry Anderson cut his political teeth within this milieu and then, initially alongside just three other junior members, set out to reorient its remnants so as to meet the challenges faced by the left in Britain in the mid 1960s and beyond.

When they took over the reins of *NLR*, Anderson and his comrades had no fully formulated strategic perspective through which they hoped to achieve this goal. They were, though, children of 1956 and as such shared many of the assumptions of the senior members of the old New Left milieu. For Anderson these included a culturalist approach to socialist politics in the West, and a Deutscherite interpretation of the Cold War. Both of these influences on his thought implied radical revisions of classical Marxism: the culturalism influenced his early idealist interpretation of the historical roots of Britain's crisis, while Deutscher's assumption of the post-capitalist character of the People's Democracies informed Anderson's revision of the central Marxist tenet of proletarian self emancipation.

As the old New Left had failed as a political movement, and as Anderson had, in any case, not been an uncritical adherent of the dominant political programme within its leadership, it was natural that he would evolve away from some elements of this politics in a reasonable attempt to avoid the repetition of earlier mistakes. The initial vector of this development led him to search the continent for a more sophisticated Marxist theory, out of which he hoped to fashion a more robust socialist perspective for Britain. The original 'Western Marxists' to whom Anderson looked for inspiration were Sartre, Gramsci and Lukács, and he utilised ideas pruned from the work of these thinkers to aid his outline of the history, sociology and politics of Britain. He concluded the strategic argument that was built upon these foundations with the hope that the left, in the short to medium-term, might critically support Harold Wilson's modernising project for Britain, so that, in the longer-term, the possibility of something akin to a proto-Eurocommunist project for Britain could be implemented. However, the reality of Labour in power repelled Anderson, and partly as a reaction to this, he began to gravitate towards classical Marxism. This trajectory was further underpinned by a developing domestic students' and workers' movement, and by what appeared to be a series of victories for the left internationally. Thus, in this period Anderson became convinced by the Leninist case for 'smashing' the bourgeois state as a necessary moment in the transition to socialism; a position which informed his break with his earlier proto-Eurocommunism. However, while he agreed with the universal applicability of Lenin's axiom, he remained convinced of the central importance of Gramsci's insight regarding the divergent structures of bourgeois power in the East and West. Gramsci claimed that the distinct structures of Eastern and Western states entailed the formulation of distinct socialist strategies for these arenas. It was to aid just this project that Anderson continued, in this period, to use *NLR* as a conduit into the Anglophone world for Marxist theory from the continent.

Anderson's attempt, in *Passages* and *Lineages*, to historically ground Gramsci's insights proved to be his most influential, yet perhaps also his most flawed work. Utilising a method that borrowed from a number of leading social theorists including Weber, in addition to Marx, Althusser and Colletti, Anderson produced a stunning work of comparative history that ranged from classical antiquity to the epoch of the bourgeois revolutions, and included substantial essays on both the Asiatic mode of production, and Japanese feudalism. However, while this bravura performance ensured Anderson's academic reputation, it was in its own terms something of a failed project. For the central focus of this work was political rather than academic: he wanted to outline a preliminary, ground-clearing theory of the state in the West to inform revolutionary practice therein. In this sense Anderson's failure to complete the subsequent volumes of his history robbed the published works of their *raison d'être*. Moreover, in as far as the published volumes did touch upon issues of contemporary revolutionary socialist strategic importance, they failed to articulate adequately the distinction between the modern Western capitalist state and the Russian state of 1917.

Partially in response to weaknesses with his application of historical materialism in *Lineages* and *Passages*, in the late 1970s Anderson gravitated towards the more orthodox interpretation of Marxism associated chiefly with G.A. Cohen. However, even at this juncture, the Deutscherite and Western Marxist legacies that he carried with him continued to inform his reception of a more orthodox interpretation of historical materialism. First, Deutscher's interpretation of Stalinism informed his re-assessment of the Marxist concept of agency, and, while Anderson outlined important weaknesses with Thompson's approach to this issue, his own solution saw him substitute, as the goal of socialist agency, a statised economy, for Marx's vision of self-emancipated workers. Second, he reinforced the tendency to downplay the role of workers in the struggle for socialism that was implied in his model of agency, by rejecting the idea that a contradiction might develop between the consciousness of the mass of the British working class and the ideology of Labourism. Moreover, while Cohen may have outlined a powerful defence of the centrality of the 1859 preface to *The Contribution to the Critique of Political Economy* to Marx's *oeuvre*, his Marxism was in many other ways very unorthodox: in particular he dismissed Marx's labour theory of value. Like Cohen, Anderson had his 'doubts' about this element of Marxism, and consequently shifted the emphasis of his reading of Marx's theory of economic crisis from the accumulation process proper to the issue of market failure. This reading of crisis theory generally reinforced his equation of socialism with statism, for it implied that the suppression of the market by the state could overcome the anarchy of capitalist production.

However, two forces were conspiring against the statist model of socialism in this period: the demise of Western Keynesianism, and the collapse of Soviet Communism. For Anderson, the latter process was especially important. In the wake of the Soviet collapse he came to agree with the generality of Fukuyama's claim that no systemic alternatives to capitalism any longer existed. Moreover, he believed that as the Western proletariat was more fragmented than it once had been, it was now less able to operate as a collective agency for the progressive reform of capitalism.

The scene was thus set for his attempt to develop a reformist strategy that would aim at a more progressive model of capitalism than the hegemonic American form, but that was not premised upon working-class agency. Anderson hoped to give this strategy some ideological shape through a fusion of the best elements of liberalism with those of socialism. He saw in the formation of the European Union a possible regional enclave that could protect a regulated European capitalism from global financial storms. This new reformist political perspective was paralleled in his more theoretical work. Indeed, the scourge of post-structuralism became a key theorist of postmodernity, and the author of the seminal obituary of Western Marxism became the champion of Jameson's neo-Adornianism.

The pessimism associated with this perspective should not, however, surprise the student of Anderson's work. For, from his unsuccessful attempts to unite the synchronic and diachronic in his 1962 essay on Portugal, to his utilisation of an undynamic model of conjunctures in his discussions of modernity and postmodernity, Anderson's use of relatively static theoretical frameworks have hampered his elucidation of realistic political perspectives. A consequence of this has been that his strategic political conclusions have been consistently impressionistic. Thus, he became, in turn, too optimistic for the perspectives for revolutionary advance in the aftermath of 1968, and then too dismissive of them once this movement went into decline. Indeed, his more moderate hopes for European reforms in the 1990s, based in any case on a very idiosyncratic interpretation of the strategy of Jacques Delors, looked increasingly forlorn as Germany, Japan and France all entered periods of protracted economic crisis. Indeed, by 2002 he had largely retreated from these earlier hopes for European integration, as the process of European widening seemed to stymie any hopes for the further deepening of the EU.

The political impressionism of Anderson's Marxism was reinforced by his acceptance of Deutscher's argument that events in the twentieth century had overthrown Marx's equation of socialism with the movement of workers from below. This position was built on the premise that the states of the Soviet Union, Eastern Europe and China were in some sense socialist. In the 1960s and '70s, not only was there an upturn in the class struggle across the West, there was also a series of regime changes in the Third World that seemed to suggest that the tide of history was with the 'Communist' system. While Anderson was aware that the proletariat had not played an important role in the creation of any these states – bar, of course, the Soviet Union – he believed that, in the West, the proletariat could both act as such an agency, and could also potentially produce a more democratic form of this type of regime. With the downturn in workers' militancy across the West from the mid 1970s, Anderson's hope for that workers might act as the agent of socialist transformation was thrown into question, but this did not entail his break with the belief that socialism was a viable alternative to capitalism. On the contrary, it was a decade later, with the collapse of the 'Communist' regimes in the East, that Anderson essentially rejected as unviable the idea of the socialist transformation of society. Indeed, since then, whatever movements of the working class have occurred, he has consistently denied that these could act as the basis for a political break with capitalism. Thus, as the Soviet Union collapsed, so too did his confidence in the socialist alternative to capitalism.

How are socialists to respond to this diagnosis of the present conjuncture?

CONCLUSION

My analysis suggests that it would be unwise for Marxists to follow Anderson in his diagnosis for a number of reasons. First, he has consistently assumed an undynamic conceptualisation of the political conjuncture. Second, he has consistently held a reified conception of the relationship between class and class consciousness, particularly in regard to the English working class. Third, his Deutscherism has meant that he has tended to transpose his conceptualisation of the key locus of the class struggle from the point of production to the Berlin Wall. Taken together these three factors have reinforced the sense of overwhelming pessimism that one gets when reading Anderson's recent work. It is to his credit, given this perspective, that he remains a staunch opponent of capitalism whose political critiques of those in power repay reading by even the most optimistic anti-capitalist. However, despite the power of some of these recent critiques of the ruling order, socialists must reject his political perspective if they are to avoid gross strategic errors. If Anderson's perspective is correct then the only principled position for a socialist to take would be one of stoical opposition to capitalism. If, however, Anderson is wrong, and the events such as the strikes in France in 1995, the anti-capitalist demonstration in Seattle in 1999, and the revolutionary upsurge in Argentina in 2002, reflect the potential for workers and others to unite together in struggles against capitalism, and through those struggles to develop the kinds of consciousness and organisations necessary to begin the process of developing the mass international opposition to neo-liberalism into a struggle for socialism, then socialists must involve themselves in this movement with the goal of aiding its evolution in a socialist direction. Indeed, once we reject any equation, however critical, of Stalinism and socialism then we might see that the parameters within which history can turn at the present conjuncture are considerably broader than Anderson's assessment allows.

Perhaps the criticism that Göran Therborn made of Marcuse's *One-Dimensional Man* can be usefully recycled as an evaluation of Anderson's latest historical perspectives. After recognising the exemplary nature of Marcuse's political record, Therborn argued that the main weakness with his book, written before the upsurge of militancy in the 1960s and 1970s, 'is not his failure to see these future tendencies, but the fact that his analysis provides no concepts by means of which he might have discovered them' (Therborn 1977b, 112). In the 1970s Anderson thought Therborn's argument important enough to publish it twice: first in *NLR* and then in *NLB* volume *Western Marxism: A Critical Reader*. Today, he might do well to re-consider these remarks, for they suggest that a willingness to explore actual and potential upsurges from below is a more creative approach than one that insists that 'what moves is only the market'.

CHRONOLOGY

1955
April – Bandung Conference.

1956
February – Twentieth congress of the Communist Party of the Soviet Union. In a 'secret session' Khruschev details some of Stalin's crimes.
July – Nasser nationalises Suez Canal.
July – Launch of *The Reasoner*.
October – Insurrection in Budapest; Anglo-French attack on Egypt.
November – Soviet invasion of Hungary.

1957
Spring – Launch of *Universities and Left Review*.
May – Launch of *New Reasoner*.
November – UK explodes its first megaton H-bomb.

1958
February – CND launched.
September – Notting Hill Race Riots.

1959
January – Cuban Revolution.

1960
January– First Issue of *NLR*, formed after merger of *New Reasoner* and *Universities and Left Review*.
October – Labour Party conference at Scarborough votes against the Party leadership to support unilateral nuclear disarmament.

1961
April – Bay of Pigs invasion of Cuba by CIA backed exiles.
October – Right overturns motion on unilateral nuclear disarmament at the Labour Party Conference.

1963
January – Sino-Soviet split becomes open.
February – Harold Wilson elected leader of Labour Party.
1964
August – Gulf of Tonkin incident – pretext for US stepping up its involvement in Vietnam.
October – Labour Party wins British General Election.
1966
March – Harold Wilson wins his second General Election in UK.
May – National Seamen's Strike begins.
June – Harold Wilson launches a red scare against National Union of Seamen.
August – Beginning of Cultural Revolution in China.
1967
March – Students occupy LSE.
May – May Day Manifesto launched by old New Left figures.
October – Anti-Vietnam War demonstration clashes with police at Grosvenor Square.
1968
January – Tet Offensive in Vietnam.
April – Enoch Powell's 'Rivers of Blood' speech.
May – *Black Dwarf* first published.
May – Clashes between students and police in France acts as catalyst that leads to a ten million strong general strike.
August – Russian invasion of Czechoslovakia.
October – Civil Rights march in Derry attacked by police.
1969
January – Publication of *In Place of Strife*, Labour's anti-union manifesto.
April – De Gaulle resigns as President of France.
August – First British Troops sent to Northern Ireland.
1970
June – Tory Party wins British General Election.
1972
Summer – Series of strikes in Britain on Docks, in Mines and elsewhere mark highpoint of post-war militancy.
1973
March – Final US troops leave Vietnam.
September – Military Coup in Chile.
1974
February/October – Labour Party wins two general election in Britain on back of high levels of working-class militancy.
April – Overthrow of fascist government in Portugal.
1975

April – First free elections in post-fascist Portugal.
November – Death of Franco.
1976
June – First election in post-fascist Spain.
1978
December – First democratic government in post-fascist Spain.
December – 'Winter of Discontent' begins in Britain.
1979
May – Thatcher wins British General Election.
December – Soviet Invasion of Afghanistan.
1980
September – Formation of Solidarity in Poland.
November – Reagan elected President of USA.
1981
May – Mitterrand becomes President of France.
1983
April – Thatcher wins second term for Tories.
1984
March – Beginning of Miners' Strike in Britain.
1985
March – Gorbachev becomes First Secretary of CPSU and announces programme of Glasnost and Perestroika.
March – End of Miners' Strike in Britain.
1987
June – Thatcher wins third term as British Prime Minister.
December – Beginning of First Intifada in Palestine.
1988
May – Soviet Troops begin to pull out of Afghanistan.
1989
June – Tiananmen Square massacre in Beijing.
July – First Solidarity government in Poland.
November – Fall of Berlin Wall.
December – Overthrow of Ceausescu regime in Romania.
1990
March – Poll Tax Riot in London.
August – Iraq occupies Kuwait.
1991
January – Gulf War.
1992
April – Major's victory in British General Election.
May – LA Riots.
September – Sterling falls out of ERM.

October/November – Pit closure announcement, followed by two massive pro-miners demonstrations in Britain.
1993
August – First Oslo Peace Agreement signed.
1995
September – Second Oslo Peace Agreement signed.
December – Public Sector Strikes in France.
1997
May – Election of Blair Government in Britain.
1998
May – Indonesian Revolution.
September – Asian economic crisis.
September – SPD win German general election.
1999
March – Oskar Lafontaine forced to resign from post as German finance minister after pressure from business circles.
March – Nato attacks Serbia.
November – Seattle anti-capitalist demonstration.
2000
January – Re-launch of *NLR*.
October – Revolution in Serbia.
October – Second Intifada begins in Palestine.
November – Bush 'wins' US presidential election.
2001
June – Blair's re-election as British Prime Minister.
July – Genoa Social Forum.
September – 9/11 attack.
October – USA and Britain attack Afghanistan.
December – Revolutionary movement erupts in Argentina.
2002
February – World Social Forum at Porto Alegre.
November – European Social Forum in Florence.
2003
February – Mass International Anti-War Protests.
March – Anglo-American Invasion of Iraq.
November – European Social Forum in Paris.
2004
January – World Social Forum in Mumbai.
January – Launch of Respect in UK.

BIBLIOGRAPHY

Works by Anderson

All books published in London unless otherwise stated.

Unpublished Essays

        1964   *Conspectus* 7pp
        1968/9 *Document A: Theory and Practice – The Coupure of May* 16pp
        1968/9 *Document B: Ten Theses* 19pp
        1969   *The Founding Moment* 137pp
        1974   *A Decennial Report* 131pp
        1980   *NLR 1975 – 1980* 92pp
        1983   *NLR 1980 – 1983* 72pp
        1983   *Charter* 11pp

Articles published under a pseudonym
Merton, R. (1968) 'Comment' *NLR* 47.
Merton, R. (1968) 'Comment' *NLR* 59.

Books and Essays by Perry Anderson
Anderson, P. (1961a) 'Sweden: Mr. Crosland's Dreamland I' *NLR* 7.
Anderson, P. (1961b) 'Sweden: Mr. Crosland's Dreamland II' *NLR* 9.
Anderson, P. (1962a) 'Introduction to the debate on the PCI' *NLR* 13/14.
Anderson, P. (1962b) 'Portugal and the End of Ultra Colonialism I.' *NLR* 15.
Anderson, P. (1962c) 'Portugal and the End of Ultra Colonialism II.' *NLR* 16.
Anderson, P. (1962d) 'Portugal and the End of Ultra Colonialism III.' *NLR* 17.
Anderson, P. (1964) 'Critique of Wilsonism' *NLR* 27.
Anderson, P. (1965a) 'The Left in the Fifties' *NLR* 29.
Anderson, P. (1965b) 'Problems of Socialist Strategy' in *NLR* ed. *Towards Socialism* Fontana Books.

Anderson, P. (1966) 'Socialism and Pseudo-Empiricism' *NLR* 35.
Anderson, P. (1967) 'The Limits and Possibilities of Trade Union Action' in Blackburn, R. & Cockburn, A. ed. *The Incompatibles* Harmondsworth, Penguin1967.
Anderson, P. (1968a) 'Introduction to Gramsci' *NLR* 51.
Anderson, P. (1968b) Editorial Introduction *NLR* 52.
Anderson, P. (1974a) *Passages From Antiquity to Feudalism* NLB.
Anderson, P. (1974b) *Lineages of the Absolutist State* NLB.
Anderson, P. (1976a) *Considerations on Western Marxism* NLB.
Anderson, P. (1976b) 'The Antinomies of Antonio Gramsci' *NLR* 100.
Anderson, P (1978) 'The Strategic Option: Some Questions' Liebich, A. ed. (1978) *The Future of Socialism in Europe* Montreal.
Anderson, P. (1980) *Arguments Within English Marxism* Verso.
Anderson, P. (1981) 'Communist Party History' Samuel, R. ed. (1981)*People's History and Socialist Theory* Routledge.
Anderson, P. (1983) *In the Tracks of Historical Materialism* Verso.
Anderson, P. (1984) 'Trotsky's Interpretation of Stalinism' Ali, T. ed. (1984) *The Stalinist Legacy* Harmondsworth, Penguin.
Anderson, P (1986) 'Social Democracy Today' *Against the Current* 1:6.
Anderson, P. (1987) 'The Myth of Hellenism' *Guardian*, 13th March 1987.
Anderson, P. (1988) 'Discussion' in Nelson, C. & Gossberg, L. eds. (1988) *Marxism and the Interpretation of Culture* Macmillan
Anderson, P. (1991) 'Gorbachev's Failure & Success' *London Review of Books* 26th Oct 1991.
Anderson, P. (1992a) *English Questions* Verso.
Anderson, P. (1992b) *A Zone of Engagement* Verso.
Anderson, P. (1992c) 'High Jinks at the Plaza' *London Review of Books* 22nd Oct 1992.
Anderson, P. (1992d) 'Origins of the Present Crisis' in Anderson 1992a. First published in *NLR* 24 1964, and reprinted in *NLR* ed. *Towards Socialism* 1965.
Anderson, P. (1992e) 'Components of a National Culture' in Anderson 1992a. First published in *NLR* 50 1968, and reprinted in Cockburn, A. & Blackburn, R. (1969) *Student Power* Harmondsworth, Penguin.
Anderson, P. (1992f) 'The Notion of a Bourgeois Revolution' in Anderson 1992a. First presented to an academic conference in 1976.
Anderson P. (1992g) 'The Figures of Descent' in Anderson 1992a. First published in *NLR* 161 1987.
Anderson P. (1992h) 'A Culture in Contraflow' in Anderson 1992a. First published in two parts in *NLR* 180 and *NLR* 182 1990.
Anderson P. (1992i) 'The Light of Europe' in Anderson 1992a.
Anderson P. (1992j) 'Geoffrey de Ste. Croix and the Ancient World' in Anderson 1992b. First published in *History Workshop Journal* 16 1983.

Anderson P. (1992k) 'Marshall Berman: Modernity and Revolution' in Anderson 1992b. First published in *NLR* 144 1984.

Anderson P. (1992m) 'The Legacy of Isaac Deutscher' in Anderson 1992b. First published as an introduction to Deutscher, I. (1985) *Marxism, Wars and Revolutions* Verso.

Anderson P. (1992n) 'Michael Mann's Sociology of Power' in Anderson 1992b. First published in *Times Literary Supplement* 12th –18th December 1986.

Anderson P. (1992p) 'The Affinities of Noberto Bobbio' in Anderson 1992b. First published in *NLR* 170 1988.

Anderson P. (1992q) 'Roberto Unger and the Politics of Empowerment' in Anderson 1992b. First published in *Times Literary Supplement* 13th –19th January 1989, and then expanded in *NLR* 173 1989.

Anderson P. (1992r) 'WG Runciman: A New Evolutionism' in Anderson 1992b. First published in *London Review of Books* 6th July 1989.

Anderson P. (1992s) 'On Emplotment: Andreas Hillgruber' in Anderson 1992b. First presented to an academic conference in 1990.

Anderson P. (1992t) 'Max Weber and Ernest Gellner: Science, Politics, Enchantment' in Anderson 1992b. First published in Hall, J. & Jarvie, I. eds. (1992) *Transition to Modernity* Cambridge, Cambridge University Press.

Anderson P. (1992u) 'Nocturnal Enquiry: Carlo Ginsburg' in Anderson 1992b. First published in *London Review of Books* 8th November 1990.

Anderson P. (1992v) 'The Pluralism of Isaiah Berlin' in Anderson 1992b. First published in *London Review of Books* 20th December 1990.

Anderson P. (1992w) 'Fernand Braudel and National Identity' in Anderson 1992b. First published in *London Review of Books* 9th May 1990.

Anderson P. (1992x) 'The Ends of History' in Anderson 1992b.

Anderson, P. (1992y) 'The Intransigent Right at the End of the Century' *London Review of Books* 24th September 1992.

Anderson P. (1993a) 'The Prussia of the East?' Miyoshi & Harootunian ed. 1993 Durham, N.C. London.

Anderson P. (1993b) 'Diary' *London Review of Books* 21st Oct 1993.

Anderson P. (1993c) 'Maurice Thompson's War' *London Review of Books* 4th Nov 1993.

Anderson, P. (1994a) 'Darkness Falls' *Guardian* 8th Nov 1994.

Anderson, P. (1994b) 'The Dark Side of Brazilian Conviviality' *London Review of Books* 24th Nov 1994.

Anderson, P. (1994c) 'Comment: Power, Politics and the Enlightenment' Miliband, D. ed. (1994) *Reinventing the Left* Cambridge, Polity.

Anderson, P. (1994d) 'Introduction to Mapping the West European Left' in Anderson and Camiller ed. Verso.

Anderson, P. (1994e) 'On John Rawls' *Dissent* Winter 1994

Anderson, P. (1996a) Introduction *London Review of Books: An Anthology*

Verso.

Anderson P. (1996b) 'Diary' *London Review of Books* 17th Oct 1996.

Anderson, P. (1997a) 'Under the Sign of the Interim' Anderson, P. & Gowan, P. eds. (1997) *The Question of Europe* Verso.

Anderson, P. (1997b) 'The Europe to Come' in Anderson, P. & Gowan, P. (eds.) (1997) *The Question of Europe* Verso.

Anderson P (1998a) *The Origins of Postmodernity* Verso.

Anderson P (1998b) 'A Belated Encounter (Part I)' *London Review of Books* 30th July 1998.

Anderson P (1998c) 'A Belated Encounter (Part II)' *London Review of Books* 20th August 1998.

Anderson P (1998d) 'Foreword' to Jameson, F. (1998) *The Cultural Turn* Verso.

Anderson, P. (1998e) 'A Sense of the Left' *NLR* 231.

Anderson, P. (1998f) 'A Reply to Noberto Bobbio' *NLR* 231.

Anderson, P. (1999a)'The German Question' *London Review of Books* 7th January 1999.

Anderson, P. (1999b) 'A Ripple of the Polonaise' *London Review of Books* 25th November 1999.

Anderson, P. (2000) 'Renewals' *NLR* 2:1.

Anderson, P. (2001a) 'Testing Formula Two' *NLR* 2:8.

Anderson, P. (2001b) 'Scurrying Towards Bethlehem' *NLR* 2:10.

Anderson, P. (2001c) 'On Sebastiano Timpanaro' *London Review of Books* 10th May 2001.

Anderson, P. (2001d) 'Reflections on the Left from the Left' at http://globetrotter.berkeley.edu/Elberg/Anderson/anderson-con0.html.

Anderson, P. (2002a) 'Land Without Prejudice' *London Review of Books* 21st March 2002.

Anderson, P. (2002b) 'Internationalism: A Breviary' *NLR* 14 March/April 2002.

Anderson, P. (2002c) 'The Age of EJH' *London Review of Books* 3rd October 2002.

Anderson, P. (2002d) 'Confronting Defeat: Eric Hobsbawm's Tetralogy' *London Review of Books* 17th October 2002.

Anderson, P. (2002e) 'Force and Consent' *NLR* 2: 17

Anderson, P. (2002f) 'The Cardoso Legacy' *London Review of Books* 12th Dec 2002

Anderson, P. (2003) 'Casuistries of Peace and War' *London Review of Books* 6th March 2003

Anderson, P. (2004) 'The River of Time' *NLR* 2:26

Anderson, P. & Blackburn, R. (1960) 'Cuba free territory of America.' *New University* 4.

Anderson, P. & Blackburn, R. (1968) 'The Marxism of Regis Debray' *Monthly*

Review Vol. 20 No 3.
Anderson, P. & Camillar, P. eds. (1994) *Mapping the West European Left* London, Verso.
Anderson, P. & Gowan, P. (eds.) (1997) *The Question of Europe* Verso.
Anderson, P. & Hall, S. (1961) 'The Politics of the Common Market' *NLR* 10.

Other Works

Achcar, G. (2000) 'The 'historical pessimism' of Perry Anderson' *International Socialism* 88.
Aglietta, M. (1979) *A Theory of Capitalist Regulation* NLB.
Ahmad, A. (1992) *In Theory* Verso.
Alexander, A. (2001) 'The Crisis in the Middle East' *International Socialism* 2: 93
Ali, T. ed. (1984) *The Stalinist Legacy* Harmondsworth, Penguin.
Ali, T. (1987) *Street Fighting Years* Collins.
Althusser, L. (1969) *For Marx* Verso.
Althusser, L. (1970) *Reading Capital* Verso.
Aronowitz, S. (1996) *The Death and Rebirth of American Radicalism* Routledge.
Aronson, R. (1985) 'Historical Materialism, Answer to Marxism's Crisis.' *NLR* 152.
Barker, C. (1982) *The Background and Significance of the Meiji Restoration of 1868* Unpublished mimeograph Manchester Polytechnic.
Barker, C. & Nicholls, D. (1988) *The Development of British Capitalist Society: A Marxist Debate* Northern Marxists Historians Group, Manchester.
Barret Brown, M. (1978) 'Considerations on Western Marxism' *Capital and Class* 5.
Barret Brown, M. (1988) 'Away with all the Great Arches' *NLR* 167.
Barnett, A. (1969) 'A Revolutionary Student Movement' *NLR* 53.
Barnett, A. (1973) 'Class Struggle and the Heath Government' *NLR* 77.
Barnett, A. (1976) 'Raymond Williams and Marxism' *NLR* 99.
Barnett, A. (1982) *Iron Britannia* Allison & Busby. A slightly shorter version of this essay was originally published as *NLR* 134.
Barnett, A. ed. (1994) *Power and the Throne* Vintage.
Barnett, A. (1997) *This Time: Our Constitutional Revolution* Vintage.
Bellamy Foster, J. (1990) 'Liberal Practicality and the US Left' *Socialist Register* 1990.
Benjamin, W. (1979) *One-Way Street* Verso.
Benn, T. (1982) *Parliament, People and Power* Verso.
Berman, M. (1984) 'The Signs in the Street: A Response to Perry Anderson' *NLR* 144.

Birchall, I. (1981) 'The Autonomy of Theory' *International Socialism* 2: 10.

Blackburn, R. (1977) 'What is the 'Democratic Road' to Socialism' *International* Vol. 3, No 4 Summer 1977.

Blackburn, R. & Cockburn, A. (1967) *The Incompatibles* Harmondsworth, Penguin.

Blackburn, R. (1971) 'The Heath Government' *NLR* 70.

Blackburn, R. (1974) 'The Test In Portugal' *NLR* 87/8.

Blackburn, R. ed. (1977) *Revolution and Class Struggle* Fontana.

Blackburn, R. ed. (1978) *Ideology in Social Science* Fontana.

Blackburn, R. (1980) 'Theory & Experience 4' *New Statesman* 18th July 1980.

Blackledge, P. (2000a) 'Perry Anderson and the End of History' in *Historical Materialism 7* Autumn 2000.

Blackledge, P. (2000b) 'Perry Anderson's Journey to Postmodernity' *Studies in Marxism* 7.

Blackledge, P. (2001a) 'Rational Capitalist Concerns: William Cail and the Amateurism of the Rugby Football Union in the 1890s' *International Journal of the History of Sport* June 2001.

Blackledge, P. (2001b) 'Realism and Renewals' *Contemporary Politics* Dec 2001.

Blackledge, P. (2002) 'Marxist Interpretations of Thatcherism' in Cowling, M. ed. *The Eighteenth Brumaire: (Post) Modern Interpretations* London, Pluto Press 2002.

Blackledge, P. (2003) 'Political Marxism: Towards an Immanent Critique' *Studies in Marxism* 9.

Bloch, E. *et al* (1977) *Aesthetics and Politics* NLB.

Bobbio, N (1998) 'At the Beginning of History' *NLR* 231.

Boggs, C. (1976) *Gramsci's Marxism* Pluto Press.

Boggs, C. (1995) *The Socialist Tradition* Routledge.

Bourdieu, P. (1998) *Acts of Resistance* Polity.

Bourdieu, P. (2000) 'The Politics of Protest' *Socialist Review 242* June 2000.

Brecher, J. (1997) *Strike* Boston, South End Press

Brenner, R. (1985) 'Agrarian Class Structures and Economic Development in Pre-Industrial Europe' TH Aston and CHE Philpin eds. 1985 Cambridge, Cambridge University Press.

Brenner, R. (1989) 'Bourgeois Revolution and the Transition to Capitalism' Brier, AL. *et al* 1989 Cambridge, Cambridge University Press.

Brenner, R. (1993) *Merchants and Revolution* Cambridge, Cambridge University Press.

Brenner, R. (1998) 'The Economics of Global Turbulence: A Special Report on the World Economy 1950-98' *NLR* 229.

Brenner, R. (2002) *The Boom and the Bubble* Verso.

Brenner, R. & Glick, M. (1991) The Regulation Approach: Theory and History *NLR* 188.

Brier, AL. *et al* (1989) *The First Modern Society* Cambridge, Cambridge University Press.
Bukharin, N. (1982) *Selected Writings* Nottingham, Spokesman.
Callinicos, A. (1980) 'Theory & Experience 3' New Statesman 27 June 1980.
Callinicos, A. (1984) 'Perry Anderson and Western Marxism' *International Socialism* 2: 23.
Callinicos, A. (1987) *Making History*. Cambridge, Cambridge University Press.
Callinicos, A. (1988) 'Exception or Symptom' *NLR* 169.
Callinicos, A. (1989) *Against Postmodernism* Cambridge, Polity.
Callinicos, A. (1990) *Trotskyism* Buckingham, Open University Press.
Callinicos, A. (1997) 'Europe: The Mounting Crisis' *International Socialism* 2: 75.
Cammack, P. (1997) 'Cardoso's Political Project in Brazil' *Socialist Register* 1997.
Carlin, N. & Birchall, I. (1983) 'Kinnock's Favourite Marxist: Eric Hobsbawm and the Working Class' *International Socialism* 2: 21.
Carr, EH. (1969) *The Interregnum* Harmondsworth, Penguin.
Chomsky, N. (2000) 'Globalising Resistance to Corporate Power' *Socialist Worker* 1696 13th May 2000.
Chossudovsky, M. (1997) *The Globalization of Poverty* Zed.
Chun, L. (1994) *The British New Left* Edinburgh University Press.
Clark, T.J. (2000) 'Origins of the Present Crisis' *NLR* 2:2.
Cliff, T. (1979) 'The Balance of Class Forces in Britain Today' *International Socialism* 2: 6.
Cliff, T. (1985) 'Patterns of Mass Strike' *International Socialism* 2: 29.
Cliff, T. (1988) *State Capitalism in Russia* Bookmarks. First published in 1948.
Cliff, T. & Gluckstein, D. (1996) *The Labour Party: A Marxist History* London, Bookmarks
Coates, D. (1975) *The Labour Party and the Struggle for Socialism* Cambridge University Press.
Coates, D. (1980) *Labour in Power* Longman
Cockburn, A. & Blackburn, R. (1969) *Student Power* Harmondsworth, Penguin.
Cohen, G.A. (1978) *Karl Marx's Theory of History: A Defence* Oxford University Press.
Cohen, G.A. (1981) The Labour Theory of Value and the concept of Exploitation, in Steedman, I. *et al* (1981) *The Value Controversy* Verso.
Colletti, L. (1972) 'Marxism: Science or Revolution' Blackburn ed. (1972) *Ideology and Social Science* Fontana.
Colletti, L. (1974a) *From Rousseau to Lenin* New York, Monthly Review Press.
Colletti, L. (1974b) 'A Philosophical and Political Interview' *NLR* ed. 1977 Verso.

Davidson, N. (1999) 'In Perspective: Tom Nairn' *International Socialism* 2:82
Davis, M. (1982) 'Nuclear Imperialism and Extended Deterrence' *NLR* ed. 1982 Verso.
Davis, M. (1986) *Prisoners of the American Dream* Verso.
Davis, M. (1990) *City of Quartz* Verso.
Debray, R. (1968) *Revolution in the Revolution* Harmondsworth, Penguin.
Debray, R. (1973) *Strategy for Revolution* Harmondsworth, Penguin.
Debray, R. (1979) 'A Modest Contribution' *NLR* 115.
Descombes, V. (1980) *Modern French Philosophy* Cambridge University Press
Deutscher, I. (1960) *The Great Contest* Oxford University Press.
Deutscher, I. (1972) *Marxism in Our Time* London, Jonathon Cape.
Deutscher, I. (1987a) *Trotsky: The Prophet Armed* Oxford University Press.
Deutscher, I. (1987b) *Trotsky: The Prophet Unarmed* Oxford University Press.
Deutscher, I. (1987c) *Trotsky: The Prophet Outcast* Oxford University Press.
Deutscher, I. (1968) *Stalin* Harmondsworth, Penguin.
Deutscher, I. (1984) *Marxism, Wars and Revolutions* Verso.
Draper, H. (1977) *Karl Marx's Theory of Revolution Vol. 1* New York, Monthly Review Press.
Draper, H. (1978) *Karl Marx's Theory of Revolution Vol. 2* New York, Monthly Review Press.
Dworkin, D. (1997) *Cultural Marxism in Post War Britain* Duke University Press.
Eagleton, T. (1976) *Criticism and Ideology* Verso.
Eagleton, T. (1986) *Against the Grain* Verso.
Eagleton, T. (1990) *The Ideology of the Aesthetic* Oxford, Blackwell.
Eagleton, T. (1991) *Ideology* Verso
Eagleton, T. (1992) 'Old Peculiar' *Guardian* 1 Oct 1992.
Eagleton, T. (1996) *The Illusions of Postmodernism* Oxford, Blackwell.
Eagleton, T. (2000) *The Idea of Culture* Oxford, Blackwell.
Eagleton, T. & Bourdieu, P. (1994) 'Doxa and Common Life: An Interview' Zizek, S. 1994.
Elliott, G. (1987) *Althusser: The Detour of Theory* Verso.
Elliott, G. (1995) 'Olympus Mislaid' *Radical Philosophy* 71.
Elliott, G. (1998) *Perry Anderson: The Merciless Laboratory of History* University of Minnesota Press.
Foot, P. (1967) 'The Seamen's struggle' Blackburn, R. & Cockburn, A. eds. 1967 *The Incompatibles* Harmondsworth, Penguin.
Foot, P. (1968) *The Politics of Harold Wilson* Harmondsworth, Penguin.
Fraser, R. (1988) *1968: A Student Generation in Revolt* Chatto & Windus.
Fukuyama, F. (1992) *The End of History and the Last Man* New York, Free Press.
Fulbrook, M. & Skocpol, T. (1984) 'Destined Pathways' Skocpol ed. 1984

Cambridge, Cambridge University Press.
Geras, N. (1976) *The Legacy of Rosa Luxemburg* Verso
Geras, N. (1977) 'Althusser's Marxism' in *NLR* ed. *Western Marxism: A Critical Reader* NLB.
Ginsborg, P. (2001) *Italy and its Discontents* Harmondsworth, Penguin.
Glucksmann, A. (1977) 'A Ventriloquist Structuralism' *NLR* ed. *Western Marxism: A Critical Reader* NLB.
Goldthorpe, J. & Lockwood, D. (1963) 'Affluence and Class structure' *Sociological Review*, July, 1963.
Gramsci, A. (1971) *Selections from the Prison Notebooks* Lawrence and Wishart.
Gramsci, A. (1977) *Selections from Political Writings 1910-1920* Lawrence and Wishart.
Gramsci, A. (1978) *Selections from Political Writings 1921-1926* Lawrence and Wishart.
Habermas, J. (1992) *Autonomy and Solidarity* Verso.
Hall, S. (1980) 'Theory & Experience' *New Statesman* 30 May 1980.
Hall, S. et al ed. (1980) *Culture, Media, Language* Routledge.
Hall, S. (1983) 'The Great Moving Right Show' Hall, S. & Jacques, M. ed. (1983) *The Politics of Thatcherism* Lawrence and Wishart.
Hall, S. (1989) 'The First New Left' in Archer, R. *et al Out of Apathy* Verso.
Hall, S. & Jacques, M. ed. (1983) *The Politics of Thatcherism* Lawrence and Wishart.
Hallas, D. (1977) 'How Can We Move On?' *Socialist Register* 1977
Halliday, F. (1976) 'Marxist Analysis and Post Revolutionary China' *NLR* 100.
Halliday, F. (1982) 'The Sources of the New Cold War' *NLR* ed. (1982) *Exterminism and Cold War* Verso.
Halliday, F. (1986) *The Making of the Second Cold War* Verso.
Halliday, F. (1994) *Rethinking International Relations* Macmillan.
Harman, C. (1982) *The Lost Revolution* Bookmarks.
Harman, C. (1985) '1984 and the Shape of Things to Come' *International Socialism* 2:29
Harman, C. (1988) *The Fire Last Time* Bookmarks.
Harrison, R. (1965) *Before the Socialists* Routledge.
Haynes, M. (2002) *Russia: Class and Power 1917-2000* Bookmarks
Heath, A. et al (2001) *The Rise of New Labour* Oxford, Oxford University Press.
Hill, C. (1990) *A Nation of Change and Novelty* Routledge.
Hill, C. (1997) *Intellectual Origins of the English Revolution Revisited* Oxford University Press.
Hilton, R. ed. (1976) *The Transition from Feudalism to Capitalism* NLB.
Hinton, J. (1965) 'The Labour Aristocracy' *NLR* 32.
Hinton, J. (1989) *Protests and Visions* Radius.
Hirst, P. (1985) *Marxism and Historical Writing* Routledge.

Hobsbawm, E. (1969) *Industry and Empire* Harmondsworth, Penguin.
Hodgson, G. (1974) 'The Theory of the Falling Rate of Profit' *NLR* 84.
Holton, R. (1985) *The Transition From Feudalism to Capitalism* London, Macmillan.
Hood, S. (1980) *On Television* Pluto Press.
Hughes, J. (1964) 'An Economic Policy for Labour' *NLR* 24.
Hutton, W. (1995) *The State We're In* Jonathan Cape.
Inglis, F. (1998) 'Marxism's Major General' *Times Higher Educational Supplement* 6th November 1998.
Jacoby, R. (1987) *The Last Intellectuals* New York, Basic Books.
Jameson, F. (1981) *The Political Unconscious* Cornell University Press.
Jameson, F. (1990) *Late Marxism: Adorno, or, the Persistence of the Dialectic* Verso.
Jameson, F. (1991) *Postmodernism, or, The Cultural Logic of Late Capitalism* Verso .
Jameson, F. (1998) *The Cultural Turn* Verso.
Jessop, B. *et al* (1988) *Thatcherism* Verso.
Jessop, B *et al* (1990) 'Farewell to Thatcherism? Liberalism and 'New Times'' *NLR* 179
Johnson, R. (1980) 'Barrington Moore, Perry Anderson and English Social Development' Hall, S. *et al* ed. (1980) *Culture, Media, Language* Routledge.
Kagarlitsky, B. (2000) 'The Suicide of *New Left Review*' *International Socialism* 2: 88
Kaye, H. (1995) *The British Marxist Historians* London, Macmillan.
Kellner, D. (1995) 'The Obsolescence of Marxism?' in Magnus, B. & Cullenberg, S. eds. (1995) *Whither Marxism?* Routledge.
Kelly, J. (1988) *Trade Unions and Socialist Politics* Verso.
Kenny, M. (1995) *The First New Left* London, Lawrence & Wishart.
Kenny, M. (1999) 'Marxism and Regulation Theory' in Gamble, A. *et al* eds. *Marxism and Social Science* Macmillan.
Krasso, N. (1967) 'Trotsky's Marxism' *NLR* 44.
Krasso, N. (1968) 'Reply to Ernest Mandel' *NLR* 48.
Kozak, M. (1995) 'How it All Began' *Socialist Register* 1995.
Lebowitz, M (1999) 'In Brenner Everything is Reversed' *Historical Materialism* 4 Summer 1999.
Lenin, V. (1970) *The April Theses* Moscow, Progress Publishers.
Liebich, A. ed. (1978) *The Future of Socialism in Europe* Montreal.
Looker, B. (1985) 'Class Conflict and Socialist Advance in Contemporary Britain' in D. Coates *et al* ed. *A Socialist Anatomy of Britain* Cambridge, Polity.
Looker, R. (1988) 'Shifting Trajectories' Barker, C & Nicholls, D. ed. 1988 Northern Marxists Historians Group, Manchester.
Löwy, M. (1979) *Georg Lukács-From Romanticism to Bolshevism* NLB.

Lukács, G. (1971) *History and Class Consciousness* Merlin.
Lukács, G. (1977) *Lenin* NLB.
Lukács, G. (1980) *The Destruction of Reason* Merlin.
Luxemburg, R. (1986) *The Mass Strike* Bookmarks.
McCarney, J. (1990) *Social Theory and the Crisis of Marxism* Verso .
McNally, D. (1997) 'Language, History and Class Struggle' in Wood, EM. & Foster, JB. ed. 1997 New York, Monthly Review Press.
Maitan, L. (1976) *Party, Army and Masses in China* NLB.
Mahamdallie, H. (1996) 'William Morris and Revolutionary Marxism' *International Socialism* 2: 71.
Mandel, E. (1968) 'Trotsky's Marxism: An Anti-Critique' *NLR* 47.
Mandel, E. (1969) 'Trotsky's Marxism: A Rejoinder' *NLR* 56.
Mandel, E. (1976) 'Revolutionary Strategy in Europe' *NLR* 100.
Mandron, G. (2001) 'Redividing Palestine?' *NLR* 2:10
Mann, M. (1984) 'Capitalism and Militarism' Shaw ed. 1984.
Mann, M. (1985) *Socialism Can Survive* Blackrose.
Mann, M. (1986) *The Sources of Social Power* Volume 1 Cambridge, Cambridge University Press.
Manning, B. (1991) *The English People and the English Revolution* Bookmarks.
Manning, B. (1992) *1649 The Crisis of the English Revolution* Bookmarks.
Manning, B. (1994) 'The English Revolution and the Transition from Feudalism to Capitalism' *International Socialism* 2: 63.
Marshall, P. (1989) *Intifada: Zionism, Imperialism and Palestinian Resistance* London, Bookmarks.
Marshall, T.H. and Bottomore, T. (1992) *Citizenship and Social Class* Pluto Press.
Marx, K. (1970) *A Contribution to the Critique of Political Economy* Moscow, Progress Publishers.
Marx, K. (1973) *The Grundrisse* Harmondsworth, Penguin.
Marx, K. (1973) 'The Eighteenth Brumaire of Louis Bonaparte' in D. Fernbach, ed. *Marx: Surveys From Exile* Penguin, Harmondsworth, Penguin.
Marx, K. (1974) *The First International and After* Harmondsworth, Penguin.
Marx, K. (1976) *Capital Volume 1* Harmondsworth, Penguin.
Marx, K. (1978) *Capital Volume 2* Harmondsworth, Penguin.
Marx, K. (1981) *Capital Volume 3* Harmondsworth, Penguin.
Marx, K. & Engels, F. (1967) *The Communist Manifesto* Harmondsworth, Penguin.
Marx, K. & Engels, F. (1970) *The German Ideology* Lawrence and Wishart.
Mayer, A. (1981) *The Persistence of the Old Regime* Croom Helm.
Mayoshi, M. & Harootunian, H. ed. (1993) *Japan in the World* Durham, N.C. London.
Merquior, JG. (1986) *From Paris to Prague* Verso.

Miliband, R. (1972) *Parliamentary Socialism* Merlin.
Miliband, R. (1983) *Class Power & State Power* Verso.
Miliband, R.(1985) 'The New Revisionism in Britain' *NLR* 150.
Moody, K. (1997) *Workers in a Lean World* Verso.
Moody, K. (2001) 'Unions' in Bircham, E. & Charlton, J. eds. (2001) *Anti-Capitalism* Bookmarks.
Morley, D. (1986) *Television, Audiences and Cultural Studies* Routledge.
Moseley, F. (1999) 'The Necessity of Value Theory' *Historical Materialism* 4 Summer 1999.
Nairn, T. (1965b) 'Labour and Imperialism' *NLR* 32.
Nairn, T. (1965c) 'The Nature of the Labour Party' *NLR* ed. Towards Socialism Fontana.
Nairn, T. (1972) 'The Left Against Europe' *NLR* 75
Nairn, T. (1977a) 'The English Working Class' Blackburn, R. ed. *Ideology in Social Science*. First published in two parts in *NLR* 27 & 28 1964.
Nairn, T. (1977b) *The Break up of Britain* NLB.
Neale, R.S. (1985) *Writing Marxist History* Oxford University Press.
New Left Review (1963) 'On internationalism' *NLR* 18.
New Left Review (1963) 'Introduction' *NLR* 20.
New Left Review (1964) 'Divide and Conquer' *NLR* 28.
New Left Review (1967) 'Che' *NLR* 46.
New Left Review (1969) Introduction to Tukhachevsky *NLR* 55.
New Left Review ed. (1965) *Towards Socialism* Fontana.
New Left Review ed. (1977) *Western Marxism a Critical Reader* Verso.
New Left Review ed. (1982) *Exterminism and Cold War* Verso.
Newman, M. (2002) *Ralph Miliband and the Politics of the New Left* Merlin.
Norris, C. (1992) *Uncritical Theory* Lawrence and Wishart.
Osborne, P. (1995) *The Politics of Time* Verso.
Palmer, B. (1990) *Descent into Discourse* Temple University Press, Philadelphia.
Palmer, J. (1988) *Europe Without America* Oxford University Press.
Parker, D. (1996) *Class & State in Ancien Regime France* Routledge.
Parkinson, G. (1977) *Georg Lukács* Routledge.
Philo, G. & Miller, D. (2001) *Market Killing* Longman.
Plekhanov, G. (1940) *The Role of the Individual in History* Lawrence and Wishart.
Poster, M. (1975) *Existential Marxism in Post War France* Princeton.
Poster, M. (1979) *Sartre's Marxism* Pluto Press.
Poulantzas, N. (1967) 'Marxist Political Theory in Great Britain' *NLR* 43.
Poulantzas, N. (1975) *Political Power and Social Class* NLB.
Przeworski, A. (1980) 'Social Democracy as a Historical Phenomenon' *NLR* 122.
Quartim, J. (1971) *Dictatorship and Armed Struggle in Brazil* NLB

Raven, J. (1989) 'British History and the Enterprise Culture' *Past and Present* 123.
Roberts, J. (2000) 'On Autonomy and the Avant-Garde' *Radical Philosophy 103* Sept/Oct 2000.
Rocha, G.M. (2002) 'Neo-Dependency in Brazil' *NLR* 2: 16.
Rosdolsky, R. (1977) *The Making of Marx's Capital* Pluto Press.
Rowthorne, B. (1965) 'The Trap of Incomes Policy' *NLR* 34.
Rowthorne, B. (1980) *Capitalism Conflict and Inflation* Lawrence and Wishart.
Runciman, W.G. (1989) *Confessions of a Reluctant Theorist* Hemel Hempstead.
Salvadori, M. (1978) *Karl Kautsky and the Socialist Revolution* Verso.
Samuel, R. ed. (1981) *People's History and Socialist Theory* Routledge.
Sartre, JP. (1960) 'Cuba' *New University* 4.
Sartre, JP. (1961) *On Cuba* Ballantine Books, New York.
Sartre, JP. (1963) *Search for a method* Vintage Books, New York.
Sartre, JP. (1968) *The Communists and Peace* Hamish Hamilton.
Sartre, JP. (1969) *The Spectre of Stalin* Hamish Hamilton.
Sartre, JP. (1974) *Between Existentialism and Marxism* NLB.
Sartre, JP. (1976) *Critique of Dialectical Reason Vol. 1* Verso.
Sartre, JP. (1991) *Critique of Dialectical Reason Vol. 2* Verso.
Saussure, F.de. (1983) *Course in General Linguistics* Duckworth.
Saville, J. (1959) 'A Note on West Fife' *New Reasoner 10* Autumn 1959.
Saville, J. (1986) 'An Open Conspiracy: Conservative Politics and the Miners' Strike of 1984-5' *Socialist Register* 1985-6.
Saville, J. (1990) 'Marxism Today: An Anatomy' *Socialist Register* 1990.
Saville, J. (2003) *Memoirs From the Left* Merlin Press
Sayer, D. (1991) *Capitalism and Modernity* Routledge.
Sedgwick, P. (1965) 'Theory at the Hour of Wilson' *International Socialism* 1: 22.
Sedgwick, P. (1976) 'The Two New Lefts' Widgery ed. *The Left in Britain* Harmondsworth, Penguin.
Shaw, M. ed. (1984) *War, State and Society* Macmillan.
Skocpol, T. ed. (1984) *Vision & Method in Historical Sociology* Cambridge, Cambridge University Press.
Smith, S. (1994) 'Mistaken Identity' *International Socialism* 2: 62.
Soboul, A. (1977) *The French Revolution* University of California Press.
Ste. Croix, G.E.M. de. (1983) *The Class Struggle in the Ancient Greek World* Duckworth.
Ste. Croix, GEM. de. (1984) 'Class in Marx's Conception of History, Ancient and Modern' *NLR* 146.
Steedman, I. (1975) 'Value, Price and Profit' *NLR* 90.
Steedman, I. *et al* (1981) *The Value Controversy* Verso.
Therborn, G. (1977a) 'The rule of Capital and the rise of democracy' *NLR* 103.

Therborn, G. (1977b) 'The Frankfurt School' in *NLR* ed. *Western Marxism: A Critical Reader* Verso.
Thomas, K. (1975) 'Jumbo History' *New York Review of Books* 17 April 1975.
Thompson, E.P. (1957b) 'Socialism and the Intellectuals' *Universities and Left Review* 1 Spring 1957.
Thompson, E.P. (1959a) 'The New Left' *New Reasoner* 9 Summer 1959.
Thompson, E.P. (1959b) 'A Psessay in Ephology' *New Reasoner* 10 Autumn 1959.
Thompson, E.P. (1959c) 'Commitment in Politics' *Universities and Left Review* 6 Spring 1959.
Thompson, E.P. (1960a) 'Revolution' in Thompson, E.P. ed. (1960) *Out of Apathy* London, Stevens and Sons.
Thompson, E.P. (1960b) 'Revolution Again' *NLR* 6.
Thompson, E.P. (1961a) 'The Long Revolution I ' *NLR* 9.
Thompson, E.P. (1961b) 'The Long Revolution II ' *NLR* 10.
Thompson, E.P. (1976a) 'Romanticism, Utopianism and Moralism: the Case of William Morris' *NLR* 99.
Thompson, E.P. (1976b) 'Through the Smoke of Budapest' in Widgery, D. ed. (1976) *The Left in Britain* Harmondsworth, Penguin
Thompson, E.P. (1977) *William Morris: Romantic to Revolutionary* Merlin.
Thompson, E.P. (1978) *The Poverty of Theory and Other Essays* Merlin.
Thompson, E.P. (1980) *The Making of the English Working Class* Harmondsworth, Penguin.
Thompson, E.P. (1982) 'Notes on Exterminism, the last stage of Civilisation' NLR ed. (1982) *Exterminism and Cold War* Verso.
Thompson, W. (1992) *The Good Old Cause* Pluto Press.
Thompson, W. (1993) *The Long Death of British Labourism* Pluto Press.
Timpanaro, S. (1975) *On Materialism* Verso.
Trotsky, L. (1904) *Our Political Tasks* downloaded from http://www.marxists.org/archive/trotsky/works/1904/1904-pt/index.htm
Trotsky, L. (1971) *1905* Harmondsworth Penguin.
Trotsky, L. (1972a) *The Revolution Betrayed* New York, Pathfinder.
Trotsky, L. (1972b) *The First Five Years of the Communist International Vol.1* New York, Pathfinder.
Trotsky, L. (1972c) *The First Five Years of the Communist International Vol.2* New York, Pathfinder.
Trotsky, L. (1973) *The Spanish Revolution* New York, Pathfinder.
Trotsky, L. (1977) *The History of the Russian Revolution* Pluto Press.
Trotsky, L. (1979) *On France* New York, Pathfinder.
Trotsky, L. (1983) *Marxism and the Trade Unions* New Park.
Trotsky, L. (1987) *The Lessons of October* Bookmarks.
Unger, R.M. (1997) *Politics: The Central Texts* Verso.

Unger, R.M. (1998) *Democracy Realised: The Progressive Alternative* Verso.
United Secretariat of the Fourth International (1978) *Socialist Democracy and the Dictatorship of the Proletariat* Toronto, Vanguard Publications.
Urwin, D. (1995) *The Community of Europe* Longman.
Volosinov, V.N. (1986) *Marxism and the Philosophy of Language* Harvard University Press.
Weber, H. (1978) 'Eurocommunism, Socialism and Democracy' *NLR* 110
Weber. H. (1979) 'Reply to Debray' *NLR* 115
Wickham, C. (1984) 'The Other Transition' *Past and Present* 103
Wickham, C. (1985) 'The Uniqueness of the West' *Journal of Peasant Studies* Vol. 12 No 2 & 3
Wickham, C. (1985) 'Historical Materialism, Historical Sociology' *NLR* 171
Wilcox, J. (1969) 'Two Tactics' *NLR* 53.
Widgery, D. ed.(1974) *The Left in Britain* Harmondsworth, Penguin.
Wiener, M. (1981) *English Culture and the Decline of the Industrial Spirit* Harmondsworth, Penguin.
Williams, G. (1975) *Proletarian Order* Pluto Press.
Williams, R. (1961) *The Long Revolution* Harmondsworth, Penguin.
Williams, R. (1965) 'Towards a Socialist Society' *NLR* ed. *Towards Socialism* 1965
Williams, R. (1977) *Marxism and Literature* Oxford, Oxford University Press.
Williams, R. (1979) *Politics and Letters* Verso.
Williams, R. (1982) *Culture and Society* Howarth Press.
Wohlforth, T. (1994) *The Prophet's Children* Humanities Press, New Jersey.
Wollen, P. (1993) *Raiding the Icebox* Verso.
Wood, E.M. (1991) *The Pristine Culture of Capitalism* Verso.
Wood, E.M. & Foster, J.B. (1997) *In Defence of History* New York, Monthly Review Press.
Worsley, P. (1960) 'Imperial Retreat' Thompson ed. (1960) *Out of Apathy* Stevens and Sons.
Wright, E. Olin. (1979) 'The Value Controversy and Social Research' *NLR* 116.
Wright, E. Olin. (1981) 'Reconsiderations' in Steedman, I. et al *The Value Controversy* Verso.
Wright, P. (1993) 'Beastly Trials of the Last Politburo' *Guardian* 17 July 1993.
Zizek, S. ed. (1994) *Mapping Ideology* Verso.

NOTES

1. Elliott writes that 'Anderson enjoys a salience within Anglophone Marxist culture that is generally acknowledged' (Elliott 1998, xi). Terry Eagleton has described him as 'Britain's most brilliant and erudite Marxist intellectual' (Eagleton 1992), while, in the *Times Higher,* he has been labelled as 'one of the most commanding figures in the British intellectual life of the past 35 years' (Inglis 1998, 31). Alex Callinicos has written that Anderson is 'perhaps the nearest British equivalent to those continental sages who have presided over the academic revival of Marxism during the past two decades' (Callinicos 1984).
2. Both Labour and Communist parties initially opposed CND's demand for unilateral nuclear disarmament (Thompson 1992, 116 and Thompson 1993, 64).
3. While Edward Thompson was not a great admirer of Deutscher, his more critical stance vis-à-vis Stalinism was less influential in the long run. Indeed Miliband, from a Deutscherite position, forced Thompson to tone down the criticisms of Stalinism he made in his essay *The Peculiarities of the English* (Kozak 1995, 274)
4. By this Deutscher meant that the 1960s would be the decade when the Soviet Union would spontaneously reform itself into a democratic socialist republic (Cf Widgery 1976, 132).
5. I am not suggesting that Anderson accepted every detail of Deutscher's analysis, especially in the early days. However, Deutscher's general understanding of the Cold War did provide the framework within which Anderson and the rest of the New Left came to comprehend the experience

of Stalinism.
6   'We shall, of course, speak colloquially about the USSR, China and the associated and disassociated states as 'socialist countries', and we are entitled to do so as long as we intend merely to oppose their regimes to the capitalist states, to indicate their postcapitalist character or to refer to the socialist origins and inspiration of their government and policies' (Deutscher 1972, 239).
7   Edward Thompson strongly criticised the implied reformism of Williams' books, and the explicit reformism of the Pilkington submission (Thompson 1961a & 1961b).
8   The three other members of the committee were Robin Blackburn, Tom Nairn and Gabriel Pearson.
9   Anderson argued that the collapse of the first New Left was a culmination of a process that began with the checking of the advance of CND in the Labour Party and included the decline in sales of *NLR* and the shrinkage in the numbers attending the New Left Clubs (Anderson 1980, 136 & 1965, 16).
10 Anderson's essays in this period were published alongside essays by Tom Nairn, his fellow editor at *NLR*, as part of an attempted coherent political intervention. Considerations of space preclude a discussion of Nairn's contribution to their thesis. For a discussion of Nairn's political evolution see Davidson 1999.
11 Sartre defended this method in *Search for a Method* and *Critique of Dialectical Reason*. In the earlier of these works he attacked what he perceived to be the Platonism of both Stalinist and Trotskyist versions of Marxism, which dissolved real history in a bath of generalising 'sulphuric acid' (Sartre 1963, 44).
12 The most sophisticated critique of this reading of Gramsci was made sometime later by Anderson; Cf chapter four below.
13 Anderson's thesis has been a key influence on both Will Hutton's 1995 bestseller *The State We're In*, and on the programme of Charter 88 (Barnett 1997, 345).
14 Indeed Dorothy Thompson, speaking at The British Marxist Historians and the New Social Movements conference at Edge Hill College in June 2002, recounted the story of the night that she, Edward Thompson, Robin Blackburn and Anderson euphorically celebrated Wilson's victory in the 1963 Labour Party leadership election. More generally Fraser has argued that with the collapse of CND, the defeat of unilateralism and the victory of Wilson 'all hopes were now focused on Labour' (Fraser 1988, 61). In contrast, some of the first New Left did hold out against the tide that pulled the majority into Wilson's orbit. Alasdair MacIntyre wrote in *International Socialism* in late 1963: 'To accept Wilsonism is to have moved to the right at least for the moment, no matter what other professions of socialism are

made' (Quoted in Foot 1968, 317)
15 The word unique is omitted from the 1992 edition (Anderson 1992d, 22).
16 Anderson argued that the British elite represented what Sartre called a 'detotalised totality': 'the dominant bloc in England can be envisaged as a narrow highly structured hegemonic class with beneath it a large diffuse polymorphous reservoir – the entrepreneurial professional and salaried middle classes. The rigorous structure of the one radically destructures the other, as access is always open to the select few from the middle to the upper class: thus the middle class in England have never produced institutions and culture of anything like a comparable distinctiveness and density to the upper or for that matter the working class' (Anderson 1992d, 20). Sartre explained his concept through the example of a market. In a market each person relates to everyone else as other, none are able to see that the market exists through them: they all perceive it as 'exteriority'. So what is in fact a totality is experienced simply as an ensemble of juxtaposed persons. The totality is thus detotalised (Sartre 1976, 285-6).
17 Lukács similarly mapped German ideological characteristics – including a 'servility and petty mean and wretched spirit' – to a certain 'blurring' between feudal and bourgeois elements (Lukács 1980, 42).
18 'It is pedantic, and parochial, to refuse a certain historical truth to the description: in a minimal ideal sense, these countries are socialist' (Anderson 1965b, 225).
19 'What our authors have done is to pick up a casual impression of the trade union conservatism and the intellectual inertia of the past fifteen years, and offer it as an interpretation of a hundred years of history' (Thompson 1978, 176).
20 More generally Thompson criticised Anderson's account of and use of Gramsci's concepts of hegemonic and corporate classes. Anderson was mistaken when he suggested that a hegemonic class had as its antithesis a corporate class, for there did not exist in Gramsci's *oeuvre*, according to Thompson, hegemonic classes but rather states that were hegemonic and whose antithesis were thus 'naked dictatorships' (Thompson 1978, 283-4). Thompson concluded that Anderson, in transposing the concepts hegemonic and corporate from states and onto classes, was in fact saying little more than that these classes were revolutionary and reformist respectively: 'We do not have any new tools of analysis here but a sophistication of the old' (Thompson 1978, 283).
21 This, as Elliott argues, 'was redolent of difficulties sidestepped' (Elliott 1998, 35). In 1992 Anderson noted that this criticism 'struck the mark' (Anderson 1992a, 4).
22 Ralph Miliband commented that Anderson's thesis was brilliant, if vicious (Newman 2002, 118).

23 Anderson's bewilderment at the tone of Thompson's critique is understandable, for the old New Left had rejected the project of building there own socialist organisation precisely because they believed that the British working class were too strongly attached to Labourism (Saville 2003, 117-8).

24 This essay was first printed anonymously in *NLR* 45 in 1967, and reprinted in the following year in *Monthly Review* under their names.

25 Moreover, the CP's slogan of 'Peace in Vietnam' was well to the right of the Vietnam Solidarity Campaign's slogan of 'Victory to the NLF' – which Anderson supported. Finally the CP's approach to youth culture was far too conservative for someone of Anderson's temperament (Waite 1995).

26 In the theory of the foco, Debray took Castro and Guevara's claim that 'it is not always necessary to wait until all the conditions for revolution are fulfilled – the insurrectionary centre can create them', and generalised it: the foco could thus be any insurrectionary centre which offered itself as a practical alternative to the status quo (Debray 1973, 39).

27 *A Decennial Report* of 1975, p29.

28 This passage is slightly amended in the version given in *English Questions* (cf Anderson 1992e, 104).

29 The word revolutionary is replaced with socialist in the 1992 edition (*NLR* ed. 1969, 277).

30 Blackburn's job at the time precluded too close an identification with actual calls for radical action. Despite his precautions he was sacked from his post as a lecturer at the LSE after defending militant action at an open meeting (cf Harman 1988, 163). That Wilcox was in fact Blackburn's pseudonym was confirmed to me by Blackburn himself.

31 *A Decennial Report*, p37 & Elliott 1998, 62.

32 In the unpublished essay *The Founding Moment* Anderson developed the thesis that the Western Communist Parties were centrist rather than reformist organisations, membership of which was not a matter of principle: Marxists could with equal validity operate inside or outside them (p127).

33 On James see A Callinicos *Trotskyism* 1990, 61 ff

34 The main body of the text was written in 1974, while the afterword was completed in 1976 (Anderson 1976a, vii).

35 The main weakness of this method is that the published essays are written at a high level of abstraction, a weakness that Anderson would have presumably attempted to overcome in the unpublished volumes.

36 This method owes much to Weber (Hirst 1985, 95-6).

37 Colin Barker, by contrast, argues that the pre-1868 Japanese regime could best be understood as a tributary rather than a feudal society. Chris Wickham argues that some non-feudal, pre-capitalist societies could be characterised using the concept of the tributary mode of production, which he classifies

as a system within which the extraction of surplus was carried out through taxation by the state rather than through rent to a lord (Wickham 1985). Wickham argues that there existed a constant tension between the central authority and regional bureaucratic elements that were intent on developing their independence from the centre. This relation explains the difference between the feudal and tributary mode in so far as the latter allowed no parcellization of sovereignty and thus disallowed the development of autonomous cities. This account provides a model against which Japan can be compared. Indeed several authors have made this comparison and argue that pre-1868 Japan was a tributary society. This isn't to say that Japan was never feudal: Barker argues that pre-Tokugawa Japan was a feudal society (Barker 1982, 1). However, Japanese social relations were reorganised at the end of the sixteenth century, such that, unlike feudal Europe, the Japanese rulers never intervened directly within the process of production – though by insisting that villagers be responsible for raising taxes they maintained high yields of surplus. Thus, 'the difference between Japan and Europe lies crucially in the simultaneous conversion of the Samurai into state bureaucrats and the peasants into members of an autonomous village community' (Barker 1982, 13). If Barker's argument that pre-Meiji Japan was a tributary rather than a feudal society is valid it has an important consequence for Anderson's work, for it undermines his view that the structure of European feudalism was insufficient to account for its transformation to capitalism. If the only developed feudal society to have existed gave birth to capitalism then no exogenous forces must of necessity be postulated to explain that mutation. This, of course, does not prove that it was not a force exogenous to feudalism's structure that caused the mutation, just that it need not have been.

38 Anderson here distanced himself from Marx who, in the *Grundrisse*, had argued that once two modes had merged their traces were abolished (Anderson 1974b, 421).

39 By contrast David Parker has argued that Roman law did not 'engender a clear sense of absolute property rights' (Parker 1996, 270). He points out that nowhere does Anderson discuss the actual 'reception and application of Roman law' (Parker 1996, 21). This is important because French absolutism was legitimated within a 'highly traditional religious teleology' rather than through a modern application of Roman law (Parker 1996, 173). Indeed Roman law 'had very little relevance to these issues' (Parker 1996, 172).

40 Anderson only implied this point. In the text itself he merely stated that the 'political lessons and implications of the fall of Tsarism ... remain to this day largely unexplored' (Anderson 1974b, 360).

41 These incoherences were related to his Anderson's method. As we saw in

the last chapter, by the early 1970s Anderson was becoming convinced by Colletti's Kantian epistemology (Anderson 1980, 6; *NLR* ed. 1977, 326). Given the direction of Colletti's research it was inevitable that he should be forced to come to terms with that great neo-Kantian social scientist Max Weber. According to Colletti, the weakness of Weber's methodology was that through his utilisation of the concept of the ideal type the 'scientific concept', as Weber himself stated, 'becomes a utopia' (Colletti 1972, 43). An ideal type, according to Colletti, was a 'purely abstract and conventional model which can never be traced in reality' (Colletti 1974a, 41) In contrast to Weber's use of ideal types, Colletti sought to solve the problem of social scientific abstractions through his concept of a determinate scientific abstraction. We have already noted Anderson's enthusiastic reception of this methodology (*NLR* 56 1969, 18). And like Colletti, Anderson rejected Weber's ideal type methodology: Weber 'lacked any historical theory proper', and his ideal types 'are in practice treated as detachable and atomic traits rather than as unified structures; consequently they can be distributed and mixed at random' (Anderson 1974b, 410). Indeed Anderson's 'unified structures' bear a close resemblance to Colletti's concept of a determinate scientific abstraction. However, while Colletti argued that this method was universally applicable, Anderson argued that it only applied to pre-capitalist modes of production; for capitalism was the first mode of production within which the extraction of a social surplus was not based upon extra-economic means. However, in his passing references to capitalism in *Lineages* he tended to define it in a generic manner. We can plausibly assume that Anderson attempted to overcome this lacuna in his specific analyses of capitalist social formations in the unpublished third and fourth volumes of his genealogy of Europe. Unfortunately, with respect to pre-capitalist societies, just as Weber's methodology ultimately led him to empiricism (Outhwaite 1987, 104), Anderson's methodology led him in the same direction. Hirst has argued that Anderson nowhere attempted to develop a general model of modes of production, and therefore he incoherently defined different modes of production variously 'by the socio-legal status of the labourer [slavery], by the form of division of state power [feudalism], and by a set of technical conditions of production [nomadic] ... None of these usages is argued for or defended theoretically' (Hirst 1985, 106). Consequently Anderson's history is marked by 'speculative empiricism' (Hirst 1985, 96). Indeed, as Anderson incorporated superstructural elements into his definition of pre-capitalist modes of production, 'the form of the state is constitutive of the social relations of production, hence modes of production are identified with and by differences in state constitutions as revealed in empirical history' (Hirst 1985, 101). Thus Anderson, in his analysis of pre-capitalist modes of production tends to equate modes of production

42 with particular social formations (Hirst 1985, 110). Similarly, Fulbrook and Skocpol argue that there is a resemblance between Anderson's concepts and Weber's ideal types. However, because 'Anderson's concepts refer to concrete sociohistoric complexes ... [they] run the danger of being nothing more than economical devices for description' (Fulbrook and Skocpol 1984, 183). This character of Anderson's model had profound consequences. In particular Anderson constantly came up against problems with his attempts to abstract models of modes of production from his descriptions of particular social formations. This fatally undermined his aim of outlining a comparative history of Eastern and Western Europe.

42 Anderson argued that 'the maturation of the Absolutist States in the 17th century now effectively dealt a death blow to the possibility of the revival of urban independence in the East' (Anderson 1974b, 205). However, he seems unaware that in arguing that such a social formation was feudal contradicts his own definition of feudalism as including parcellized sovereignty which allowed for autonomous urban developments (Anderson 1974a, 150). As Runciman argues; 'on Anderson's own evidence the distinctive role of the cities of Western Europe is such as seriously to qualify his own conclusions about Absolutism' (Runciman 1989, 207).

43 This, as Michael Mann has argued, 'is a little difficult to believe' (Mann 1984, 27). Indeed, Anderson has recently argued that 'the Darwinian struggle between firms has an inherent tendency to escalate to the level of states' (Anderson 2002e, 20).

44 Elliott links this reconfiguration of Anderson's concept of bourgeois revolution to his reception of Brenner's thesis on the transition from feudalism to capitalism (Elliott 1998, 80). I shall discuss this further in the next chapter.

45 From an interview originally commissioned as part of the Fourth International's attempt to come to grips with the aftermath of the Portuguese Revolution.

46 This position contrasts with that taken by a number of other members of *NLR*'s editorial committee who joined the Trotskyist International Marxist Group (IMG) in the 1970s. In particular Robin Blackburn published a defence of the IMG's politics in a debate with Geoff Roberts of the CPGB in the IMG's magazine *International* in 1977. Blackburn argued that a viable socialist strategy for contemporary Britain demanded that socialists develop an electoral alternative to the Labour Party in the context of the Social Contract (Blackburn 1977, 23). This dovetailed with the Fourth International's general stress on the importance of taking bourgeois democracy seriously, as expressed in the policy document they produced in the aftermath of the Portuguese Revolution. In this document the FI stressed that socialism could only be won through the dictatorship of the proletariat

but that this should be understood not in the Stalinist sense of the dictatorship of the General Secretary through the party, but as the full flowering of democracy unconstrained by economic fetters that so curtail it in the West. Thus, as against the Stalinists, they stressed the democratic nature of the dictatorship of the proletariat while, as against the Eurocommunists, they stressed the continued relevance of a revolutionary strategy. However, the FI was still left with the problem of explaining how the East could be regarded as socialist and yet be without even a minimum level of democracy (United Secretariat of the Fourth International 1978). In 1983 Anderson, rehearsing an argument that perhaps underpinned his unwillingness to join the FI in the 1970s, suggested that this position 'failed to synthesise the contending positions, each with its contradictory share of the truth, into any cogent or innovative strategy. The Fourth International lost its way at the crossroads of the Portuguese Revolution' (Anderson 1983, 80).

47 These arguments were both built upon the analysis of bureaucratic conservatism outlined by Rosa Luxemburg (Luxemburg 1986).
48 The phrase 'super optimism' was used by Chris Harman to describe this general phenomenon (Harman 1985, 82-7). This essay greatly impressed Anderson when it was first published.
49 We shall discuss Anderson's analysis of this remaking in the next chapter.
50 This placed Anderson at the borderline between the right wing of Trotskyism and the left wing of Communism, in a position similar to that taken by the unorthodox Trotskyist Michael Pablo in the 1950s. Pablo had argued that 'objective conditions were forcing the Stalinists to act in a revolutionary fashion, and we Trotskyists needed to be inside the Stalinist organisations where we could influence this process' (Wohlforth 1994, 94).
51 We shall see in the next chapter this theoretical heritage helped to undermine his attempts to develop dynamic models of the modern and postmodern conjunctures.
52 This implication is confirmed in the document *NLR 1980-83*, in which Anderson made clear his disagreements with Tariq Ali's and Quentin Hoare's decisions to join the Labour Party. (p12 & p18 & p41).
53 The SWP believed that the Soviet Union was a form of bureaucratic state capitalism (Cliff 1988) and carried on the masthead of its paper, *Socialist Worker*, the slogan *Neither Washington nor Moscow but International Socialism*.
54 This was the strategy of taking on the working class section by section, in a salami fashion, starting with the weakest groups and culminating with an attack on the miners (Saville 1986).
55 When I questioned Ste Croix regarding his discussion of women in antiquity at a meeting organised by the London Socialist Historians in 1997 he said that he accepted Anderson's critique.

56 Anderson's term is 'regulative intelligence'. This, as Callinicos points out, is evidence of the influence upon Anderson of the ideas of the French regulation school (Callinicos 1988, 103). I shall return to this issue below.
57 Compare this argument with his equally mechanical discussion of the relationship of ideology to the changing structure of the workers movement in his recent discussion of internationalism (Anderson 2002b, 10-13).
58 The *London Review of Books* and the *Times Literary Supplement*.
59 Anderson relates Thatcher's downfall solely to the crisis over her strategic and tactical relationship to Europe. While this was very important, Anderson misses the point: the issue of Europe could play such an important part in Thatcher's downfall only because the Poll Tax had already made her the most unpopular Prime Minister in history. Heath *et al* are closer to the mark when they write that the Poll Tax 'played a crucial role in her downfall' (Heath *et al*. 2001, 1).
60 Compare Anderson's more recent comments on *Marxism Today*: 'It is obvious that on a minor scale *Marxism Today* – journalistically lively, but with no intellectual or political stamina ... – played the role of sorcerers apprentice, not least in preparing the cult of Thatcher as a model of radical government that was taken over with a vengeance by New Labour' (Anderson 2002c, 7).
61 See also Anderson's discussion of 'Margaret Thatcher's authoritarian populism' in Themes *NLR* 134. Jessop *et al* had challenged Stuart Hall's conceptualisation of Thatcher's 'authoritarian populism' on the pages of *NLR* in 1984. However, they criticised Hall more for what he didn't say than for what he did. Thus, they argued that Hall concentrated on ideological factors at the expense of economic factors, and concluded that 'whilst the authoritarian populist approach has been able to suggest certain necessary conditions for rethinking left strategy in Britain, it is far from establishing the sufficient conditions for a successful alternative strategy'. In particular Jessop *et al* agreed with Hall that Thatcher's 'unique success with skilled workers enabled her to arrest – even to reverse in the short term – the structural decline in Tory support' (Jessop *et al*. 1988, 98 & 86). Despite their disagreements Jessop, Hall and Anderson all came to share a broadly similar pessimistic appraisal of the perspectives for a radical break, by the English working class. (Blackledge 2002)
62 This essay was, in the main, a history of the idea of the end of history. Anderson traced this concept in a magisterial survey from Hegel through Cournot and Kojève to de Man, Gehlen, Habermas and finally to Fukuyama. He then moved on to a discussion of the contemporary relevance of the idea of socialism. I shall confine my comments to this last point for considerations of space.
63 These included, most importantly, Michael Barret Brown (1988), Ellen

Meiksins Wood (1991), Alex Callinicos (1988) and Bob Looker (1988).

64 The naivety of Anderson's hopes for ex-leftists in government is perhaps best illustrated in his 1994 discussion of the prospects for Cardoso's incoming government in Brazil. Cardoso, he argued, was likely to confound his leftwing critics, who 'delude themselves if they imagine he will neglect' Brazil's desperately poor (Anderson 1994b, 8). Indeed, Cardoso was likely to be 'the best President Brazil has ever had' (Anderson 1994b, 6). Unfortunately, the reality of Cardoso's government was far more predictable: 'in power, he has accommodated himself to the archaic state which his earlier analysis had consistently condemned, and it is that capitulation, more than anything else, which has stripped the social democratic promise from his project, and reduced it to a recipe for the consolidation of neo-liberalism in practice' (Cammack 1997, 242). More prescient in their support for Cardoso were the bankers who, after hearing him tell the business community to 'forget everything I have written', supported him in the hope that he would supply Brazil with a 'soft Pinochet government' (Chossudovsky 1997, 182 & 185). In fact, two terms of Cardoso's government has led to 'real measures of deindustrialisation', combined with increasing unemployment, poverty, inequality, while much of Brazil's infrastructure has been sold off to Western multinationals (Rocha 2002). Anderson has recently written his own evaluation of Cardoso's legacy (Anderson 2002f).

65 Anderson did not accept regulation theory uncritically, however, his work in the early 1980s can be best understood to share with the regulation school a general methodological approach (Kenny 1999, 35).

66 Cohen's remarks on this page refer to the Soviet Union, but imply that national correctives to the market could prevent crises

67 Murry Smith has noted 'the affinity of Brenner's account to 'disproportionality' theories of capitalist crisis', which posit 'a much more 'manageable' contradiction' than that which is to be found in Marx's writings (Smith 1999, 154 & 160). Lebowitz argues that Brenner's 'implicit solution' to the crisis of capitalism is a 'depression cartel': 'Regardless of [Brenner's] own political perspective, the methodology permeating his analytical model drives him in the direction of a political strategy in which the logic is not one of class struggle but, rather, of a search for transnational agencies to stabilise the competition of capitals' (Lebowitz 1999, 127).

68 Jameson based his economic analysis on Ernest Mandel's *Late Capitalism* (Jameson 1991, 3). The problem with this approach, as many of Jameson's critics have pointed out, is that Mandel argued that the break in the history of capitalism occurred around 1945, while for Jameson the transformation is dated to the 1960s (Mandel 1975, 118-121; Davis 1985, 107). Marxist critics of Jameson's thesis have thus tended to downplay the impact of economic changes from around the late sixties, and have instead concentrated

upon delivering a political history of the postmodernist movement. Thus, as we noted above, both Terry Eagleton and Alex Callinicos have analysed postmodernism as the bastard child of the defeated radicalism of the generation of 1968. Other Marxists, drawing on the regulation school, have made more of the economic changes from the early 1970s in explaining postmodernism. So, for David Harvey, the move towards postmodernism is predicated upon the shift from a Fordist regime of accumulation to a flexible regime of accumulation. However, even Harvey concedes that one must be very careful not to overstate the case for this change (Harvey 1990, 189-197). Jameson has more recently attempted to strengthen his economic analysis by borrowing from Giovanni Arrighi's *The Long Twentieth Century* (Jameson 1998, 136ff; Anderson 1998, 126).

69 Compare this with Anderson's discussion of this conjuncture in *Arguments*: 'It was the reactionary consolidation of the 50s that dominated our consciousness. That 'base period' ... was marked throughout the West by Cold War mobilisation at every institutional and ideological level. In Britain its major idiom was glutinously chauvinist ... The bulk of the working class was passive and integrated into the national 'consensus' ... The UK appeared a stable bastion of the Free World (Anderson 1980, 147): Anderson's glass seems to be perpetually half-empty!

70 Compare this statement to the concluding lines of the foreword to *English Questions*: 'Gramsci's strength of mind was to bring moral resistance and political innovation together. In related circumstances, this is the combination needed today' (Anderson 1992a, 11).

71 In a later essay Anderson noted a difference between the Clinton and Bush administrations in that the latter 'showed a certain impatience with the fiction that the 'international community' was an alliance of democratic equals'. However, this 'shift in style signified no change in the fundamental aims of American global strategy' (Anderson 2002e, 11). What September 11 gave the Bush administration was the perfect opportunity to mobilise domestic opinion in favour of a more strident foreign policy. Moreover, this opinion could be protected from the shock of a Vietnam style homecoming for thousands of Americans in body bags because of the 'revolution in military affairs'. Anderson notes that these two changes accompanied a third ideological shift from Clinton's 'construction of a democratic peace' to Bush's 'war on terrorism' (Anderson 2002e, 11-13).

72 Brenner, as we noted in the last chapter, does not hold an optimistic perspective for the future of the world economy. Like all serious commentators he recognises both that the US economy has acted as the powerhouse of the world economy over the last few years, and that the US is in a very precarious position at the moment. Today, 'the deflation of the stock market bubble is propelling the US economy, heavily burdened by manufacturing

overcapacity, towards a serious recession, and in the process detonating further recession all across the advanced capitalist world that is similarly held down by superfluous productive power' (Brenner 2002, 282).

73 More specifically John Roberts has criticised both Anderson and Jameson for what he argues is a systematic confusion in their work between 'the end of the avant-garde as the positivisation of the revolutionary transformation in action ... and the avant-garde as the continuing labour of negation on the category of art and the representations and institutions of capitalist culture'. While the former may have been crushed by the combined forces of fascism and Stalinism, thus easing the process of the post-war incorporation of modernism, the latter continues 'inexorably to exert its demands and responsibilities' (Roberts 2000, 26l; cf Eagleton 1990, 372). T.J. Clark makes similar criticisms of both Anderson's and Jameson's conceptualisations of postmodernism, however his argument that the critic must be aware of continuities as well as change over the period of rupture located by them is less emphatic than that of Roberts' (Clark 2000, 93-6; Roberts 2000, 27).

74 For instance Jeremy Brecher quotes Gloria Harris – a thirty-nine-year-old single mother in Chicago – who through her experience in the 1997 UPS strike argued 'we now feel more like brothers and sisters than co-workers', and 'we all learned something about color. It comes down to green' (Brecher 1997, 361).

75 Ste Croix has pointed out that Weber's conceptualisation of class was unable to account for historical change (de Ste Croix 1981, 90).

76 Anderson's top down and static approach to the politics of social class, and his a priori dismissal of the potential class struggle to generate viable alternatives to the status quo can be seen in three recent essays. In *Internationalism: A Breviary* he dismisses contemporary anti-capitalist internationalism: internationalism today, he writes, is synonymous with its American meaning as 'the reconstruction of the globe in the American image', while 'resistances to this new dispensation still appear, for the most part, as chaff in the wind' (Anderson 2002b, 24). Similarly, in his discussion of Berlusconi's Italy, while basing his narrative on Ginsborg's history from below of Italy's developing crisis over the last two decades, Anderson has written a superior top-down political history within which the working class makes only a fleeting and superficial appearance (Anderson 2002a & cf Ginsborg 2001). Finally, in his discussion of the immediate political context to the Anglo-American invasion of Iraq, Anderson explains the size and militancy of the international anti-war demonstrations of 15th February 2003 through a combination of European pro-Clinton/Gore anti-Republicanism, poor pro-war rhetorical imagery, and popular fear of Islamic terrorism. This argument, while containing much insight into mainstream European

politics, appears ignorant of the mechanisms through which the preceding anti-capitalist milieu partially morphed into and provided much of the local and international leadership for the anti-war movement, ensuring, contra Anderson's claims that 'current debates so interminably invoke the "international community" and the "United Nations", that calls for the UN to lead action against Iraq were very much in the minority on the anti-war demonstrations and within the anti-war movement more generally: in Britain at least the anti-war protestors marched behind banners proclaiming 'No Blood for Oil: Freedom for Palestine' , suggesting an anti-capitalist, and anti-imperialist component to the movement that Anderson implicitly dismisses (Anderson 2003).

77 Mike Haynes has made a similar, if more depressing, reading of the class struggle in post transition Russia. Like Anderson, he notes the catastrophic collapse of the living standards of working-class Russians over the last decade and a half. However, unlike Anderson, Haynes attempts to analyse the ebb and flow of the class struggle in Russia at its ideological, economic, and political levels. He concludes, contra Anderson, that the Russian calamity has created a class struggle backlash, but that these movements have suffered from ideological and organisational constraints as a consequence of a the combined legacy of Stalinism, and the incredible difficulties involved in attempting to organise in such dire circumstances. In particular, Haynes suggests that the 'railway wars' of 1998 exhibited the potential of workers to act as an alternative to the status quo that sent 'shudders' down Yeltsin's back (Haynes 2002, 214-219). It is precisely Anderson's schematic presentation of the issue of class consciousness that blinds him to these eddy currents against the general picture; eddy currents that should be the starting point of a socialist counter offensive against capitalism.

78 Christopher Norris similarly rejects Jameson's declaration that those who refuse the term postmodernism make a category-mistake similar to those who reject bad weather. Norris argues that it is only because Jameson blurs the distinction between postmodernism, understood either as an epoch or as a set of philosophical theories, that he is able to condemn attempts to make moral judgements of it. This conflation of two senses of the term postmodernism is only possible, Norris argues, if Jameson's controversial 'Hegelian notion of postmodernism as an all-pervasive spirit of the times' is accepted (Norris 1992, 161-2; cf Eagleton 1986, 73).

79 Ironically Anderson began to accept these arguments just as Bourdieu began to reject them. Thus, in the last years before his death, and in the context of the renewed struggles of the French working class, Bourdieu asked 'is it reasonable to expect that the extraordinary mass of suffering produced by such a political and economic regime could one day give rise to a movement capable of stopping the rush into the abyss?' (Bourdieu 1998, 102). He an-

swered in the affirmative. Indeed he argued that it would be 'facile' to label the struggles against the neo-liberal revolution as 'conservative'. Rather, he suggested that these struggles could become 'subversive forces – so long as we know how to conduct the symbolic struggle against the incessant work of the neo-liberal 'thinkers'' (Bourdieu 1998, 103). He thus suggested that 'our dream, as social scientists, might be for part of our research to be useful to the social movement' (Bourdieu 1998, 58). Moreover, 'the French movement can be seen as the vanguard of a worldwide struggle against neo-liberalism and against the new conservative revolution' (Bourdieu 1998, 53). In this struggle the postmodernists in their 'scholastic games' at best 'wrap themselves up in a verbal defence of reason and rational dialogue, or, worse, offer a supposedly postmodern but in fact 'radical chic' version of the ideology of the end of ideology, with the condemnation of the great explanatory narratives or the nihilist denunciation of science' (Bourdieu 1998, 42; cf Bourdieu 2000).

80 Kellner makes the point that the collapse of the Soviet Union means an end for only a specific interpretation of Marxism: something he misleadingly calls 'orthodox Marxism' (Kellner 1995, 16).

INDEX

1917 - see Russian Revoltion
1968 (General Strike in France), 35, 61, 54, 64, 68, 79

absolutism, 70-5
Adorno, Theodor, 163, 170
agency, 95-7, 114
Aglietta, Michel, 137, 144, 145
Ahmad, Aijaz, 148-9
Albania, 100
Alexander, Anne, 159-60
Ali, Tariq, 48, 52
alienation, 58
Althusser, Louis, 37, 55, 56-9, 72, 82, 94, 98, 105, 163, 168
   criticised by Thompson, 91-2
   on history, 93
   on totality, 40-1, 59, 67
Anderson, Perry
   on 1968, 54
   on absolutism, 70-75
   Althusser and, 57-8, 67
   Anderson-Nairn thesis, 40-1, 43
   anti-capitalism and, 165-6
   on Brenner, 122-3, 145
   Cold War and, 99-100
   Communist Party and, 22, 46, 48-9
   on Cuba, 5-6
   on Europe, 7-8, 24, 141
   on feudalism, 69-74
   functionalism of, 10
   Gramsci and, 15, 16-7, 20, 80-3
   on imperialism, 19-21
   isolation from left, 110-1
   on Jameson, 152-5, 164
   on Labour Party, 30, 33
   on Leninism, 72, 96, 126
   on Mann, 108-11
   nationalism and, 15
   NLR and, ix-x, 147, 155-7
   as Olympian, x
   on parliament, 6-7, 23, 33, 82
   on PCI, 8
   post-structuralism critique, 104-6
   professorship, 147
   as postmodernist, 169-70
   reform versus revolution, ix-x, 133-4, 138-40
   on Soviet Bloc, 29
   Scarborough 1961 and, 14-5
   Soviet collapse and, 134-6, 166, 169, 170
   on students, 52-3
   Thompson critique, 35-40, 42-3, 91-7, 99, 100-2, 127-8
   on trade unions, 44-7
   Trotsky and, 49-50, 64-5, 68-9, 82-3, 106, 126, 138, 148
   on Western Marxism, 152
   on Wilson, 23, 25-7, 64

WORKS: A Critique of Wilsonism, 118; A Culture in Contraflow, 118, 128-31, 134-5; A Decennial Report, 51; A Ripple of the Polonaise, 157; *Arguments Within English Marxism*, 93-7, 100-3, 116, 118, 131, 160, 162; Communist Party History, 133; Components of a National Culture, 40, 51-3, 128; *Considerations on Western Marxism*, 60-6, 93, 104; Critique of Wilsonism, 23, 25-7; Cuba, Free Territory of America (with Blackburn), 5-6; *English Questions*, 118; Geoffrey de Ste. Croix and the Ancient Greek World, 114-5; High Jinks at the Plaza, 143; *In the Tracks of Historical Materialism*, 93, 97-8, 104-6, 132, 151; Introduction to Colletti, 60; Introduction to Tukhachevsky, 56; *Lineages of the Absolutist State*, 69-73, 75, 95, 109, 168-9; *Mapping the West European Left*, 134; Marshall Berman: Modernity and Revolution, 114-6, 126, 153, 154; *Origins of Postmodernity*, 150-5; Origins of the Present Crisis, 14-24, 39, 118, 119, 126, 138; *Passages From Antiquity to Feudalism*, 69-70, 95, 168-9; Portugal and the End of Ultra-Colonialism, 9-11; Problems of Socialist Strategy, 17, 23-4, 29-34, 118; Renewals, 155-6; Scurrying Towards Bethlehem, 157-8; Social Democracy Today, 118, 132-3, 134; Socialism and Pseudo-Empiricism, 14, 35-40, 43, 93; Testing Formula Two, 157; The Antinomies of Antonio Gramsci, 80-3, 93, 100; The Ends of History, 135-7, 141; The Figures of Descent, 118-20, 126-8, 133, 134, 137, 138, 140, 145; The German Question, 144-5; The Left in the Fifties, 27-9; The Light of Europe, 118, 130, 139-42, 145; The Limits and Possibilities of Trade Union Action, 44-5; The Marxism of Regis Debray (with Blackburn), 47-50; The Notion of a Bourgeois Revolution, 75, 118, 126; The Politics of the Common Market (with Hall), 7-8; Trotsky's Interpretation of Stalinism, 99-100; Under the Sign of the Interim, 142-3

Angola, 9
anti-capitalism, 162, 165-6
Anti-Nazi League, 111
anti-Semitism, 157-8
anti-war movement, 202-3
Argentina, 171
Aronowitz, Stanley, 148
Ash, Timothy Garton, 157

Bachelard, Gaston, 37
Balibar, Etienne, 58
Bandung Asia-Africa Conference (1955), 1, 2
Barnett, Anthony, 76-7, 87, 91
Barratt Brown, Michael, 85, 125
Bauer, Otto, 62
Benn, Tony, 88, 111, 112
Berman, Marshall, 150, 164
Bernstein, Eduard, 62
Birchall, Ian, 57, 132
Black Wednesday (1992), 113
Blackburn, Robin, ix, 5-6, 47-9, 53, 76-7
Blackledge, Paul, 88, 121, 131
Bobbio, Noberto, 138
Boggs, Carl, 84
Bordiga, Amadeo, 81
Bourdieu, Pierre, 162, 164
Brenner, Robert, xii, 121-3, 144-6
Bukharin, Nikolai, 62, 74
Bush, George W., 156, 157

Callinicos, Alex, 132, 147, 150, 154, 155, 160, 162
  on American left, 148
  on postmodernism, 162
  on state, 115-6
  on UK economy, 124-5
Carlin, Nora, 132
Carr, Edward Hallett, 63
Castro, Fidel, 48
Ceylon, 57
Chamberlain, Neville, 124-5
Charter 88, 130, 140-1
Chartism, 19, 126-7

INDEX

China, 98, 100
Chomsky, Noam, 158-9, 162
Christianity, 109
citizenship, 139
City of London, 124-5
Civil War, 122
class consciousness, 94
Cliff, Tony, 13, 87-9
CND (Campaign for Nuclear Disarmament), 1, 13-4, 27-8, 107-8, 110-1, 112
Coates, David, 44, 78, 111
Cohen, Gerry A., xii, 66-7, 93-5, 117-8, 127-8, 137, 144, 169
Cold War, 1, 7-8, 28, 98-9
    70s escalation of, 107
Colletti, Lucio, 57-60, 93, 168
Communist Party (CPGB), 1, 22, 46, 48, 111
Cousins, Frank, 46
Cuba, 5-6, 47
Cultural Revolution, 35

Daly, Lawrence, 13
Darwin, Charles, 36, 38
Davis, Mike, 107-8, 147, 163
Debray, Regis, 47-50, 53, 55, 79
deconstruction, 106, 129
Delors, Jacques, 142-4, 170
democracy, 79-80
deregulisation, 120-1
Derrida, Jacques, 130-1
desire, 101-2
Deutscher, Isaac, 3-4, 50, 63, 64, 98, 107, 167, 169, 170, 171
    on Anderson, 15
    on classical Marxism, 61
    on revolution, 96
    on Soviet Union, 3-4, 99
disarmament – see CND
Draper, Hal, 4
Dworkin, Dennis, 3

Eagleton, Terry, 91, 106, 131, 148, 149-50, 154, 155, 162, 164
Elliott, Gregory, xi, 23-4, 56, 93, 99, 118, 137, 148

Engels, Friedrich, 61, 93
English Revolution, 18, 36, 121-4
Enlightenment, 104, 106, 151-2
Etzioni, Amatai, 151
Eurocommunism, 17, 79, 81, 98, 104, 106
Europe, 24, 141-4
    Anderson and Hall on, 7-8
    Heath and, 76
exterminism, 107, 110

Fabians, 22, 91
feminism, 32-3, 106, 130, 131
feudalism, 69-74
Fielder, Leslie. 151
Fine, Ben, 67
Foot, Paul, 46
Foster, John Bellamy, 149
Foucault, Michel, 105, 130
Fourth International, 64, 106
Fukuyama, Francis, 93, 135-6, 137, 138, 169
Fulbrook, Mary, 72

Gamble, Andrew, 87-8
Gates, Bill, 154
Geras, Norman, 57-9, 78, 80
German Revolution (1918-23), 62-3
Giddens, Anthony, 131
Glick, Mark, 144
globalisation, 145-6, 161-2
Glorious Revolution (1688), 119
Glucksmann, Andre, 57-9
Gluckstein, Donny, 13
Goldthorpe, John, 31
Gore, Al, 157
Gramsci, Antonio, x, 15, 16-7, 20, 54-6, 80-3, 80-5, 164-5, 168
    on trade unions, 84
    war of position, 85
Guevara, Che, x, 47, 53

Habermas, Jürgen, 104, 106, 151-2
Hague, William, 157
Hall, Stuart, 7, 9, 87-9
Halliday, Fred, 107, 108, 111
Harman, Chris, 54, 62, 68, 113
Harris, Lawrence, 67

Harrison, Roydon, 39
Hayek, Friedrich von, 143
Haynes, Mike, 203
Heath, Edward, 76-7
Hegel, Georg Wilhelm Friedrich, 35, 52, 56-8, 67, 136
hegemony, 17, 20-3, 42-3, 80-5
Hill, Christopher, 123-4
Hinton, James, 39-40, 43
Hirst, Paul, 75
Hobsbawm, Eric, 88, 116, 125
Hodgson, Geoff, 66
Holton, Robert, 74
Home, Alec Douglas, 27
Hood, Stuart, 163
Howe, Irving, 151
Hughes, John, 44

IMG (International Marxist Group), 88, 197-8
imperialism, 19-20
intelligentsia, 32
intentionality, 94-5
irrationalism, 101, 104, 106
IS (International Socialism) Group, 39
Israel, 157-9

Jacoby, Russell, 147-8, 149
Jacques, Martin, 87-8
James, C.L.R., 65
Jameson, Fredric, xii, 149-50, 170
    flaw of, 162
    postmodernism and, 150-5
Japan, 70
Jessop, Bob, 87, 89-90
Jones, Jack, 46

Kant, Immanuel, 58
Kautsky, Karl, 61, 62
Kaye, Harvey, 97
Kellner, Douglas, 204
Kelly, John, 84
Kenny, Michael, 5, 13
Keynesianism, 139, 169
Kinnock, Neil, 132
Kozak, Marion, 3
Krasso, Nicolas, 50-1, 56

Labour Party, 1, 6, 26, 30-1, 111,
    Scarborough conference (1961), 13-4, 27-8
labour theory of value, 66-7, 117-8, 169
Labriola, Antonio, 62
Lacan, Jacques, 37
left in US, 147-50
Lenin, V.I., 61, 62, 74-5, 96, 126
Lévi-Strauss, Claude, 10, 52, 98, 105
Liberal Party, 127
liberalism, 138-40
Lipietz, Alain, 144
Lockwood, David, 31
Looker, Bob, 15, 89, 127-8
LRB (*London Review of Books*), 129, 130
Lukács, Gyorgi, 16, 20-1, 103, 168
Luxemburg, Rosa, 61, 62
Lyotard, Jean-François, 151

Maastricht Treaty (1991), 143-4
Machiavelli, Niccolo, 69
MacIntyre, Alasdair, 39, 192
Mahamdallie, Hassan, 103
Major, John, 113, 153
Mandel, Ernest, 15-6, 51, 64
    Trotsky and, 56-7
    on democracy, 79-80
Mandron, Guy, 158
Mann, Michael, 108-11, 139
Manning, Brian, 123
Mao Tse Tung, 48, 49, 56
Maoism, x, 98, 104, 106
    NLR and, 57
Marcuse, Herbert, 171
Marshall, Phil, 139, 158
Marx, Karl, 61, 165
    WORKS: 1844 Manuscripts, 60; *Grundrisse*, 69; preface to *The Contribution to the Critique of Political Economy*, 93, 169
Marxism Today, 88-90, 113, 131-2, 134
Marxism
    classical, 61
    cultural, 5
Mayer, Arno, 115-6, 119
Mehring, Franz, 62
Merquior, Jose G., 10

INDEX

Miliband, Ralph, 74, 113, 127, 132
militarism, 108-10
Miller, David, 164
Mills, C. Wright, 149, 151
Milward, Alan, 142-3
Miners' Strike, 113, 131-2, 141
Mitterand, François, 133
modernisation, 24-5, 34
modernism, 115-7
modes of production, 74-5
Monnet, Jean, 142
Monthly Review, 149
Moody, Kim, 161-2
Morley, David, 163-4
Morris, William, 101-3
    News From Nowhere, 102, 103

N30 – see Seattle protest
Nairn, Tom, 40, 41, 43
Nationwide, 163
NATO (North Atlantic Treaty Organisation), 156-7
neo-liberalism, 155-6, 161-2
New Cold War, 107-8
New Left
    birth of (1956), 1-2, 167
    Leninism and, 12
NLR (*New Left Review*), 129
    Anderson and, ix-x
    birth of, 1-2, 167
    relaunch (2000), ix-x, 155
    Wilsonism and, 44
Norris, Christopher, 150

Olson, Charles, 151
Onis, Federco de, 151
organic intellectuals, 65
Osborne, John, 2
Osborne, Peter, 116-7, 160

Palestine, 157-9
parliament, 48, 82
Parsons, Talcott, 38, 41
PCF (French Communist Party), 16
    1968 and 54
PCI (Italian Communist Party), 8-9
Petras, James, 161

Philo, Greg, 164
Pilkington Committee on Television, 5, 27
Plekhanov, Georgi, 61
Poll Tax, 113, 130
Portugal, 9-11, 68, 77, 78, 87, 87, 106, 170
post-structuralism, 104-6, 112, 130-1
postcolonial theory, 154
Poster, Mark, 10
postmodernism, 112, 131, 132, 150-5, 160
Poulantzas, Nicos, 40-4, 119
Preobrazhensky, Evgeny, 62
public schools, 121

red bases, 53
Rees Mogg, Lord, 141
reformism, 132, 138-40, 169
revolution, 133-4
Ridley plan, 113
Roman law, 70
Rosdolsky, Roman, 64, 118
Rowthorn, Bob, 44
Russia, 71-2, 75
Russian Revolution, 74-5
    agency and, 96

Sartre, Jean-Paul, 55, 56, 98, 105, 168
    on PCF, 15-6
    WORKS: *Critique of Dialectical Reason*, 94; *The Communists and Peace*, 99
Saussure, Ferdinand de, 10, 106, 116
Saville, John, 13, 39, 132
Scanlon, Hugh, 46
Scarborough Labour Party conference (1961), 13-4, 27-8
Scargill, Arthur, 78
Schumpeter, Joseph A., 145
Seattle protest (30 November 1999), 156, 162, 171
Second International, 62, 13
Sedgwick, Peter, 3, 5, 14, 39
Serbia, 157
sexuality, 34
Sino-Soviet dispute, 98, 108
Skocpol, Theda, 72
slavery, 114
Smith, Adam, 36, 38

Smith, Sharon, 149
Soares, Mario, 78
Social Contract, 89, 113
social democracy, 132-3, 138
sociology, 52
Soviet Bloc, 29
Soviet Union
    collapse of, 134-5, 166, 169, 170
    nature of, 29, 99-100
Stalin, Josef, 92
Stalinism, 61-2, 92-3, 99, 169, 171
    Thompson and, 101
Ste. Croix, Geoffrey de, 114
Stedman Jones, Gareth, 3
Steedman, Ian, 66
Stone, Norman, 116
Strachey, John, 32
structuralism, 10
students, 52-3
SWP (Socialist Workers' Party), 88, 111

Tawney, R.H., 22
television, 5, 27, 154, 162, 163-5
The Value Controversy (conference 1978), 66
Therborn, Göran, 78-9, 171
Third International, 133
Third Way, 156, 157, 160
Thompson, Edward P., 15, 18, 35-9, 74, 119, 169
    Anderson's critique of, 91-7, 99, 100-2
    New Cold War and, 107-8, 110
    on party, 12-3
    Stalinism and, 101
    WORKS: *The Poverty of Theory*, 91-2; *The Making of the English Working Class*, 94, 127-8; *William Morris*, 101
Thompson, Willie, 46
Timpanero, Sebastiano, 93, 96-7
totality, 40-1, 52, 67, 162
Toynbee, Arnold, 151
trade unions, 44-7, 84-5
Trotsky, Leon, x, 49-51, 56, 68-9, 80, 96, 106, 126
    Anderson's turns to, 49-50, 64-5, 82-3
    criticised by Anderson, 138
    Deutscher and, 3

    on Germany, 63
    on Soviet Union, 99
    on trade unions, 84-5
    on united front, 82-3
    rediscovery of, 61

Unger, Roberto M., 137-8
united front
    Anderson on, 86
    Trotsky on, 82-3
utilitarianism, 21-2
utopia, 103

Vietnam, 35, 52-3, 78, 100
Volosinov, Valentin, 10

Weber, Max, 108, 122, 153, 161
Weber, Henri, 79
Wickham, Chris, 109
Widgery, David, 3
Wilcox, James, 53
Williams, Raymond, 3, 4-5, 21, 22, 34, 84, 131
    on Scarborough 1961, 14
    Politics and Letters, 91
Wilson, Harold, 18, 25-9, 34, 35, 39, 64, 168
    NLR and, 44
Wohlforth, Tim, 148
Wollen, Peter, 153
women, 32-3, 106, 130, 131
working class, 126-8, 130
    Anderson on, 19-20, 22, 31-2
    revolutionary consciousness and, 40
    white vs blue collar, 32
    Williams on, 4-5
Worsley, Peter, 3
Wright, Erik Olin, 66

Yugoslavia, 100

Zionism, 157-9